D1446455

Autobiography

THE GREENHAVEN PRESS COMPANION TO
Literary Movements and Genres

Autobiography

Lawrence Kappel, *Book Editor*

Bonnie Szumski, *Editorial Director*

Scott Barbour, *Managing Editor*

David M. Haugen, *Series Editor*

Greenhaven Press, Inc., San Diego, CA

Every effort has been made to trace the owners of copyrighted material. The articles in this volume may have been edited for content, length, and/or reading level. The titles have been changed to enhance the editorial purpose. Those interested in locating the original source will find the complete citation on the first page of each article.

Library of Congress Cataloging-in-Publication Data

Autobiography / Lawrence Kappel, book editor.
    p.   cm. — (Greenhaven Press companion to
literary movements and genres)
    Includes bibliographical references and index.
    ISBN 0-7377-0673-2 (hardcover : alk. paper) —
ISBN 0-7377-0672-4 (pbk. : alk. paper)
    1. Autobiography. I. Kappel, Lawrence. II. Series.
CT25 .A946 2001
920.02—dc21   00-050351

Cover photo: Art Resource
Dover Publications, 72
Library of Congress, 63, 84, 148, 185, 195, 204
North Wind Picture Archives, 129, 178

Copyright © 2001 by Greenhaven Press, Inc.
PO Box 289009
San Diego, CA 92198-9009
Printed in the U.S.A.

CONTENTS

Chapter 1: Forms of Autobiography

   Autobiography is not universally present in all cultures,
   but only where there are highly developed concepts of
   individualism, freedom, and self-consciousness, as in
   modern Europe and the United States. The primary
   Euro-American religion, Christianity, fostered autobiography through its emphasis on individual spiritual
   self-examination.

   The medieval precursor of autobiography is confession.
   While the original context is religious, as in the classic
   Confessions of St. Augustine, confession as a narrative
   mode can be purely literary as well, as in Coleridge's
   poem "The Rime of the Ancient Mariner." Modern autobiography is more secular than its predecessor and lacks
   the penitence of its roots in Christian confession.

   In recording his own private, subjective thoughts directly
   in the new "essay" form he had created, sixteenth-century
   Frenchman Michel de Montaigne established a major
   autobiographical genre. This genre focused on the writer's
   thought process—rather than on his spiritual history or
   the external events of his life—as the essence of himself.

   Memoir is a third form of autobiography (after confession
   and essay). Traditionally, it emphasizes recollections of
   events and people who are important beyond their connection with the autobiographer; the modern definition, however, emphasizes the subjective quality of these memories.

Contemporary American memoirist Annie Dillard focuses on the intersection of the two realities—when the awakening self recognizes a world independent of itself.

Chapter 2: Anglo-American Autobiographies

Chapter 4: Women's Autobiographies

FOREWORD

The study of literature most often involves focusing on an individual work and uncovering its themes, stylistic conventions, and historical relevance. It is also enlightening to examine multiple works by a single author, identifying similarities and differences among texts and tracing the author's development as an artist.

While the study of individual works and authors is instructive, however, examining groups of authors who shared certain cultural or historical experiences adds a further richness to the study of literature. By focusing on literary movements and genres, readers gain a greater appreciation of influence of historical events and social circumstances on the development of particular literary forms and themes. For example, in the early twentieth century, rapid technological and industrial advances, mass urban migration, World War I, and other events contributed to the emergence of a movement known as American modernism. The dramatic social changes, and the uncertainty they created, were reflected in an increased use of free verse in poetry, the stream-of-consciousness technique in fiction, and a general sense of historical discontinuity and crisis of faith in most of the literature of the era. By focusing on these commonalities, readers attain a more comprehensive picture of the complex interplay of social, economic, political, aesthetic, and philosophical forces and ideas that create the tenor of any era. In the nineteenth-century American romanticism movement, for example, authors shared many ideas concerning the preeminence of the self-reliant individual, the infusion of nature with spiritual significance, and the potential of persons to achieve transcendence via communion with nature. However, despite their commonalities, American romantics often differed significantly in their thematic and stylistic approaches. Walt Whitman celebrated the communal nature of America's open democratic society, while Ralph Waldo

Emerson expressed the need for individuals to pursue their own fulfillment regardless of their fellow citizens. Herman Melville wrote novels in a largely naturalistic style whereas Nathaniel Hawthorne's novels were gothic and allegorical. Another valuable reason to investigate literary movements and genres lies in their potential to clarify the process of literary evolution. By examining groups of authors, literary trends across time become evident. The reader learns, for instance, how English romanticism was transformed as it crossed the Atlantic to America. The poetry of Lord Byron, William Wordsworth, and John Keats celebrated the restorative potential of rural scenes. The American romantics, writing later in the century, shared their English counterparts' faith in nature; but American authors were more likely to present an ambiguous view of nature as a source of liberation as well as the dwelling place of personal demons. The whale in Melville's *Moby-Dick* and the forests in Hawthorne's novels and stories bear little resemblance to the benign pastoral scenes in Wordsworth's lyric poems.

Each volume in Greenhaven Press's Companions to Literary Movements and Genres series begins with an introductory essay that places the topic in a historical and literary context. The essays that follow are carefully chosen and edited for ease of comprehension. These essays are arranged into clearly defined chapters that are outlined in a concise annotated table of contents. Finally, a thorough chronology maps out crucial literary milestones of the movement or genre as well as significant social and historical events. Readers will benefit from the structure and coherence that these features lend to material that is often challenging. With Greenhaven's Literary Movements and Genres in hand, readers will be better able to comprehend and appreciate the major literary works and their impact on society.

INTRODUCTION

The telling of an individual person's life story, or biography, was traditionally viewed as a minor kind of literature when compared to the three major genres: poetry, drama, and fiction. When a person wrote his or her own biography, called autobiography, it was seen as a minor variation on a minor genre. But this view changed dramatically during the last three or four decades of the twentieth century. Now autobiography is taken more seriously and is given more respect than in the past.

A primary reason for autobiography's new dignity is an increased recognition of the many African American autobiographies, from the slave-era *The Narrative of the Life of Frederick Douglass* (1845) to the civil rights–era *The Autobiography of Malcolm X* (1965). These books began to gain recognition as more than the stories of extraordinary individuals, told with the unique authority of their own voices. They were also seen as representative of the experience of an entire people, from the people's own point of view, and thus a crucial historical record.

Following the civil rights movement of the 1960s were similar democratic movements on behalf of other American ethnicities and women. Autobiographies by members of these groups—such as the Native American N. Scott Momaday's *The Way to Rainy Mountain* and the Jewish woman radical Emma Goldman's *Living My Life*—were seen as uniquely valuable documents of the lives of whole categories of people who had been underrepresented and misrepresented by traditional historians.

At the same time that autobiography was gaining social and historical weight, it was also acquiring aesthetic stature. In fact, two classics of American literature share the common characteristic of being extravagant autobiographies: Walt Whitman's "Song of Myself" and Henry David Thoreau's *Walden*. Literature critics and scholars, such as James Olney

(*Metaphors of Self*) and Paul John Eakin (*Fictions in Autobiography*), emphasize that in writing the story of one's own life, the autobiographer creates and projects a personality and a self in a profound psychological and artistic act. In contrast to the old idea of autobiography as simply making a record of a life that is coincidentally one's own, this idea of autobiography as a complex interconnection of writing and living is more worthy of respect and thoughtful study.

This study has brought the realization that the category of autobiography is inclusive rather than narrow. It begins with personal spiritual histories and religious confessions as its historical source. It may include modern memoirs, such as Annie Dillard's *An American Childhood,* which do not attempt to chronicle the author's whole life but instead may focus on a particular period of it and may be wholly subjective. Another autobiographical mode is the essay, in the true sense of recording the individual writer's unique, subjective thought process. And poetry, drama, and fiction are often significantly autobiographical in content, as in James Joyce's "The Dead" and *A Portrait of the Artist as a Young Man.*

This recognition of the genre has focused new attention beyond a modern American classic like Norman Mailer's *The Armies of the Night* to traditional American autobiographical classics such as *The Education of Henry Adams* and *The Autobiography of Benjamin Franklin.* And beyond Franklin, the modern student of autobiography uncovers an older European tradition that begins with the *Confessions* of St. Augustine and includes the *Essays* of Michel de Montaigne and the *Confessions* of Jean-Jacques Rousseau.

This anthology of essays on autobiography, written by the most distinguished critics of the genre, includes theoretical and historical discussions as well as specific analyses of the most well known individual examples of European, Anglo-American, ethnic American, and women's autobiographies. It also includes a chronology of significant dates in the history of autobiography and a selected bibliography for use in further study. The purpose of this collection is to enhance the reader's understanding and enjoyment of autobiography as a rich and powerful genre of literature.

A HISTORICAL OVERVIEW
OF THE AUTOBIOGRAPHY

Autobiography is a broad genre that has developed over the centuries to encompass a variety of writing styles. From its roots in ancient biography to the modern-day memoir, it has evolved into a creative literary form.

The concept and the word *autobiography* are based on *biography*, or a written history of a person's life. Early biographies emphasized history—a complete unfolding of external events and the subject's role in those events. Chronicling the lives of prominent generals and leaders of the Greek and Roman world, Plutarch's *Lives*, written in the first century A.D., was one of the first such biographies.

ST. AUGUSTINE AND SPIRITUAL AUTOBIOGRAPHY

But it would be several centuries before writers began chronicling their *own* lives. An autobiography is a biography of an individual narrated or written by that person. Through one's own personal history, the writer's values, opinions, and personality are explained. Although the ideal of self-knowledge had been a Western tradition dating back to Socrates in ancient Greece, the first major autobiographical work, known as the *Confessions,* was written in the fourth century by St. Augustine, a North African colonial Roman.

With the advent of Christianity in the first centuries A.D., a new emphasis was placed on looking internally at the self. This early soul-searching related primarily to God and to man's proper behavior and place in the religious universe. Known as a spiritual autobiography, St. Augustine's book is humbly addressed to God and represents a true confession in the religious sense; the disclosure of personal weaknesses and sins serves as a penance, and the writer seeks forgiveness, redemption, and a closer relationship with his creator. Written in the form of a prayer that reflects his moral struggle, St. Augustine concludes:

Too late have I loved thee, O beauty ever ancient and ever new, too late have I loved thee! And behold! Thou wert within and I without, and it was without that I sought thee. Thou wert with me, and I was not with thee. . . . Thou didst call . . . thou didst gleam forth . . . thou didst banish my blindness; thou didst send forth thy fragrance, and I drew breath and yearned for thee . . . and I was on flame to find thy peace.

Like traditional biographies, the *Confessions* emphasizes St. Augustine's history, beginning with his sinful youth and young adulthood and ending with his ultimate salvation as a grown man.

Such soul searching carried into the Middle Ages (A.D. 400–1400), whose culture focused on intense religious piety and devotion. Through the centuries spiritual autobiographies have remained a tool for writers to explore the issues of faith, grace, and a personal bond with God. Significant spiritual autobiographies were produced during the Renaissance by Margery Kempe in the fifteenth century and St. Teresa of Avila in the sixteenth century; they continued to be produced during the Reformation by Protestant ministers John Bunyan in the seventeenth century and Jonathan Edwards in the eighteenth century. Moving forward in time, the American writer Henry David Thoreau's *Walden* is recognized as a landmark nineteenth-century spiritual autobiography. And even in the twentieth century, spiritual autobiographies remain a vital part of the autobiographical tradition, as in those of the Indian spiritual and political leader Mahatma Gandhi (*The Story of My Experiments with Truth*) and the American priest Thomas Merton (*The Seven Storey Mountain*). All autobiographers wrote about themselves, but the stories that unfolded revolved around their relationships with God and church, as did St. Augustine's *Confessions.*

MOVEMENT TOWARD THE SECULAR

In the era of St. Augustine and the Middle Ages that followed, it was uncommon for autobiographers to write specifically about themselves and their own thoughts; such self-serving writing was believed by some to violate a self-sacrificing communion with God. During the Renaissance of the fifteenth and sixteenth centuries, however, autobiographers began to experiment with a wider variety of themes than those dealt with in early spiritual autobiographies. Hence, the emphasis on strictly religious themes shifted to non-religious, or secular, themes. These included not only political and social themes, but also the raw ideas, concepts, and musings of the writers.

Two significant autobiographers of the Renaissance who pushed the boundaries of autobiography further from the church were the Frenchman Michel de Montaigne and the Italian Benvenuto Cellini. Written in the sixteenth century, their works are milestones not only because of their roles in secularizing the spiritual autobiography but also because each of them established another basic form of autobiography in addition to the confession: the essay, in the case of Montaigne; and the memoir, in the case of Cellini.

Montaigne and the Essay

Montaigne invented the essay as an informal and intimate window into the thinking of the writer. An essay stands as a demonstration of the human mind, processing observations and thought, making sense of experience, and developing ideas to be tested by further experience. Thus, essayists are not just concerned with facts and dates; they are also interested in their own perceptions of and notions about this factual and historical information. Essayists sift through this information, discuss it, mull it over, and interpret it. The reader acts as the proverbial fly on the wall, a voyeur who, in the course of reading the work, becomes privy to the writer's innermost thoughts.

Although there is a historical emphasis in traditional biographies and early confessional autobiographies, which serve as chronicles, Montaigne departs from this tradition and makes no attempt to produce anything like a detailed narrative history of his external life. Rather, in the essay the reader experiences the writer's ideas intimately; they are not finished events or occurrences, but living thoughts that are ever changing as the essay progresses. In his essays Montaigne appeals to the reader's humanity as he confronts his own weaknesses (as in spiritual autobiographies) as well as his strengths (unlike spiritual autobiographies). In discussing his self, thoughts, and strengths so freely, Montaigne can be credited with taking autobiographical writing out of the medieval church, where Augustine had started it.

CELLINI AND THE MEMOIR

Benvenuto Cellini, Montaigne's sixteenth-century contemporary, also wrote about his life outside of the context of religious confession or spiritual autobiography. In contrast to previous spiritual works, Cellini's ego loomed large in his writing, his own observations taking priority over religious insight.

Cellini followed the traditional historical organization more closely than Montaigne did. However, the distinctive feature of his life's presentation is not a simple chronicling of events, but an emphasis on the important people and events that he witnessed in the course of his life. In addition to being the subject of his book, Cellini functions as a journalist of his day or a Renaissance tour guide. Along with the memoirists who followed him, he has a sense of history and is concerned with recording observations of significant public events and personalities. Typically, the subject of the memoir is preceded by "The Life and Times of" in the work's title. Cellini's work thus established the tradition of the memoir, a form of autobiographical writing distinct from the confession of St. Augustine and the essay of Montaigne.

ROUSSEAU AND THE APOLOGY

Moving even further away from God and the church than Montaigne and Cellini was the Frenchman Jean-Jacques Rousseau. Rousseau's eighteenth-century autobiography, like St. Augustine's fourteen hundred years earlier, is entitled *Confessions;* but despite their shared title, the two books are opposites in many ways. Whereas Augustine's book is humbly addressed to God, Rousseau's is proudly addressed to humankind. And whereas St. Augustine's work is a true confession in the religious sense, Rousseau's use of the word *confession* is ironic because he confesses nothing to God and asks no forgiveness for his conduct. He is not concerned with divine judgment, and unlike St. Augustine, he seeks no personal salvation. Instead, Rousseau's style is more centered on human feeling and spontaneous emotions:

> What style can I assume to unravel the immense chaos of sentiments, so diverse, so contradictory, often so vile and sometimes so sublime, which have agitated me without respite? . . . I shall always put down what comes to me, I shall change it according to my humor without scruple, I shall say each thing as I feel it, as I see it, without study.

The traditional name given to Rousseau's kind of anticonfession is *apology*, meaning a personal self-defense or justification. The author of the apology accepts no guilt for his or her thoughts or actions, seeking only vindication through honest disclosure of the self. Although Montaigne began steering autobiography away from the medieval church two hundred years earlier, Rousseau mocks his predecessor's modesty as dishonest and commits himself to a fuller disclosure of his sentiments, a more extreme self-revelation. In this sense, Rousseau's departure from traditional autobiography was dramatic.

Rousseau's *Confessions* marked the beginning of an alternative tradition of autobiography as self-affirmation and self-celebration associated with the romantic movement of the early nineteenth century, which Rousseau so profoundly influenced. The romantic self that he celebrates is filled with subjective feeling. It is focused on a quest for its own natural innocence, lately tarnished by corrupting social experience. The strong influence of Rousseau and this romantic autobiographical tradition of self-assertion and pride, if not boasting, can be seen in many later autobiographies, including present-day works. Some good examples are Walt Whitman's *Leaves of Grass* and Norman Mailer's *Advertisements for Myself.*

REVOLUTION AND AUTOBIOGRAPHY

Not until the occurrence of two important events in world history did the ideals of democracy, personal freedom, and individualism become primary concerns for citizens or writers. As desirable values worth fighting for, they did not come into play in a major way until the American Revolution of 1776 and the French Revolution of 1789. In both conflicts, common citizens who wanted more autonomy and better opportunities for themselves fought against established monarchies that were both privileged and absolute in their ruling powers. Also in both wars, the common man triumphed, overthrowing the old aristocratic order and therefore making the potential significance of each unique life unlimited, regardless of class or status. Ordinary people were suddenly empowered with the newfound notion that their own lives and ideas were meaningful.

In fact, the term *autobiography* did not come into use until a few decades after the American and French Revolutions. (The first documented use of the word was in an article by Robert Southey in the *Quarterly Review* in 1807, and the first work to call itself by that name was W.P. Scargill's *The Autobiography of a Dissenting Minister,* published in 1834.) Shortly after the revolutions came Benjamin Franklin's autobiography, in which he establishes himself as an American, a self-made man of the world, free to choose his careers, residences, social causes, and political alliances. Being the first of its kind, Franklin's work is a landmark in autobiographical literature.

ANGLO-AMERICAN AUTOBIOGRAPHY

In addition to Franklin, many other American writers helped establish the young, democratic United States as a hotbed for various forms of autobiography. When the revolutions of the late 1700s ushered in the use of the word *autobiography,* the affinity between autobiography as a form and the American values of democracy, rugged individualism, and self-reliance had already been established. This has given personal narratives a special prominence in American culture.

The European foundations of the genre—the confession, the essay, the memoir, and the apology—were in place when the Pilgrims landed in the New World. The Puritans, who endured untold hardships in search of new lives and religious freedom, began the American autobiographical tradition with pious spiritual autobiographies in the manner of St. Augustine. The tradition continued and evolved in the nineteenth century with religious philosopher Ralph Waldo Emerson. As a minister, Emerson was intimately concerned with his relationship with God; but he had other concerns as well, notably his relationship with his self and with nature. His sermons and writings addressed personal introspection, self-consciousness, and the godlike quality of spiritual humankind. A well-read scholar, Emerson was aware of the subjectivity of human interpretation and the difficulties of writing autobiography in an unbiased way: "These novels will give way, by and by, to diaries or autobiographies— captivating books, if only a man knew how to choose among what he calls his experiences that which is really his experience, and how to record truth truly." Emerson inspired two prominent writers who followed in the nineteenth century:

Henry David Thoreau and Walt Whitman. The United States was still young and full of possibility, and these two men personified forward thinking, exuberance, and even a certain arrogance in their writing. Thoreau's *Walden,* written in the 1850s, is an American milestone that represents not a chronicle of the author's life but a philosophical search for the truth of his inner self. Taking place in a one-year period that uses the four seasons as a metaphor for living, the work examines the cycles of life, death, and rebirth as they relate to the human soul. *Walden* is recognized as a nineteenth-century spiritual autobiography and is classified as an apology, in the tradition of Rousseau. It also has the texture of an essay, in the tradition of Montaigne, because Thoreau presents for the reader his own thoughts and interpretations in a way that transcends pure facts and history.

Walt Whitman, Thoreau's contemporary and a fellow Emerson disciple, also shows the affinity between autobiography and American ideals in his rhapsodic identifications in *Leaves of Grass.* In "Song of Myself," one of the most famous poems in this lengthy autobiographical work, Whitman honors not only his mental/spiritual being but also his physical being. Like Rousseau in his *Confessions,* Whitman is nothing if not self-assured and proud:

I celebrate myself. . . .

I loafe and invite my Soul,
I lean and loafe at my ease, observing a spear of summer grass. . . .

The atmosphere is not a perfume, it has no taste of
    the distillation, it is odorless;
It is for my mouth forever—I am in love with it,
I will go to the bank by the wood, and become
    undisguised and naked,
I am mad for it to be in contact with me.

Moving toward modern times, Henry Adams's complex experience of the forces of history is painstakingly detailed in his *Education,* published in 1918. Not only was Adams the great-grandson of one of America's founding fathers and early presidents, John Quincy Adams, but he was also a student of art, architecture, science, philosophy, history, and politics. His work is a historical reference that incorporates all of these elements; but perhaps more interestingly, it includes Adams himself and his own ideas on the larger historical picture.

TWENTIETH-CENTURY ANGLO-AMERICAN AUTOBIOGRAPHY

The twentieth century has produced an abundance of Anglo-American autobiographical writing. Many of the works are novels with characters and events that are based on the authors' personal histories, or "literary autobiographies." One of the more famous American literary autobiographers is Ernest Hemingway, who wrote numerous novels based on his life and travels. Among them are books about his experiences in Italy during World War I (*A Farewell to Arms*), in Paris and Spain (*The Sun Also Rises*), and in Spain during the Spanish Civil War (*For Whom the Bell Tolls*). In these, as in Hemingway's other novels and short stories, the author's own life and history are always bubbling just beneath the surface.

Like Hemingway, other twentieth-century American writers have mined their own lives for the raw materials for their works. James Agee's *A Death in the Family* is an autobiographical novel about his father's death in an automobile accident. Agee deals with the intensely personal issues of death, family ties, and perseverance in the face of adversity. The novel's six-year-old character is, in fact, the author at that age, and his childlike confusion about his family's situation is a prominent characteristic of the book. Similarly, each of Jack Kerouac's novels represents a specific period in his life, but unlike many chronological works, the order in which they were written is completely different from the order in which they were lived. Only by fitting them together like pieces in a puzzle does the coherent picture of Kerouac's life emerge.

Although these are all autobiographical novels, two unusual examples of Anglo-American autobiographical writing that are not novels are Frederick Exley's *A Fan's Notes* (1968) and Robert Pirsig's *Zen and the Art of Motorcycle Maintenance* (1974). Both are so original and unconventional that they are hard to categorize, but they have in common a strong first-person autobiographical element.

NEW JOURNALISM

In addition to literary autobiographies, another significant use of autobiography in modern American writing is in the field of journalism. Journalistic technique has traditionally emphasized objectivity and a nonpartisan way of reporting that makes the writer invisible. In the 1960s and 1970s writers and reporters experimented with these techniques, basically turning them upside down. Some writers became highly visible participants in the events they covered, and their stories became closer to editorials than to strictly factual news articles.

Although Norman Mailer, for example, is a novelist, *The Armies of the Night* is not a novel. It is the account of a public demonstration in the country's capital against American involvement in the Vietnam War in the 1960s. He wrote it while covering the news event as a reporter for *Harper's*, a national monthly magazine. Mailer acts out a nation's inner conflict over its participation in an unpopular war in Asia by acting out his own inner conflicts that bedevil him as he records the demonstration. The fact that Mailer was a very public participant in the event he was covering makes his report unconventional journalism, or "New Journalism," as it was called. Mailer uses his skills as a novelist to conceive and present his firsthand experience as a concrete form of the event. In his opening to *The Armies of the Night,* he writes,

> From the outset, let us bring you news of your protagonist. The following is from *Time* magazine, October 27, 1967.
>
> "A Shaky Start"
>
> Washington's scruffy Ambassador Theater, normally a pad for psychedelic frolics, was the scene of an unscheduled scatological solo last week in support of the peace demonstrations. Its anti-star was author Norman Mailer, who proved even less prepared to explain Why Are We In Vietnam? than his current novel bearing that title. . . .
>
> Now we may leave *Time* in order to find out what happened.

Referring to the technique as "gonzo journalism," Hunter Thompson uses the same basic style in *Fear and Loathing in Las Vegas* (1974), in which he is an active participant instead of a conventional reporter.

Another remarkable example of this autobiographical kind of New Journalism, in which the reporter becomes part of the story and makes it personal, was actually written well before the 1960s. James Agee's *Let Us Now Praise Famous Men* was a precursor to Mailer's work and explored some of the same techniques the New Journalists would make famous. On assignment from *Fortune* magazine, Agee was to write an article on tenant farming in Alabama during the

Great Depression of the 1930s. Agee and Walker Evans, the photographer assigned to the story, lived with two families in the most dire conditions of poverty for several weeks, and Agee became deeply involved with the subjects of his research for the article. His original article was rejected by the magazine, but Agee continued to work on it for years. The book-length, poetic work, eventually published in 1941, was an experimental and subjective expression of his intimate encounter with the human face of hunger and poverty. In this sense, Agee worked in the spirit of the Shakespearean determination to "expose thyself to feel what wretches feel," taking autobiography further away from a simple chronicling of events. Both Agee's and Mailer's works thus were significant landmarks in the recent development of autobiography.

ETHNIC AMERICAN AUTOBIOGRAPHY

American autobiography has by no means been limited to white males such as Agee and Mailer, Thoreau and Whitman, Franklin and Adams. There is a rich tradition of ethnic autobiography as well, beginning with African American slave narratives such as those by Frederick Douglass and Harriet Jacobs. Slave narratives were used as powerful tools by the pre–Civil War abolitionist movement in exposing the injustice and cruelty of slavery. After emancipation in the late 1800s, succeeding generations of African Americans recorded their experiences in such works as Booker T. Washington's *Up from Slavery* and the autobiographies of W.E.B. DuBois and Malcolm X. These testimonial-style African American autobiographies, as critic Elizabeth Schultz calls them, are largely shaped by the ideas they are trying to convey through the lives they describe. Although they are written by individuals about their own experiences, they are also works that speak about and for an entire group of people, giving them a communal voice.

On the other hand, there is a countertradition of African American autobiography, which Schultz refers to as the blues style, including Richard Wright's *Black Boy* (1945) and Zora Neale Hurston's *Dust Tracks on a Road* (1942). These maintain more characteristics of the oral, non-European culture (verbal storytelling) within the European form of the written autobiography. The blues autobiography is similar to the literary autobiography in that the author is more concerned with the subjective accuracy of the experience in his or her personal voice than with the objective validity and urgency of an idea in a communal voice, as in the testimonial autobiography. These works focus more on the individual and his or her own experience than the author's ethnic group and the group's experience.

The paradox of using European-style autobiography to represent and preserve a culture that may be incompatible with European culture is a major issue in Native American autobiographies such as *The Way to Rainy Mountain* (1969) and *The Names* (1976) by N. Scott Momaday and *Storyteller* (1981) by Leslie Marmon Silko. One reason for this incompatibility is that Native American culture de-emphasizes individual experience in favor of communal experience. Importance is attached to the way in which history and experience affects the native tribe as a whole. Native American writers are therefore less familiar with writing first-person narratives. In addition, most Native American tribes had no written language until recently, so they have no longstanding written tradition; their personal and communal narratives were traditionally passed down verbally from generation to generation.

Both Momaday and Silko are aware of the European autobiographical traditions on one hand and are consciously committed to maintaining their Native American heritage and identity on the other, resulting in highly unconventional autobiographies that preserve the tone of traditional Native American oral storytelling, but in written form. In a culture in which identity itself is so differently understood, autobiography is bound to be radically altered and enriched.

MINORITY AUTOBIOGRAPHY BRANCHES OUT

The field of ethnic American autobiography has been so highly cultivated over the last generation that African American and Native American autobiographies are only two of the five major branches that have been recognized and studied. The other three branches are Latino American (Piri Thomas, Richard Rodriguez, Gloria Anzaldua), Asian American (Jade Snow Wong, Maxine Hong Kingston), and Jewish American (Abraham Cahan, Henry Roth, Alfred Kazin). Each has its own substantial bibliography, its own set of conventions, and its own unfolding history.

Like numerous African American autobiographies, many ethnic American autobiographies either directly or indirectly address the wrongs and hardships their groups have endured as minorities. Ethnic authors have found it therapeutic to write about and share their burdens with others, and ethnic readers have found comfort in discovering that they are not alone in their circumstances. These readers have often embraced autobiographers as ethnic spokespeople for their groups. Ethnic autobiographies have also served as sources of information for many recent immigrants, who are more familiar with their culture of origin than with mainstream American culture. In the American "melting pot," the questions of origins, national identity, and assimilation have always been issues with minority groups. Ethnic autobiographies have addressed these issues and have given their writers and readers a greater sense of belonging in this diverse country. As long as cultural diversity is a recognized ideal of American society, ethnic autobiography will be an important tool of affirmation and awareness.

Although not ethnic in nature, gay and lesbian autobiography has more recently become an important branch of minority autobiography as well. A remarkable book in this category that clearly predates the late-twentieth-century gay liberation movement is Jean Genet's *The Thief's Journal* (1949). In it, Genet celebrates his homosexuality, violently antisocial attitudes, and criminal lifestyle, not his accomplishments as a novelist and playwright or his common humanity. In this extreme example of literary autobiography—in which a self is created rather than reflected—Genet constructs a self as an attack on society. Just as ethnic autobiographies affirm the experiences and identities of the oppressed, offering dignity and liberation through self-recognition, so do gay autobiographies such as those by Martin Duberman (*Cures: A Gay Man's Odyssey*), Paul Monette (*Becoming a Man*), and Mary Meigs (*Lily Briscoe, a Self-Portrait: An Autobiography by Mary Meigs*).

WOMEN'S AUTOBIOGRAPHIES

Whereas ethnic autobiographies are complicated by the simultaneous presence and the interplay within a single life of diverse cultures, the same can be said of many women's autobiographies. These books have revealed within a male-dominated society a female culture that calls into question conventional values and attitudes. According to critic Estelle

C. Jelinek, a comparative study of the autobiographies of men and women reveals that whereas a man tends to see his life as a unified story of an individual acting publicly in the world, a woman is inclined to see her life as a discontinuous and episodic series of relationships understood from within. Jelinek also notes that the tone of many men's autobiographies is bold and assertive, frequently focusing on their professional successes. Women's writings, on the other hand, are often understated, mirroring a quiet and private perseverance rather than a public conquest:

> Men tend to idealize their lives or to cast them into heroic molds to project their universal import. They may exaggerate, mythologize, or monumentalize their boyhood and their entire lives. . . . Women tend to write in a straightforward and objective manner. . . . They also write obliquely, elliptically, or humorously in order to camouflage their feelings, the same techniques used to play down their professional lives.

Some women's autobiographies, such as *An Unfinished Woman* (1969) and *Pentimento* (1973) by Lillian Hellman, reveal the conscious strategy of choosing male attitudes and values as a means of liberation. Hellman pursued activities traditionally reserved for men, including writing; she also embraced attitudes traditionally considered male attitudes, including a competitive nature. Other autobiographies, such as the *Diaries* (1966–1974) of Anaïs Nin, reveal the opposite strategy of exaggerating the female style in pursuit of freedom. Writing frankly about sex, for example, Nin uses her feminine wiles to gain attention and sympathy from men.

In choosing a life of radical activism, the Russian-American feminist Emma Goldman personified rebellion in the early part of the twentieth century. In the male-dominated world of politics, she was an anarchist and a public speaker who lobbied for social and Communist causes. Having been exiled from the United States for her political beliefs, Goldman wished to return as she worked on her autobiography, *Living My Life,* in the late 1920s. She used her writing to redefine herself and put herself in a more positive light by American standards. According to critic Blanche H. Gelfant, Goldman's autobiography helped her revise her image by projecting a more pro-American political attitude, by softening her attitudes toward violence and sex, and by taking on a more nurturing, less aggressive tone.

Anthropologist Margaret Mead's autobiography, *Blackberry Winter* (1972), demonstrates the profound influence of her mother and grandmother in teaching the female values of relatedness, nurturing, and inner strength, which served her well in later life experiences. Other major women's autobiographies are *Out of Africa* (1937) by the Danish Karen Blixen, known by the pseudonym Isak Dinesen; *Memories of a Catholic Girlhood* (1957) by the American Mary McCarthy; and *Memoirs of a Dutiful Daughter* (1958) by the French Simone de Beauvoir. All of these autobiographies are written in a way that, according to Jelinek, is more honest and introspective than traditional male autobiographies.

Maya Angelou's *I Know Why the Caged Bird Sings* (1970) is an autobiography that speaks urgently to a variety of issues: ethnicity, sexuality, gender, abuse, victimization, and, ultimately, triumphant self-creation. Although Angelou is an actress, poet, and critic, it is her remarkable African American woman's autobiography that has earned her the most attention—and, indeed, made her a celebrity. It is through her autobiography that Angelou is known by the world, as the self that came into being through the book. In addition, it is an African American blues-style autobiography in which an individual voice is developed within a communal voice; *I Know Why the Caged Bird Sings* speaks not only for and about Angelou but also indirectly for and about millions of African Americans. And it is a woman's autobiography, focused on the traditionally female and maternal theme of relationships, from the bond with her brother at the beginning of the book to the bond with her baby at the end.

AUTOBIOGRAPHICAL STAGES OVER THE CENTURIES

Angelou's book and autobiographies dating back to St. Augustine fall into one or more loosely defined categories that have been established to describe this broad genre. According to critic William Spengemann, the development of autobiography occurred in four basic stages. In stage one, when the concept and word appeared, there was an emphasis on a chronology of events, as in early biographies. These chronological narratives are explanations of a person's life and are known as historical autobiographies. A prominent example is Benjamin Franklin's *Autobiography.*

Historical autobiographies like Franklin's were soon augmented by a new emphasis on the inner life of philosophy. In stage two, works that tackled not only the tangible and chronological but also the intangible issues of the inner mind were called philosophical autobiographies. Autobiographical works such as Thoreau's *Walden* would present themselves not as an explanation of the events in their lives but as a search for the ultimate truth of the writer's inner self. These works do not just present facts; they ask questions about the nature of God, man, and existence. They are concerned with the spiritual lives of their authors. Rousseau's forms of soul-searching and extreme self-revelation make his *Confessions* an early example of the philosophical autobiography. Likewise, many testimonial-style African American autobiographies, which focus on the larger picture of conveying the writers' main ideas instead of just recounting events, are also philosophical autobiographies.

In stage three, these philosophical autobiographies took a turn further inward in the development of subjective and imaginative works, or literary autobiographies. For example, Irishman James Joyce's "The Dead," written in the early twentieth century, is neither a historical explanation nor a philosophical search but rather a literary expression of Joyce's self. Joyce himself is not a character in "The Dead," but he is clearly represented in his leading male character. He expresses notions about himself and his ideals, along with those of people he has known in his real life, through the actions of his characters. As mentioned earlier, the American writers Hemingway, Agee, and Kerouac, among others, have played a major role in the development of the philosophical autobiography.

In stage four, the self is neither explained, searched for, nor expressed; it is created in the second kind of literary autobiography—because a particular persona of a particular writer exists nowhere else but in his or her autobiography. The first three stages assume that a writer's identity exists independently of and prior to the autobiography; these stages differ in how they reveal that identity (explaining, searching, expressing). But in the fourth and final stage—as in American Sylvia Plath's 1966 book of poems, *Ariel,* for example—the self is so profoundly reshaped by the autobiography that it cannot be said to exist in its ultimate form prior to or independently of the creation of the autobiography. The intensely personal creative process inherent in writing autobiography has shaped its author's ideas and personality in the course of writing it. Angelou's *I Know Why the Caged Bird Sings* is a major example of Spengemann's second kind of literary autobiography, in which the self is actually created in the autobiography. By the end of the book, Angelou is neither a poor orphaned child nor a downtrodden black woman; she is a self-assured American who embraces her life and her experiences in order to move forward in a positive way.

AUTOBIOGRAPHY VERSUS AUTOBIOGRAPHICAL WRITING

Spengemann's four stages show that the evolution of autobiographical writing goes well beyond the original concept of the word *autobiography*, a narrow label meaning the author's life story as a kind of nonfiction history. Numerous examples demonstrate that autobiographical writing has often come to transcend the original definition as a simple chronicle. But regardless of how the genre has changed over the centuries, it is clear that writers' experimentation with or manipulation of their content does not change the work's autobiographical nature.

Traditional autobiography covered a person's life from birth to the time of writing, yet Thoreau's *Walden* makes virtually no reference to his childhood, his family, or his development as a person. Rather, it is concerned exclusively with a single two-and-a-half-year experience in his life. Traditional autobiography is also rooted in facts and dates, yet in the book Thoreau falsifies the experience (for artistic reasons) as having taken a single year; therefore, it is no kind of history, and it is not even, strictly speaking, nonfiction.

Walden thus demonstrates how various forms of autobiography have evolved and branched out into other literary forms. Joyce's "The Dead" is a short story, and Plath's *Ariel* is a collection of poems. In addition to autobiographical fiction and poetry, there is autobiographical drama as well, such as Eugene O'Neill's classic American play *Long Day's Journey into Night* (1956). This play involves a leading character who is a wife and a mother addicted to morphine; O'Neill's mother was also a morphine addict. Although these literary works would not be classified in the autobiography section of a bookstore, they are all profoundly autobiographical in their source material and in their projections of complex selves.

Similarly, two of Charles Dickens's most well known works—*David Copperfield* and *Great Expectations*—are classic autobiographical novels of this nature. Both the protagonists and the plots are modeled after Dickens's own experience. And the themes of poverty, class, and upward mobility—major issues in Dickens's own life—are at the center of each novel. Following Dickens a century later, among the great literary autobiographers of the twentieth century are Marcel Proust, Thomas Mann, and Virginia Woolf.

NEWER FORMS OF AUTOBIOGRAPHICAL WRITING

Like other forms of autobiography, the memoir shifted somewhat in the twentieth century away from its origins with Cellini five centuries earlier. Just as the autobiography in general has turned from external history to internal thought, philosophy, and psychology in defining the author's identity, the specific genre of the memoir has shifted in emphasis from the outside world of public affairs and personalities to the writer's own subjectivity. Contemporary memoirs are rarely historically organized; instead, the writer typically chooses a particular narrow period of his or her life and tries to recall it. This attempt to recapture his or her past is not in order to recover the objects of perception, but rather to recover the perceptions themselves and ultimately the elusive past self of the writer. In the 1970s Annie Dillard attracted attention to the literary memoir with her *Walden*-like *Pilgrim at Tinker Creek,* followed in the 1980s by her memoir of growing up, *An American Childhood.* Likewise, two of the most celebrated books of the 1990s were memoirs of this type: *The Liars' Club* by Mary Karr and *Angela's Ashes* by Frank McCourt.

The present state of autobiography also reflects the impact of women's culture in the emergence of "collaborative" autobiographies, written by more than one author. These are not stories told by individuals about their professional conquests, as in the traditional male-oriented autobiography; rather, they are by and about two partners in a relationship (husband/wife, siblings, parent/child, etc.), as in a more traditionally female-oriented context. A pioneering example of the relationship-focused autobiography is Gertrude Stein's *The Autobiography of Alice B. Toklas* (1933). As opposed to traditional autobiographies that focus on an individual's experience, collaborative autobiographies de-emphasize the individual as experiencer and writer. In this way, they are similar to Native American autobiographies, frequently focusing on communal rather than individual experience.

The genre's greater inclusiveness is also reflected in the appearance of autobiographical works in new and unconventional media, among them comic books. Fifty years after World War II, Art Spiegelman collaborated with his parents to create *Maus*, which details his parents' lives in the concentration camps of Nazi Germany. In it, his characters are represented as animals: The Jews are mice, and the Nazi guards are cats. Harvey Pekar's *American Splendor* is another autobiographical comic book, and in *Our Cancer Year* he collaborates with his wife in writing about his discovery of and medical treatments for cancer. Both comic books were published in the 1990s. The colorful and playful medium of comics may seem an unlikely outlet for such weighty subjects as the Holocaust and cancer, but as with other forms of autobiography (particularly ethnic American works), writing about and sharing the burden of painful experiences can be used in a therapeutic way.

THE FUTURE OF AUTOBIOGRAPHY

As evidenced in the variety of autobiographical writing styles, the future of autobiography seems to be aimed at still greater inclusiveness and an ever wider range of autobiographical forms. Once considered a minor subgenre, autobiography has grown into a major literary form with many of its own subgenres. From the reverential *Confessions* of St. Augustine to comic books of the late twentieth century, autobiography has steadily developed in new, if not surprising, ways. But regardless of the form, all autobiographies have at their core a strong focus on the authors' lives, ideas, and attitudes about what they have done and witnessed.

Autobiography's increasing significance corresponds to its historical pattern of development: growing more broadly and creatively as a concept and finding ever newer forms. The vitality of this dynamic process points to autobiography's continued importance, both as a way of writing and thinking and as a literary genre.

CHAPTER 1

Forms of Autobiography

 Autobiography

The Cultural Values Necessary for the Creation of Autobiography

Georges Gusdorf

Georges Gusdorf, professor emeritus of philosophy at the University of Strasbourg, identifies the specific cultural values necessary for the creation of autobiography—personal freedom, self-knowledge, and the potential heroism of any individual human life. These are the values of post-Renaissance European and American democracies. St. Augustine's fifth-century *Confessions* exemplifies how Christian confession became a medium for autobiographical writing long before the term "autobiography" was used. Later French pioneers of first-person writing— Michel de Montaigne in the sixteenth century and Jean Jacques Rousseau in the eighteenth century— secularized the confession, leading to the first autobiographies to be called by that name.

First of all, it is necessary to point out that the genre of autobiography seems limited in time and in space; it has not always existed nor does it exist everywhere. If Augustine's *Confessions* offer us a brilliantly successful landmark right at the beginning, one nevertheless recognizes immediately that this is a late phenomenon in Western culture, coming at that moment when the Christian contribution was grafted onto classical traditions. Moreover, it would seem that autobiography is not to be found outside of our cultural area; one would say that it expresses a concern peculiar to Western man, a concern that has been of good use in his systematic conquest of the universe and that he has communicated to

Excerpted from Georges Gusdorf, "Conditions and Limits of Autobiography," in *Autobiography: Essays Theoretical and Critical*, edited by James Olney. Copyright © 1980 Princeton University Press. Reprinted with permission from Princeton University Press.

men of other cultures; but those men will thereby have been annexed by a sort of intellectual colonizing to a mentality that was not their own. When Gandhi tells his own story, he is using Western means to defend the East.

THE INDIVIDUAL VERSUS THE COMMUNITY

The concern, which seems natural to us, to turn back on one's own past, to recollect one's life in order to narrate it, is not at all universal. It asserts itself only in recent centuries and only on a small part of the map of the world. The man who takes delight in thus drawing his own image believes himself worthy of a special interest. Each of us tends to think of himself as the center of a living space: I count, my existence is significant to the world, and my death will leave the world incomplete. In narrating my life, I give witness of myself even from beyond my death and so can preserve this precious capital that ought not disappear. The author of an autobiography gives a sort of relief to his image by reference to the environment with its independent existence; he looks at himself being and delights in being looked at—he calls himself as witness for himself; others he calls as witness for what is irreplaceable in his presence.

This conscious awareness of the singularity of each individual life is the late product of a specific civilization. Throughout most of human history, the individual does not oppose himself to all others; he does not feel himself to exist outside of others, and still less against others, but very much *with* others in an interdependent existence that asserts its rhythms everywhere in the community. No one is rightful possessor of his life or his death; lives are so thoroughly entangled that each of them has its center everywhere and its circumference nowhere. The important unit is thus never the isolated being—or, rather, isolation is impossible in such a scheme of total cohesiveness as this. Community life unfolds like a great drama, with its climactic moments originally fixed by the gods being repeated from age to age. Each man thus appears as the possessor of a rôle, already performed by the ancestors and to be performed again by descendants. The number of rôles is limited, and this is expressed by a limited number of names. Newborn children receive the names of the deceased whose rôles, in a sense, they perform again, and so the community maintains a continuous self-identity in spite of the constant renewal of individuals who constitute it.

It is obvious that autobiography is not possible in a cultural landscape where consciousness of self does not, properly speaking, exist. But this unconsciousness of personality, characteristic of primitive societies such as ethnologists describe to us, lasts also in more advanced civilizations that subscribe to mythic structures, they too being governed by the principle of repetition. Theories of eternal recurrence, accepted in various guises as dogma by the majority of the great cultures of antiquity, fix attention on that which remains, not on that which passes. "That which is," according to the wisdom of Ecclesiastes, "is that which has been, and there is nothing new under the sun." Likewise, beliefs in the transmigration of souls—beliefs to be found throughout the Indo-European sphere—grant to the nodes of temporal existence only a sort of negative value. The wisdom of India considers personality an evil illusion and seeks salvation in depersonalization.

Autobiography becomes possible only under certain metaphysical preconditions. To begin with, at the cost of a cultural revolution humanity must have emerged from the mythic framework of traditional teachings and must have entered into the perilous domain of history. The man who takes the trouble to tell of himself knows that the present differs from the past and that it will not be repeated in the future; he has become more aware of differences than of similarities; given the constant change, given the uncertainty of events and of men, he believes it a useful and valuable thing to fix his own image so that he can be certain it will not disappear like all things in this world. History then would be the memory of a humanity heading toward unforeseeable goals, struggling against the breakdown of forms and of beings. Each man matters to the world, each life and each death; the witnessing of each about himself enriches the common cultural heritage.

The curiosity of the individual about himself, the wonder that he feels before the mystery of his own destiny, is thus tied to the Copernican Revolution: at the moment it enters into history, humanity, which previously aligned its development to the great cosmic cycles, finds itself engaged in an autonomous adventure; soon mankind even brings the domain of the sciences into line with its own reckoning, organizing them, by means of technical expertise, according to its own desires. Henceforth, man knows himself a responsible agent:

gatherer of men, of lands, of power, maker of kingdoms or of empires, inventor of laws or of wisdom, he along adds consciousness to nature, leaving there the sign of his presence. The historic personage now appears, and biography, taking its place alongside monuments, inscriptions, statues, is one manifestation of his desire to endure in men's memory. Famous men—heroes and princes—acquire a sort of literary and pedagogical immortality in those exemplary "Lives" written for the edification of future centuries.

A SPIRITUAL REVOLUTION

But biography, which is thus established as a literary genre, provides only an exterior presentation of great persons, reviewed and corrected by the demands of propaganda and by the general sense of the age. The historian finds himself removed from his model by the passage of time—at least, this is most often true, and it is always true that he is at a great social distance from his model. He is conscious of performing a public and official function similar to that of the artist who sculpts or paints the likeness of a powerful man of the day, posed most flatteringly as determined by current conventions. The appearance of autobiography implies a new spiritual revolution: the artist and the model coincide, the historian tackles himself as object. That is to say, he considers himself a great person, worthy of men's remembrance even though in fact he is only a more or less obscure intellectual. Here a new social area that turns classes about and readjusts values comes into play. Montaigne had a certain prominence, but was descended from a family of merchants; Rousseau, no more than a common citizen of Geneva, was a kind of literary adventurer; yet both of them, in spite of their lowly station on the stage of the world, considered their destiny worthy of being given by way of example. Our interest is turned from public to private history: alongside the great men who act out the official history of humanity, there are obscure men who conduct the campaign of their spiritual life within their breast, carrying on silent battles whose ways and means, whose triumphs and reversals also merit being preserved in the universal memory.

This conversion is late in coming insofar as it corresponds to a difficult evolution—or rather to an *in*volution of consciousness. The truth is that one is wonderstruck by everything else much sooner than by the self. One wonders at what one sees, but one does not see oneself. If exterior space—the stage of the world—is a light, clear space where everyone's behavior, movements, and motives are quite plain on first sight, interior space is shadowy in its very essence. The subject who seizes on himself for object inverts the natural direction of attention; it appears that in acting thus he violates certain secret taboos of human nature. Sociology, depth psychology, psychoanalysis have revealed the complex and agonizing sense that the encounter of a man with his image carries. The image is another "myself," a double of my being but more fragile and vulnerable, invested with a sacred character that makes it at once fascinating and frightening. Narcissus, contemplating his face in the fountain's depth, is so fascinated with the apparition that he would die bending toward himself. According to most folklore and myth, the apparition of the double is a death sign.

THE REFLECTION IN THE MIRROR

Mythic taboos underline the disconcerting character of the discovery of the self. Nature did not foresee the encounter of man with his reflection, and it is as if she tried to prevent this reflection from appearing. The invention of the mirror would seem to have disrupted human experience, especially from that moment when the mediocre metal plates that were used in antiquity gave way at the end of the Middle Ages to silver-backed mirrors produced by Venetian technique. From that moment, the image in the mirror became a part of the scene of life, and psychoanalysts have brought out the major role that this image plays in the child's gradual consciousness of his own personality. From the age of six months, the human infant is particularly interested in this reflection of himself, which would leave an animal indifferent. Little by little the infant discovers an essential aspect of his identity: he distinguishes that which is without from his own within, he sees himself as another among others; he is situated in social space, at the heart of which he will become capable of reshaping his own reality.

The primitive who has not been forewarned is frightened of his reflection in the mirror, just as he is terrified by a photographic or motion-picture image. The child of civilization, on the other hand, has had all the leisure necessary to make himself at home with the changing garments of appearances that he has clothed himself in under the alluring influence of the mirror. And yet even an adult, whether man or woman, if he reflects on it a little, rediscovers beyond this confrontation with himself the turmoil and fascination of Narcissus. The first sound image from the tape recorder, the animated image of the cinema, awaken the same anguish in the depths of our life. The author of an autobiography masters this anxiety by submitting to it; beyond all the images, he follows unceasingly the call of his own being. Thus with Rembrandt, who was fascinated by his Venetian mirror and as a result endlessly multiplied his self-portraits (like Van Gogh later)—witnessings by himself about himself and evidence of the impassioned new disquiet of modern man, fierce to elucidate the mystery of his own personality.

THE RISE OF CHRISTIANITY AND SELF-EXAMINATION

If it is indeed true that autobiography is the mirror in which the individual reflects his own image, one must nevertheless acknowledge that the genre appeared before the technical achievements of German and Italian artisans. At the edge of modern times, the physical and material appeal of the reflection in the mirror bolsters and strengthens the tradition of self-examination of Christian asceticism. Augustine's *Confessions* answer to this new spiritual orientation by contrast to the great philosophic systems of classical antiquity—Epicurean, for example, or Stoic—that contented themselves with a disciplinary notion of individual being and argued that one should seek salvation in adhering to a universal and transcendent law without any regard for the mysteries (which anyway were unsuspected) of interior life. Christianity brings a new anthropology to the fore: every destiny, however humble it be, assumes a kind of supernatural stake. Christian destiny unfolds as a dialogue of the soul with God in which, right up to the end, every action, every initiative of thought or of conduct, can call everything back into question. Each man is accountable for his own existence, and intentions weigh as heavily as acts—whence a new fascination with the secret springs of personal life. The rule requiring confession of sins gives to self-examination a character at once systematic and necessary. Augustine's great book is a consequence of this dogmatic requirement: a soul of genius presents his balance sheet before God in all humility—but also in full rhetorical splendor.

During the Christian centuries of the Western Middle Ages, the penitent, following in the footsteps of Augustine, could scarcely do anything but plead guilty before his Creator. The theological mirror of the Christian soul is a deforming mirror that plays up without pity the slightest faults of the moral personality. The most elementary rule of humility requires the faithful to discover traces of sin everywhere and to suspect beneath the more or less appealing exterior of the individual person the horrid decay of the flesh, the hideous rotting of Ligier Richier's *Skeleton:* every man is uncovered to reveal a potential participant in the *Dance of Death.* Here again, as with primitives, man cannot look on his own image without anguish. It was to require the exploding of the medieval Romania—the Renaissance and the Reformation—before man could have any interest in seeing himself as he is without any taint of the transcendent. The Venetian mirror provides the restless Rembrandt with an image of himself that is neither twisted nor flattering. Renascent man puts forth on the oceans in search of new continents and men of nature. Montaigne discovers in himself a new world, a man of nature, naked and artless, whose confessions he gives us in his *Essays,* but without penitence.

The *Essays* were to be one of the gospels of the modern spirituality. Freed of all doctrinal allegiance, in a world well on its way to becoming secularized, the autobiographer assumes the task of bringing out the most hidden aspects of individual being. The new age practises the virtue of *individuality* particularly dear to the great men of the Renaissance, champions of free enterprise in art as in morals, in finance and in technical affairs as in philosophy. The *Life* of Cellini, artist and adventurer, testifies to this new freedom of the individual who believes that all things are permitted to him. Beyond the rediscovered disciplines of the classical period, the Romantic era, in its exaltation of genius, reintroduced the taste for autobiography. The virtue of individuality is completed by the virtue of *sincerity,* which Rousseau adopts from Montaigne: the heroism of understanding and telling all, reenforced even more by the teachings of psychoanalysis, takes on, in the eyes of our contemporaries, an increasing value. Complexities, contradictions, and aberrations do not cause hesitation or repugnance but a kind of wonderment. And in a profoundly secular sense, Gide repeats the Psalmist's exclamation: "I praise thee, O my God, for making me a creature so marvellous."

The Literary Confession and Its Religious Model

Susanna Egan

Susanna Egan, an English professor at the University of British Columbia and the author of two books on autobiography, outlines the features of the eighteenth- and nineteenth-century literary confession that were borrowed from earlier religious confessions. One is the focus on a guilty narrator who gets relief through telling his story and knowing himself, but who must describe states of mind normally kept private. Another is the feeling of dramatic tension between the narrator and God or the devil in religious confessions, and between the narrator and his audience in literary confessions.

We can say of confession . . . that it derives from situations common to the human psyche . . . and we can also describe equivalences and analogues that explain the usefulness of this form to the nineteenth-century autobiographer who has an entirely personal story to tell. Like conversion, confession receives its most immediate definition from Christianity, specifically from Catholicism. As with conversion, the process of confession need have no connection with religion beyond the contribution of religion to the metaphor. . . . For [Samuel Taylor Coleridge's poetic character] the Ancient Mariner who stoppeth one of three, revealing or confessing his soul consists simply in catching his audience, however busy that audience may otherwise be, and telling his story. So urgent is the story to be told that the anxious wedding guest sits down on a stone to listen; he cannot choose but hear. [French philosopher Jean Jacques] Rousseau appends a paragraph to his *Confessions* describing the occasion on which he read his *Confessions* to an illustrious assembly

Excerpted from Susanna Egan, *Patterns of Experience in Autobiography*. Copyright © 1984 The University of North Carolina Press. Reprinted with permission from the publisher.

and then challenged anyone present to find him a dishonorable man. Notably, everyone "was silent.". . .

THE BURDEN OF GUILT AND NEUROSES

The Mariner is burdened with terrible guilt after killing the albatross. His story is a form of confession; its narration acts as catharsis equivalent to absolution. Rousseau, too, is burdened with many specific instances of private guilt and with imputations by society of guilt where he feels himself to be innocent; he, too, derives considerable satisfaction from making his story known. [German poet and novelist Johann Wolfgang von] Goethe recognizes the parallel between the relief enjoyed by the absolved Catholic and the relief that can be found in literary confession; in a letter to [his colleague] Göttling dated Weimar, 4 March 1826, he suggests that Protestants may be more prone to autobiography than Catholics who can turn to a confessor.

Whereas the Catholic repents his sin and seeks absolution to relieve him of its burden, literary confession simply eliminates the burden of sin or guilt, or translates it into the burden of neuroses. Literary confession may express regret. It may demonstrate the painful acquisition of maturity, which in terms of character formation may be equated with amendment, but it does not need to share the assumption that what is found in the soul is sinful. Literary confession, in other words, shares with religious confession the pursuit of truth about the self through rigorous self-examination, but it does not need to share the contrition or penance.

The psyche needs salving as urgently as the soul needs saving, and the story that one tells follows essentially the same pattern, whether it is told to the priest, or the analyst, or as literary confession before many witnesses. . . .

Literary confession shares with religious confession a central emphasis on the (guilty) self. Literary and religious confession alike travel from sin to redemption and enact their own penance and thanksgiving. ("The sacrifices of God," sings the contrite King David, "are a broken spirit: a broken and a contrite heart, O God, thou wilt not despise.") . . . Literary and religious confession describe places and states of mind that are radically different from the present. Their perspective on the past helps to shape the narrative.

Saint Augustine has established the model for examination of conscience, for rigorous pursuit of thoughts and feelings back to their source in the depths of his psyche. Examination of conscience and confession of what is found there distinguishes confessional literature, like confessional speech, from the general run of communication between people; it says that which is not normally said, shares that which is usually hidden. William Hale White [author of *The Autobiography of Mark Rutherford*] describes both the urgency and the intimacy that are appropriate: "Direct appeal to God," he writes, "can only be justified when it is passionate. To come maundering into His presence when we have nothing particular to say is an insult, upon which we should never presume if we had a petition to offer to any earthly personage." Confession recognizes appropriate times for saying certain things about oneself that one would not normally say. The occasion is filled with awe, the account is in some way prodigious. "For behold," Saint Augustine tells God, "Thou lovest the truth, and he that doth it, cometh to the light. This would I do in my heart before Thee in confession: and in my writing, before many witnesses."

It becomes necessary at this point to establish that confession represents more than a statement of past sin. The fact of its existence presupposes a faith. Confession can mean simply a profession of faith: "Every tongue shall confess that Jesus Christ is Lord, to the glory of God the Father" [Philippians 2:11], or, "I will confess his name before my Father, and before his angels" [Revelation 3:5]. Confession, then, merges with testimony, which is a motivating force for works as different as those by Saint Augustine, [English spiritual writer John] Bunyan [*Grace Abounding*], and Rousseau. Persecution of early Christians and of seventeenth-century sectarians provides a common cause for such a testament, so that confession can also imply a righteous defense of oneself in the light of the faith one wishes to promulgate and glorify. . . .

THE IMPORTANCE OF THE AUDIENCE

We have seen how literary and religious confessions share the emotional need to unburden the self by exploring states of mind. (In general, as Saint Augustine realizes, "men go abroad to admire the heights of mountains, the mighty billows of the sea, the broad tides of rivers, the compass of the ocean, and the circuits of the stars, and pass themselves by.") Unburdening, however, is not effective without an audience, and the audience needs to be clearly established by or within the text. Confession is necessarily a dialogue: the Catholic penitent talks to God through the priest; Saint Augustine speaks to God with a human audience as witness; [Italian poet] Petrarch turns to Saint Augustine and the silent witness of the Lady Truth; Rousseau turns to society; and George Moore, in his *Confessions of a Young Man,* positively attacks his "hypocrite lecteur."

One final, important connection between religious and literary confession may be described as dramatic conflict or tension. This can take the form of dramatic confrontation: between Saint Augustine and God, Bunyan and the devil, Petrarch and Saint Augustine. Such conflict is an aspect of the dialogue form and of that perspective on the past that enables a known result to be juxtaposed with the difficulties preventing its achievement. It is seen at its most direct in *The Confessions of Saint Augustine* and in Bunyan's *Grace Abounding,* where past sins and present graces are most directly perceived. Rousseau and [English essayist and critic Thomas]

CONFESSION AND COMMUNITY

Poet and critic Stephen Spender, in his article "Confessions and Autobiography," asserts that a confession always comes from an isolated individual seeking wholeness with the human community.

All confessions are from subject to object, from the individual to the community or creed. Even the most shamelessly revealed inner life pleads its cause before the moral system of an outer, objective life. One of the things that the most abysmal confessions prove is the incapacity of even the most outcast creature to be alone. Indeed, the essence of the confession is that the one who feels outcast pleads with humanity to relate his isolation to its wholeness. He pleads to be forgiven, condoned, even condemned, so long as he is brought back into the wholeness of people and things. . . .

But no one confesses to meanness, cowardice, vanity, pettiness: or at least not unless he is assured that his crime, instead of excluding him from humanity, brings him back into the moral fold.

Stephen Spender, "Confessions and Autobiography" in *Autobiography: Essays Theoretical and Critical.* Ed. James Olney. Princeton, NJ: Princeton University Press, 1980, pp. 120–21.

De Quincey exercise a subtler form of tension that is woven less visibly into the narrative in the form of fate or "echo-augury" controlling their lives. Tension is also an aspect of the need to unburden oneself of sin. De Quincey, rating his own *Confessions* in this respect above those of Saint Augustine and Rousseau, believes that the very idea of breathing a record of human passion into the confessional suggests an impassioned theme. . . .

Saint Augustine begins book 2 by calling to mind "my past foulness, and the carnal corruptions of my soul; not because I love them, but that I may love Thee, O my God." Petrarch is notably less God-centered, but he is still concerned with the state of his soul. His dialogue ends with the wish that "I may raise up no cloud of dust before my eyes; and with my mind calmed down and at peace, I may hear the world grow still and silent, and the winds of adversity die away." Bunyan's purpose, like Saint Paul's, is specifically hieratic: "Indeed I have been as one sent to them from the dead; I went my self in chains to preach to them in chains, and carried that fire in my own conscience that I perswaded them to beware of." His *Grace Abounding* represents the spoils of his battle with the devil now dedicated to "maintain the house of God."

THE CONFESSION MOVES TOWARD THE NOVEL

These three stand in marked contrast to Rousseau, who is entirely concerned with himself in a social rather than a divine context. Rousseau exonerates personal guilt by displaying himself as he has been:

> as vile and despicable when my behaviour was such, as good, generous, and noble when I was so. . . . So let the numberless legion of my fellow men gather round me, and hear my confessions. Let them groan at my depravities, and blush for my misdeeds. But let each one of them reveal his heart at the foot of Thy throne with equal sincerity, and may any man who dares, say "I was a better man than he."

Moore may not have read Rousseau, but he virtually echoes him: "You, hypocritical reader, who are now turning up your eyes and murmuring 'horrid young man'—examine your weakly heart, and see what divides us." In his 1917 preface, Moore claims that he had not known of Rousseau at the time of first writing his *Confessions* and so wrote without a model, but he pays direct homage to De Quincey and writes in the

1889 preface: "St. Augustine wrote the story of a god-tortured soul; would it not be interesting to write the story of an art-tortured soul?"

These more modern confessions are secular, even anti-religious, and essentially self-centered. Addressed to the public rather than to God, they move closer to the novel in tone and emphasis.

Montaigne's *Essays:* A Method of Knowing the Self

James Olney

James Olney, Voorhies professor of English and professor of French and Italian at Louisiana State University, has been one of the most influential and admired commentators on autobiography, from his *Metaphors of Self* (1972) to his *Narrative and Memory* (1998). In this excerpt, Olney explains that sixteenth-century essayist Michel de Montaigne's commitment to subjectivity, his insistence that reality is mental, establishes a cornerstone of modern Western philosophy. Montaigne's *Essays* offer a vivid self-portrait that is so profoundly autobiographical and universal that it feels as though it is the reader's own self-portrait.

[I]t is not his subjects or even his thought that make Montaigne peculiarly available to us in the twentieth century and that make him uniquely valuable in a discussion of autobiography and art. Though the later essays in particular are extraordinarily attractive in the quality of their philosophy, what draws and holds our attention is less Montaigne's thought than his practice and the implications of that practice; it is the bent of his character, his special viewpoint, the way he thinks that speaks so much to us and that, across four centuries, brings him closer to us and our temper than many writers who are much nearer in time. . . . As Montaigne made himself in making his book—and in revisions remade both together—so the reader creates and recreates himself (not Montaigne) in his response to the *Essays*. We go with Montaigne into himself and—fortuitous paradox—find there ourselves. As Montaigne, portraying the way of his life, discovers how to live, so we can follow his portrait in humanity to rediscover the way (which may properly be quite different from Montaigne's way) for ourselves. Or, perhaps more accurately, we should say that Montaigne is leading the moral life in the very search for it, and that, following his search, searching too, we likewise come finally to realize that the search *is* the moral life and the way, therefore, the end. This, I think, is why we reread the *Essays*—and there can be no better reason—and each time find them almost infinitely rich and continuously new. . . .

THE STYLE IS THE MAN

Montaigne takes for his subject his complete but constantly changing self: whatever the title of individual pieces (titles that are often irrelevant to Montaigne's intention and practice), the book is *Essays* in thinking, in feeling, and in being, *Essays* trying or testing the nature of reality as subjectively, privately experienced, *Essays* that record Montaigne's experiments in living and his alone. "Le style," the French proverb says, "c'est l'homme" ["the style is the man"], and since Montaigne takes "l'homme" for his subject, the terms are endlessly intertwined and bound up together in the essential process of self-realization and self-projection: Montaigne's subject is his self, his self is his style, and his style and his subject are one. "In modeling this figure upon myself," Montaigne declares . . .

> I have had to fashion and compose myself so often to bring myself out, that the model itself has to some extent grown firm and taken shape. . . . I have no more made my book than my book has made me—a book consubstantial with its author, concerned with my own self, an integral part of my life ("Of giving the lie").

Montaigne thus lands, not half-heartedly or half-way but with both feet and right in the center, on the subject that has preoccupied modern philosophy, modern poetry, modern psychology—and, as Alfred North Whitehead points out in *Science and the Modern World*, even modern theology:

> Modern philosophy is tinged with subjectivism, as against the objective attitude of the ancients. The same change is to be seen in religion. In the early history of the Christian Church, the theological interest centered in discussion on the nature of God, the meaning of Incarnation, and apocalyptic forecasts of the ultimate fate of the world. At the Reformation, the Church was torn asunder by dissension as to the individual experiences of believers in respect to justification. The individual subject of experience had been substituted for the total drama

of reality. Luther asked, "How am I justified?"; modern philosophers have asked, "How do I have knowledge?" The emphasis lies upon the subject of experience.

Montaigne does not precisely "substitute," and so push the "total drama of reality" out of the realm of philosophy, but in the view that he gives us the "subject of experience"—the self or the "I"—is the only subject realistically accessible to human study. Individual experience becomes the only source of knowledge that is at all sure, and that too is dangerously touchy and uncertain. . . . In the theatre of the individual, "the total drama of reality" is enacted for Montaigne, and the viewpoint of his modern philosophy constitutes not so much a substitution as an identification, not so much a turning aside from the study of reality as a sharpened refocusing inward before outward, or outward only through the inward.

How, one might ask, does Montaigne come to spring thus full-blown, with a single leap and unaided, into modern subjectivity? The full answer is there to be followed in the *Essays.* "In fine," Montaigne says of his book in his last and greatest essay, "all this fricassee that I am scribbling here is nothing but a record of the essays of my life" ("Of experience"). His essence as an autobiographer and his value in a discussion of autobiographic art may well lie in this: that Montaigne's philosophy is one of enactment rather than precept. . . .

SELF-AWARENESS AS A PRECURSOR TO AUTOBIOGRAPHY

It is the given condition of life for each of us to go on "flowing and rolling unceasingly," watching all things flash by smudged and clouded windows of observation, unable to grasp the least of them in sure judgment. One thing only is constant in the process, one thing only accompanies unceasingly the flow and roll: consciousness. But the self and consciousness are inseparable, for coherent self is the result of the process of consciousness. The two go on simultaneously, or, more truly, they go on without regard to limits of time and space: the self comes into existence as it becomes conscious or aware of itself, and self-awareness comes about and advances only as it has an object, the self, to be aware of. Since he must forever roll anyway, Montaigne chooses to roll where rolling is best, and he mounts the drama of all reality on a new stage, an epitome stage of the self, on which one might view the "total drama" in summary and symbolic form:

The world always looks straight ahead; as for me, I turn my gaze inward, I fix it there and keep it busy. Everyone looks in front of him; as for me, I look inside of me; I have no business but with myself; I continually observe myself, I take stock of myself, I taste myself. Others always go elsewhere, if they stop to think about it; they always go forward; as for me, I roll about in myself ("Of presumption"). . . .

The whole duty of man lies in the making of the self according to its own natural laws and necessities: to say that this is an exclusively modern philosophy would not be quite just (the Greeks, after all, are said to have thought of everything first, and in this particular idea they had the assistance of the Delphic oracle: "Know thyself"). But to found, in the Montaignesque way, all philosophy in autobiography; to plunge into subjectivity as wholly and intensely as Montaigne does; to refuse any other subject than the self as completely as he does—this symbolizes the historical tendency of philosophic concerns since the Reformation. . . .

KNOWING MONTAIGNE AND KNOWING OURSELVES

Montaigne is the writer who tells us everything about himself—we know this is so because he tells us that he tells us everything. He is said to be the man that we know as well as ourselves and better than our friends. Can this be so, and in what sense? Surely it goes directly against our normal understanding. . . . The effect of his art—and the reason why he does not describe actions or deeds but tries instead to capture mental and spiritual quality in a manner and a style, in anecdote and argument—is to make the reader identify with Montaigne's essential self, not in the life but in the autobiographical art, so that we do not respond to what he did in the past but to what he is in the present of his book. As with any work of art, we tend to live into the experience of the *Essays* and come to identify that experience with our own, which would only be possible if Montaigne were creating a coherent, artistic portrait, valid for the reach of humanity, rather than a record of events true only for one man. Whereas our lives and those of our friends may be incoherent as experienced, in order to draw our response Montaigne's portrait, though it be of inconsistent and variable spirit, must be coherent in capturing that inconsistency and unified in its portrayal of that essential quality of human nature. . . . Nor is Montaigne a moralist concerned with the ideal and possessed of a Mosaic tablet of laws to be handed down; he is rather the artist engaged in the real who describes the philosopher enacting the pursuit of himself. "Others form man," he says; "I tell of him, and portray a very particular one" ("Of repentance"). And, as he says in another place, his has been the queerest preoccupation in the world: "And then, finding myself entirely destitute and void of any other matter, I presented myself to myself for argument and subject. It is the only book in the world of its kind, a book with a wild and eccentric plan" ("Of the affection of fathers for their children"). Montaigne is the only man who ever made himself the entire subject of his book—the only one, that is, except for all poets, and other artists. . . .

What, in fact, do we know of Montaigne from his portrait? He gives a myriad details: he could eat nearly anything, but could not tolerate beer; he dressed in black and white; he had an astonishingly weak memory ("if I were to live a long time, I do not doubt that I would forget my own name"); he loved poetry, but could not write it, and after poetry, biography; he hated hypocrisy and, more than any other vice, cruelty; he had a rather low opinion of women intellectually; he was below medium height; he lost his virginity at such an early age that, looking back, he could not recall the event (or was this only weak memory again?); he suffered sometimes from prematurity in sexual congress but, in the same encounters, he retained sense and discretion ("a little excitement, but no folly"); he could not "make a child except before going to sleep, or make one standing up"; he was overscrupulous in keeping promises; he was a good horseman; and a hundred other details. To recognize these details, however, and to add them together is hardly to know Montaigne in the sense that we know a friend. Yet, if we do not know Montaigne as we know a friend, we do come to know him in a way that is strikingly analogous to the way in which we know ourselves: what we experience in the *Essays* is like what we experience as the inner processes that go to make up the self. Montaigne's subject might, in fact, be said to be this process of the self, inconsistent but evolutionary and imperfectly perfect from moment to moment. Hence all these pieces and details are necessary to the portrait, not so much for themselves as for the pattern they establish and for what their very telling, and the manner of that telling, reveals to us about Montaigne. What we can perceive in the *Essays* is not the substance of a character but a mode of proceeding, and what we finally observe is not the person of Montaigne but a style revealing a set, an attitude, a point of view, a mind-in-operation, a self-in-becoming—all of which, having realized it through our reading, we identify in the end with ourselves.

The artist's defense for not giving us general truth direct, and Montaigne's defense, or one of them, for not even trying, is that the universal is real in the particular, and not otherwise nor elsewhere. The faithful specificity of the artist, nowhere better illustrated than in the rich mental, physical, and moral precision of Montaigne's self-portrait, ensures the reality of the embodied universal on the one hand, the energy of the reader's emphatic response on the other. In Montaigne's artistic portrait, all the concentric circles of abstractions and universals—that he was "Man," "Frenchman," "Gascon," "de Montaigne," for example—live and have their being only in the central particularity, only in *this* man, *this* Frenchman, *this* Gascon, *this* de Montaigne: in the unique, unrepeated and unrepeatable, but artistically viable, existence of Michel Eyquem de Montaigne. Within the self and the portrait, each of the abstractions is made real, so that eventually the first and last circles, the circumference and the center, Man and this man, are one and the same, neither existing, either "impossible and unnatural," without the other. . . .

The greatness of Montaigne's achievement in autobiography lies in the wholeness and balance of his view of life, in the fidelity of his portrait of the questing spirit, in the stylistic verve which exactly mirrors the process of becoming, in the multifold consciousness and self-consciousness, the profound subjectivity that goes so deep that it becomes transformed into an objective vision of the human condition, a vision finally indistinguishable from revelation of the divine.

Memoir: The Interior Life Meets the Exterior World

Annie Dillard

Annie Dillard, the author of the autobiographical classic *Pilgrim at Tinker Creek* and the memoir *An American Childhood*, emphasizes the subjectivity of memoir by listing what she included and excluded from hers. This subjectivity was a matter of her choices based on her interests, preferences, and personality. The list of inclusions becomes a mini-memoir in itself. Dillard notes that memoir differs from autobiography because, although the speaker is recounting personal experiences, the subject of the writing is the experiences and not the author. She closes with the ironic observation that to preserve memories in a memoir is to lose them as memories.

I'm here because I'm writing a book called *An American Childhood*, which is a memoir—insofar as a memoir is any account, usually in the first person, of incidents that happened a while ago. It isn't an autobiography, and it isn't "memoirs." I wouldn't dream of writing my memoirs; I'm only forty years old. Or my autobiography; any chronology of my days would make very dull reading—I've spent about thirty years behind either a book or a desk. The book that I'm writing is an account of a childhood in Pittsburgh, Pennsylvania, where I grew up.

The best memoirs, I think, forge their own forms. The writer of any work, and particularly any nonfiction work, must decide two crucial points: what to put in and what to leave out.

So I thought, "What shall I put in?" Well, what is the book about? *An American Childhood* is about the passion of childhood. It's about a child's vigor, and originality, and eagerness, and mastery, and joy.

It's about waking up. A child wakes up over and over again, and notices that she's living. She dreams along, loving the exuberant life of the senses, in love with beauty and power, oblivious of herself—and then suddenly, bingo, she wakes up and feels herself alive. She notices her own awareness. And she notices that she is set down here, mysteriously, in a going world. The world is full of fascinating information that she can collect and enjoy. And the world is public; its issues are moral and historical ones.

THE MEMOIR TAKES SHAPE

So the book is about two things: a child's interior life—vivid, superstitious and timeless—and a child's growing awareness of the world. The structural motion of the book is from the interior landscape—one brain's own idiosyncratic topography—to the American landscape, the vast setting of our common history. The little child pinches the skin on the back of her hand and sees where God made Adam from spit and clay. The older child explores the city on foot and starts to work on her future as a detective, or an epidemiologist, or a painter. Older yet, she runs wild and restless over the city's bridges, and finds in Old Testament poetry and French symbolist poetry some language sounds she loves.

The interior life is in constant vertical motion; consciousness runs up and down the scales every hour like a slide trombone. It dreams down below; it notices up above; and it notices itself, too, and its own alertness. The vertical motion of consciousness, from inside to outside and back, interests me. I've written about it once before, in an essay about a solar eclipse, and I wanted to do more with it.

For a private interior life, I've picked—almost at random—my own. As an aside, this isn't as evident as it may seem. I simply like to write books. About twelve years ago, while I was walking in Acadia National Park in Maine, I decided to write a narrative—a prose narrative, because I wanted to write prose. After a week's thought I decided to write mostly about nature, because I thought I could make it do what I wanted, and I decided to set it all on the coast of Maine. I decided further to write it in the third person, about a man, a sort of metaphysician, in his fifties. A month or so later I decided reluctantly to set the whole shebang in Virginia, because I knew more about Virginia. Then I decided to write it in the first person, as a man. Not until I had written the first chapter and showed it around—this was *Pilgrim at Tinker Creek*—did I give up the pretext of writing in the first person as a man. I wasn't out to deceive people; I just didn't like the idea of writing about myself. I knew I wasn't the subject.

So in this book, for simplicity's sake, I've got my own interior life. It was a lively one. I put in what it was that had me so excited all the time—the sensation of time pelting me as if I were standing under a waterfall. I loved the power of the life in which I found myself. I loved to feel its many things in all their force. I put in what it feels like to play with the skin on your mother's knuckles. I put in what it feels like to throw a baseball—you aim your whole body at the target and watch the ball fly off as if it were your own head. I put in drawing pencil studies of my baseball mitt and collecting insects and fooling around with a microscope.

In my study on Cape Cod, where I write, I've stuck above my desk a big photograph of a little Amazonian boy whose face is sticking out of a waterfall or a rapids. White water is pounding all around his head, in a kind of wreath, but his face is absolutely still, looking up, and his black eyes are open dreamily on the distance. That little boy is completely alive; he's letting the mystery of existence beat on him. He's having his childhood, and I think he knows it. And I think he will come out of the water strong, and ready to do some good. I see this photograph whenever I look up from my computer screen.

So I put in that moment of waking up and noticing that you've been put down in a world that's already under way. The rushing of time wakes you: you play along mindless and eternal on the kitchen floor, and time streams in full flood beside you on the floor. It rages beside you, down its swollen banks, and when it wakes you you're so startled you fall in.

When you wake up, you notice that you're here.

WHAT TO INCLUDE?

"Here," in my case, was Pittsburgh. I put in the three rivers that meet here. The Allegheny from the north and the Monongahela from the south converge to form the Ohio, the major tributary of the Mississippi, which, in turn, drains the whole continent east of the divide via the Missouri River rising in the Rocky Mountains. The great chain of the Alleghenies kept pioneers out of Pittsburgh until the 1760s, one hundred and fifty years after Jamestown.

I put in those forested mountains and hills, and the way the three rivers lie flat and moving among them, and the way the low land lies wooded among them, and the way the blunt mountains rise in the darkness from the rivers' banks. I put in Lake Erie, and summers along its mild shore. I put in New Orleans, the home of Dixieland jazz, where my father was heading when he jumped in his boat one day to go down the river like Huck Finn.

I put in the pioneers who "broke wilderness," and the romance of the French and Indian Wars that centered around Fort Duquesne and Fort Pitt. I put in the brawling rivermen—the flatboatmen and keelboatmen.

I put in the old Scotch-Irish families who dominate Pittsburgh and always have. The Mellons are Scotch-Irish, and so were Andrew Carnegie and Henry Clay Frick. They're all Presbyterians. I grew up in this world—at the lunatic fringe of it—and it fascinates me. I think it's important. . . .

My sisters and I grew up in this world, and I put it in *An American Childhood.* I put in our private school and quiet club and hushed neighborhood where the houses were stone and their roofs were slate. I put in dancing with little boys at dancing school, and looking at the backs of their interesting necks at Presbyterian church.

Just to make trouble, I put in money. My grandmother used to tell me never to touch money with my bare hands.

I put in books, for that's where this book started, with an essay I wrote for the *New York Times Magazine* on reading books. Almost all of my many passionate interests, and my many changes of mind, came through books. . . .

I had the notion back then that everything was interesting if you just learned enough about it. Now, writing about it, I have the pleasure of learning it all again and finding that it *is* interesting. I get to inform myself and any readers about such esoterica as rock collecting, which I hadn't thought about in almost thirty years.

When I was twelve a paperboy gave me two grocery bags full of rock and mineral chunks. It took me most of a year to identify them. . . .

Now, in this memoir, I get to recall where the romance of rock collecting had lain: the symbolic sense that underneath the dreary highways, underneath Pittsburgh, were canyons of crystals—that you could find treasure by prying open the landscape. . . .

My father was a dreamer; he lived differently from other men around him. One day he abruptly quit the family firm—when I was ten—and took off down the Ohio River in a boat by himself to search out the roots of jazz in New Orleans. . . .

My mother was both a thinker and what one might call a card. . . . She was interested in language. Once my father and I were in the kitchen listening to a ballgame—the Pirates playing the New York Giants. The Giants had a utility infielder named Wayne Terwilliger. Just as Mother walked through the kitchen, the announcer said, "Terwilliger bunts one." Mother stopped dead and said, "What was that? Was that English?" Father said, "The man's name is Terwilliger. He bunted." Mother thought that was terrific. For the next ten or twelve years she made this surprising string of syllables her own. If she was testing a microphone, or if she was pretending to whisper a secret in my ear, she said, "Terwilliger bunts one." If she had ever had an occasion to create a motto for a coat of arms, as Andrew Carnegie had, her motto would have been "Terwilliger bunts one." Carnegie's was "Death to privilege.". . .

I've learned a lot by writing this book, not only about writing but about American history. Eastern woodland Indians killed many more settlers than plains Indians did. . . . I put in early industry, because it was unexpectedly interesting. Before there was steel, everything was made out of wrought iron—which I find just amazing. . . .

I learned about the heyday of the big industrialists and the endless paradox of Andrew Carnegie, the only one of the great American moguls who not only read books but actually wrote them. . . .

Editing Yourself Out of Your Memoir

And what to leave out?

Well, I'm not writing social history. This is not one of those books in which you may read the lyrics or even the titles of popular songs on the radio. Or the names of radio and TV programs, or advertising slogans or product names or clothing fashions. I don't like all that. I want to direct the reader's attention in equal parts to the text—as a formal object—and to the world, as an interesting place in which we find ourselves.

So another thing I left out, as far as I could, was myself. The personal pronoun can be the subject of the verb: "I see this, I did that." But not the object of the verb: "I analyze me, I discuss me, I describe me, I quote me."

In the course of writing this memoir I've learned all sorts of things, quite inadvertently, about myself and various relationships. But these things are not important to the book and I easily leave them out. Since the subject of the book is not me, other omissions naturally follow. I leave out many things that were important to my life but of no concern for the present book, like the summer I spent in Wyoming when I was fifteen. I keep the action in Pittsburgh; I see no reason to drag everybody off to Wyoming just because I want to tell them about my summer vacation. You have to take pains in a memoir not to hang on the reader's arm, like a drunk, and say, "And then I did this and it was so interesting." I don't write for that reason.

On the other hand, I dig deeply into the exuberant heart of a child and the restless, violent heart of an adolescent— and I was that child and I was that adolescent.

I leave out my private involvement with various young men. I didn't want to kiss and tell. I did put in several sections, however, about boys in general and the fascination they exerted. I ran around with one crowd of older boys so decadent, so accustomed to the most glittering of social lives, that one of them carried with him at all times, in his jacket pocket, a canister of dance wax so that he could be ready for anything. Other boys carry Swiss Army knives for those occasions which occur unexpectedly; this boy carried dance wax for the same reason. He could just sprinkle it on the dining room floor and take you in his arms and whirl you away. These were the sort of boys I knew; they had worn ties from the moment their mothers could locate their necks.

I tried to leave out anything that might trouble my family. My parents are quite young. My sisters are watching this book carefully. Everybody I'm writing about is alive and well, in full possession of his faculties, and possibly willing to sue. Things were simpler when I wrote about muskrats.

No Place for Grievances

Writing in the first person can trap the writer into airing grievances. When I taught writing I spent a lot of time trying to convince young writers that, while literature is an art, it's not a martial art—that the pages of a short story or a novel are no place to defend yourself from an attack, real or imagined, and no place from which to launch an attack, particularly an attack against the very people who painstakingly reared you to your present omniscience.

I have no temptation to air grievances; in fact, I have no grievances left. Unfortunately, I seem to have written the story of my impassioned adolescence so convincingly that my parents (after reading that section of my book) think I still feel that way. It's a problem that I have to solve—one of many in this delicate area. My parents and my youngest sister still live in Pittsburgh; I have to handle it with tongs.

As a result of all of this, I've promised my family that each may pass on the book. I've promised to take out anything that anyone objects to—anything at all. When I was growing up I didn't really take to Pittsburgh society, and I was happy to throw myself into any other world I could find. But I guess I can't say so, because my family may think that I confuse them with conventional Pittsburgh society people in the '50s.

I know a writer who cruelly sticks his parents into all his short stories and still pleases them both, because his mother is pleased to see his father look bad and his father is pleased to see his mother look bad. I had, I thought, nothing but good to say about all named people, but I'll make all that better yet. I don't believe in a writer's kicking around people who don't have access to a printing press. They can't defend themselves.

MEMOIR REPLACES MEMORIES

My advice to memoir writers is to embark upon a memoir for the same reason that you would embark on any other book: to fashion a text. Don't hope in a memoir to preserve your memories. If you prize your memories as they are, by all means avoid—eschew—writing a memoir. Because it is a certain way to lose them. You can't put together a memoir without cannibalizing your own life for parts. The work battens on your memories. And it replaces them.

It's a matter of writing's vividness for the writer. If you spend a couple of days writing a tricky paragraph, and if you spend a week or two laying out a scene or describing an event, you've spent more time writing about it than you did living it. The writing time is also much more intense.

After you've written, you can no longer remember anything but the writing. However true you make that writing, you've created a monster. This has happened to me many, many times, because I'm willing to turn events into pieces of paper. After I've written about any experience, my memories—those elusive, fragmentary patches of color and feeling—are gone; they've been replaced by the work. The work is a sort of changeling on the doorstep—not your baby but someone else's baby rather like it, different in some way that you can't pinpoint, and yours has vanished.

Memory is insubstantial. Things keep replacing it. Your batch of snapshots will both fix and ruin your memory of your travels, or your childhood, or your children's childhood. You can't remember anything from your trip except this wretched collection of snapshots. The painting you did of the light on the water will forever alter the way you see the light on the water; so will looking at Flemish paintings. If you describe a dream you'll notice that at the end of the verbal description you've lost the dream but gained a verbal description. You have to like verbal descriptions a lot to keep up this sort of thing. I like verbal descriptions a lot.

Autobiographical Fiction: James Joyce and the Artistic Transformation of Fact

Suzanne Nalbantian

Suzanne Nalbantian, a professor of English and comparative literature at Long Island University, traces autobiographical elements in an early short story and in the first novel of twentieth-century Irishman James Joyce. Nalbantian argues that in the short story "The Dead," Joyce reflects himself and his wife in the characters of Gabriel and Gretta Conroy. Yet the story draws its power from resonances and meanings created by Joyce that go beyond his personal recollections. Similarly in *A Portrait of the Artist as a Young Man*, Joyce incorporated people and events of his younger days into his novel, but subjugated them to a larger artistic message.

For most biographical critics, James Joyce's life has been intimately tied to his fiction. Characters in *Dubliners* have been identified with real-life counterparts. Associations have been drawn between Michael Furey of 'The Dead' and both Michael Feeney and Michael Bodkin, the first loves in Galway of Nora Barnacle, who became Joyce's wife. More and more parallels have been drawn between Nora and Molly Bloom [from Joyce's *Ulysses*], even to the point of refashioning the real-life woman after the fictional one. Some critics have continued to read *A Portrait of the Artist as a Young Man* as pure biography up to the time of Joyce's departure from Ireland in 1902 despite the objections to such literal interpretation, the most forceful being that of Joyce's brother, Stanislaus, who may have been his most discerning critic. . . . Stanislaus seemed to have been analytical about the nature of his [brother's] autobiographical work. For in his record of Joyce's life to the year 1904, *My Brother's Keeper*, Stanislaus remarked that actually Joyce 'exploited the minute, unpromising material of his immediate experience.' We can observe how, over and over again, Joyce stylised the quotidian from his recollection of the everyday drab world of Dublin.

BEYOND DUBLIN

The parallels may indeed be interesting between the life and the work, but they circumscribe the texts instead of highlighting the way Joyce expanded outward, like [Marcel] Proust, from the limited experiences and locale he drew from. For Joyce it was one wife and one city. And having moved at least 20 times within Dublin during his childhood because of his father's financial instability, he knew that city well. Later as Joyce travelled as a vagabond writer from Trieste to Rome, Zurich and Paris, rejecting Ireland, his main intent remained that of memorialising Dublin, the city in which he lived until the age of 20 and visited three times later only briefly until his self-imposed exile became permanent. With the playwright [Henrik] Ibsen as his model, Joyce had written a university essay 'Drama and Life', in which he stated: 'Even the most commonplace, the deadest among the living, may play a part in a great drama'. Like Ibsen, Joyce was to heighten Naturalistic detail onto a dramatic plane of symbolic art.

If, on the one hand, the autobiographical ingredient was very much a part of Joyce's artistry, it was consciously recast in a mode of depersonalisation, objectification and mythification. To have stayed on the personal level would have been Romantic and lyrical for him, a tendency he rejected from his university years onwards, as he strove toward epic proportions and dramatic intensity. Again, his brother who had been following his life most closely, observed his passage from autobiography into fiction. In his diary notation of 2 February 1904, Stanislaus recalls that *Stephen Hero*, the title he had suggested for the first version of *A Portrait*, was to be 'almost autobiographical':

> Jim told me his idea for the novel. It is to be almost autobiographical . . . He is putting a large number of his acquaintances into it, and those Jesuits whom he has known.

In a subsequent note of 29 March 1904, commenting on several chapters he had read of *Stephen Hero*, Stanislaus described the style of that narrative as 'altogether original' and a 'lying autobiography'. In a later comment on *A Portrait*, Stanislaus emphasised the distinction he perceived between his brother and the evolving persona of Stephen Dedalus:

> My brother was not the weak, shirking infant who figures in *A Portrait of the Artist*. He has drawn, it is true, very largely upon his own life and his own experience. . . . But *A Portrait of the Artist* is not an autobiography; it is an artistic creation. As I had something to say to its reshaping, I can affirm this without hesitation.

FROM CLAY TO ART

Such successive comments made by his brother suggest that as Joyce had taken many incidents from his everyday experience, he had also altered and refashioned them. Instead of a formal diary . . . Joyce assembled a collection of raw life materials primarily in the years 1900 to 1903 in a book of what he called 'epiphanies'. He defined the term 'epiphany' while using some in *Stephen Hero* as 'a sudden spiritual manifestation, whether in the vulgarity of speech or of gesture or in a memorable phase of the mind itself.' His brother Stanislaus likened the collection to the sketchbook of an artist. These fragments of life experience, 40 of which are preserved, whether they were a recorded vulgar overheard conversation or a trivial incident, were some of the clay from which he proceeded to mould his fiction. . . .

The various themes woven into Joyce's works stem from his own life in Dublin, but the itinerary through the recognisable streets and places take on extra personal dimensions. As far as place is concerned, Joyce retained all the real names of streets and places in his exclusive treatment of Ireland, and most especially Dublin. A traveller today can readily identify the places in his fiction. . . . [T]he attention to 'microscopic' detail in Joyce's work, as it might be the particular behaviour of little people in relatively insignificant places, is at the source of the transformation process. For proceeding from the 'insignificant' characters in *Dubliners* who inhabit these drab, real Dublin streets and frequent the dead alleys or corners, Joyce transforms the ordinary and everyday into the aesthetic. . . .

GABRIEL CONROY—OR JAMES JOYCE?

'The Dead' has been considered the most transparent story, autobiographically speaking, and has been fully probed for parallels by such critics as Lionel Trilling, Harry Levin and Richard Ellmann. But what has not been discerned is the aesthetic moulding of such parallels. Let us first recall the story and then its referential components. The narrative describes a Christmas party to which Gabriel Conroy and his wife are invited. It is an annual dance given by two spinster sisters, the Morkans, who live in a dark, gaunt house at Usher's Island. The same guests reappear at this event each year, certain musical performances are given, a grand festive dinner is consumed, and a certain nostalgia for the past and old Irish values is always prevalent. Viewing the scene as an outsider is Gabriel, the devoted nephew of the Morkans who, as an intellectual of sorts set against Irish nationalism, looks toward Ireland's future. He gives an ambivalent speech, tolerates the niceties of the evening, and then retires to a hotel room with his wife. But in this second scene at a Dublin hotel, a crisis of consciousness occurs, in which he suddenly realises that his wife clings to the memory of a past dead lover named Michael Furey, who is suggestive of the Ireland of the past. Such a surprising revelation and disillusionment gives Gabriel an identity crisis, as he senses the ever-presence of the dead and the past.

James Joyce

As has been readily seen, 'The Dead' is actually a composite of facts stemming from Joyce's relationship with Nora. Actually, Joyce's letters of 1904–9 refer to the raw material of the story. Early in their relationship Joyce had been aware that Nora had had a lover in Galway who had died as a young boy. Joyce wrote to Stanislaus in 1904: 'She has had many love-affairs, one when quite young with a boy who died.' Later, Joyce doubted (but only for a short period) Nora's fidelity to him because of a false accusation by his university friend Vincent Cosgrave. While travelling apart from Nora in 1909, Joyce communicated this fear in a letter to her:

> At the time I used to meet you at the corner of Merrion Square
> and talk out with you and feel your hand touch me in the dark
> and hear your voice . . . every second night you kept an ap-
> pointment with a friend of mine outside the Museum . . . you
> lifted your face and kissed him.

It is clear that Joyce's infatuation with Nora, accentuated
during his visit to Dublin, had prompted jealousy to emerge
as a dominant emotion. At this very time, Joyce clearly communicated to Nora that she was indeed the woman in 'The
Dead': 'Do you remember the three adjectives I have used in
'The Dead' in speaking of your body. They are these: "musical and strange and perfumed". . . my jealousy is still smoul-
dering in my heart.'

Joyce confirmed that another ingredient had nourished
the story. Following the above letters to Nora, Joyce had proceeded to Galway. There he was introduced to Nora's mother,
Mrs Thomas Barnacle, who apparently sang to him the tan-
talising song *The Lass of Aughrim*. Joyce reported this to
Nora in another letter: 'She sang for me *The Lass of Aughrim*'.
But days later he called it Nora's song since it was actually
from her that he had first heard the ballad: 'I was singing an
hour ago your song *The Lass of Aughrim*. The tears come into
my eyes and my voice trembles with emotion when I sing
that lovely air.' This cluster of references makes it clear that
Nora was to be identified with Gretta Conroy of the story as
the Galway girl. But in the story, Joyce [uses] the identifiable
song . . . as a vehicle to provoke memory. In the climactic
scene, Gretta admits to her husband: 'It was a young boy I
used to know . . . named Michael Furey. He used to sing that
song, *The Lass of Aughrim*. He was very delicate.' This memory, initially identified with Gretta's or Nora's personal past,
is transformed and universalised into the collective memory
of Ireland's past as viewed by the writer figure who is looking into Ireland's future: 'His soul had approached that re-
gion where dwell the vast hosts of the dead.'

Joyce locates the story in the identifiable place of Usher's
Island. Those who have visited Dublin know that Usher's Island is actually a quay on the south bank of the river Liffey
with a full view of the Wellington monument. By the power
of association, Joyce connects the snow on the Wellington
monument with another real locale, though far away, Galway: 'It was falling, too, upon every part of the lonely
churchyard on the hill where Michael Furey lay buried.' It is

interesting that Joyce visited Galway only after having written the story and that in 1912 he actually visited the graveyard of 'The Dead' and wrote to his brother: 'I cycled to Oughterard on Sunday and visited the graveyard of "The Dead". It is exactly as I had imagined it.'. . . In Joyce's story, the compounding of the near and the faraway place conflates the past and the present in the view of Ireland—the living and the dead. . . .

At the time he was writing 'The Dead' in 1907, Joyce was obviously contemplating the dilemma of flight which he was conceiving in the Stephen Dedalus persona. Writing this story near the beginning of his self-imposed exile, he gave vent to speculations on what he would have been had he personally forgone that flight and remained in his country. Like Joyce, Gabriel writes book reviews for the Dublin *Daily Express*, wears glasses, has chosen an Irish Galway girl as his life companion and is interested in the progressive ideas of Europe. Yet the fictionalisation of the life material turns the domestic story into an archetypal one. Contrasting the purely Irish Galway element of Michael Furey and Gretta to the Europeanised inclination of Joyce himself, Joyce creates a dialectic of death and life, of the old and the new. The Galway lover, though identifiable, is symbolic of Ireland's past. Gabriel, though linked with the author, is the consciousness of the future. Joyce adds the element of snow, symbolic of natural process, as the all-inclusive element which mediates between the past and the present.

MINING HIS PAST FOR RAW MATERIALS

After writing 'The Dead' Joyce returned to his life materials to remake his image in *Stephen Hero* and then again in *A Portrait*. In fact, Joyce returned to the narrative of his life, which he had not yet attempted to reconstruct in the stories. In the process of relating key experiences of his childhood, Joyce seems to have surveyed his life for facts which could be exploited in his art. In fact, his brother Stanislaus's account *My Brother's Keeper*, ending in 1904, along with his diary ending in 1905, substantiates many of the facts which are transposed in the fiction. What is considered to be the draft for *A Portrait, Stephen Hero*, in the surviving fragment of the Harvard manuscript, parallels only the first two years of Joyce's university life (1898–1900) and reads like a crisis autobiography, chronicling the youth's rebellion against the Catholic religion and his domestic life. It is, in this sense, reminiscent of Victorian autobiography. . . . *Stephen Hero* introduces certain artistic theories pertaining to the development of the artistic figure, Stephen. Along with the definition of epiphany, it describes the process of transposition that is crucial to the artist:

> The artist who could disentangle the subtle soul of the image from its mesh of defining circumstances most exactly and re-embody it in artistic circumstances chosen as the most exact for it in its new office, he was the supreme artist.

It would seem that this process of poetic transformation of fact had not yet occurred in *Stephen Hero* and was awaiting the mythical substratum which would be added to *A Portrait*. For 'Stephen Hero' merely declares in flatly unpoetic ways that he would be an artist, lacking the actual epiphany at 'The Bull', which occurs in *A Portrait*. . . .

The manuscript of *Stephen Hero* ends abruptly with a reference to a scene in the North Bull area of Dublin, where Stephen expresses his disappointment with his university and an awareness of his future vocation as an artist. Yet the epiphany connected with this scene and the dramatisation of it is waiting to be elaborated in *A Portrait*.

MYTH VERSUS REALITY—RE-CREATING LIFE OUT OF LIFE

Stephen Daedalus of *Stephen Hero* turns into Stephen Dedalus of *A Portrait*. Despite the alteration of the spelling from the Greek original, the second Stephen becomes much more linked to the Greek archetype and the theme of the myth. For in *A Portrait* the exploitation of the Daedalus reference enriches the recasting of Joyce's life by adding a mythic dimension to it. The focus on *A Portrait*, which was not evident in the draft, is upon the flight of the persona with which Joyce identifies. Joyce had attempted to move the subject matter of his life from the lyrical to the dramatic in the ten years that separate *Stephen Hero* from *A Portrait*. And although *A Portrait* contains much more of the immediate 'I' than *Stephen Hero* does, that 'I' is at once personal and de-personalised in the transformation of the alienated Irish boy into the generalised artist figure. The Daedalus-Icarus myth serves Joyce's purposes for suggesting a threefold situation of constriction, art and flight. After all, in the celebrated myth, Daedalus was the supreme artificer who had constructed the labyrinth on the island of Crete to house the monstrous minotaur. He had also created the wings with which his son Icarus sought to fly. Appropriately, then, Joyce adapts the myth to his modern purposes as Stephen focuses upon birds and flight: 'He watched their flight; bird after bird; a dark flash, a swerve, a flash again, a dark aside, a curve, a flutter of wings.'

As is well known, an entire section of the fourth chapter focuses on Stephen's recognition of his identity through an association with the mythical figure. An extended epiphany is created in the scene at North Bull Island, a real site which Joyce must have visited many a time in his youth. As an island on Dublin Bay, it is connected to the mainland by the wooden bridge of the Bull. Walking beyond the bridge to the breakwater, one has views of the commanding Howth Head, rolling distant mountains and Dublin port. One leaves behind in the distance Dublin, which becomes barely visible, and one can suddenly be overtaken by nature. By contrast to the confines of the city, there all the senses are assaulted by the vaulted sky full of clouds, the fresh sea breeze, the brackish red seaweed which is baked into the spongy sand. The strand where Stephen sees the wading girl is readily visible today and one can actually reincarnate the scene by replacing the wading girl with any passer-by looking out towards Dublin Bay and beyond. It is especially striking that patches of clouds above the Bull can very well pertain to the poetic phrase which Stephen utters: 'A day of dappled seaborne clouds.'

From this realistic setting, there is a transposition from sight to insight. A pleasurable experience emerges from the use of language. . . . [T]he artistic calling is associated with the transfer to language. Stephen is uplifted in an ecstasy of flight:

> His heart trembled; his breath came faster and a wild spirit passed over his limbs as though he were soaring sunward. His heart trembled in an ecstasy of fear and his soul was in flight. His soul was soaring in an air beyond the world . . .

The image of a wading girl in the distance is the intermediary through which the artistic awakening is experienced.

Such is the re-presentation of poetic inspiration, which writers have often associated with some muse, but in this case is identified with a concrete place to which Joyce himself had fled for solace from the confines of his restrictive environment. Within the work, however, it continues to be suggested that the material that the artist 'forges' is the 'sluggish matter of the earth', since the artist's ultimate task is to 'recreate life out of life'. For, after all, Joyce was using the 'dregs' of his childhood and adolescent experiences as the raw material of his art.

CHAPTER 2

Anglo-American Autobiographies

 Autobiography

History as Personal Experience

Alfred Kazin

A distinguished American critic, Alfred Kazin is the author of three celebrated memoirs: *A Walker in the City* (1951), *Starting Out in the Thirties* (1965), and *New York Jew* (1978). In this essay, he reviews the many American autobiographical writers who inspired him. Kazin notes the Puritan background in New England that established a tradition of self-examination, and the transcendentalist or romantic impulse of Ralph Waldo Emerson and his followers Henry David Thoreau and Walt Whitman to discover and create a higher self. But for Kazin, American autobiographies are not characterized merely by self-analysis, but by a rather self-aggrandizing desire to show the author's involvement with important historical events or people. That is, the American autobiographer is stressing the notion that he or she has, in Kazin's words, "lived history."

In my experience, Americans sooner or later bring any discussion around to themselves. The American writers with whom, more than any others, I have lived my spiritual life tend to project the world as a picture of themselves even when they are not writing directly about themselves. No doubt this has much to do with the emphasis on the self in America's ancestral Protestantism. Theology in America tends to be Protestant. The self remains the focal point of American literary thinking. From Jonathan Edwards to [Ernest] Hemingway we are confronted by the primitive and unmediated self arriving alone on the American strand, then battling opposing selves who share with us only the experience of being an American.

THE INDIVIDUAL SOUL IN AMERICA

The deepest side of being an American is the sense of being like nothing before us in history—often enough like no one else around us who is not immediately recognized as one of our tradition, faith, culture, profession. *"What do you do, bud?"* is the poignant beginning of American conversation, "Who are *you? * What am I to expect from *you?"* put into history's language, means that I am alone in a world that was new to begin with and that still feels new to me because the experience of being so *much* a "self"—constantly explaining oneself and telling one's own story—is as traditional in the greatest American writing as it is in a barroom.

What is being talked about is inevitably oneself as a creature of our time and place, the common era that is the subject of history. Every American story revolving around the self, even Henry Miller as a derelict in Paris, is a story of making it against a background symbolically American. Miller made it to Paris after years of being an indistinguishable big-city nobody. In Paris this American nobody wrote himself up as somebody, a symbol of the free life. The point of the story—as it was for Ben Franklin arriving in Philadelphia, Emerson crossing "a bare common" in ecstasies at his newly recognized spiritual powers, Whitman nursing the helpless wounded soldiers in the Civil War hospitals, Henry Adams in awe of the dynamo at the 1900 Paris exposition, E.E. Cummings observing his fellow prisoners in *The Enormous Room,* Hemingway in Parisian cafes writing about his boyhood in Upper Michigan—is that he is making a book out of it, a great book, an exemplary tale of some initiating and original accomplishment that could have been imagined only in an American book. The background seems to say that although the creative spirit is peculiarly alone in America, it is alone *with* America. Here the self, the active, partisan, acquisitive self, born of society, is forever remaking itself. . . .

We tend to emphasize the self as a creature of history and history as a human creation. Even Emerson, the last truly religious, God-oriented writer we have had, the last to believe that the world exists entirely *for* the individual and that "Nature is meant to serve," even Emerson wobbles on the ultimate existence of the individual soul, feels easier with a universal cloud cover called the "Oversoul" than he does with the traditional religious soul in God's keeping. . . . What he habitually says is that he has taken himself out of the church, out of formal Christianity, in order to prove that one man, by himself, can be a bridge to divine truth.

THE LAND OF OPPORTUNITY

And that man is you, my fellow American. You can become as great an artist in words as Ralph Waldo Emerson: All you have to do is become a church to yourself and preach from your own immortal genius. July 15, 1838, a Sunday evening before the senior class at Divinity College, Harvard:

> And now, my brothers, you will ask, What in these desponding days can be done by us? . . .
>
> Wherever a man comes, there comes revolution. The old is for slaves. When a man comes, all books are legible, all things transparent, all religions are forms. . . . Yourself a newborn bard of the Holy Ghost, cast behind you all conformity and acquaint man at first hand with Deity . . . Live with the pleasure of the immeasurable mind.

America itself seemed immeasurable in opportunity: "Nature," which meant everything outside of man, existed to serve man on this continent. An American armed with the primacy of the self can do anything. Especially in words. Like Emerson,

Ralph Waldo Emerson

he can invent a religion just for free spirits and call it literature. Like Thoreau, he can turn a totally lonely life, the death of his beloved brother John, his penny-pinching, lung-destroying, graphite-owning family, into the most beautiful prose fable we have of man perfectly at home with nature. Like Whitman, who took self-revelation as his basic strategy, he can propose a whole new self—which for millions he has become. Whitman, who wrote a great book in the form of a personal epic, compelled and still compels many readers to believe him not only the desperado poet he was but one of the supreme teachers of a troubled humanity. And then in prose, this worldly failure used the Civil War as an abundant backdrop to his picture of himself as tending the wounded soldiers, an American St. Francis who reincarnated himself as a poet, thanks to war and the assassination on Good Friday of his beloved Lincoln. Henry Adams in the *Education,* reverses his loneliness as a widower, his isolation as an historical imagination, into the exquisite historical myth of a Hamlet kept from his rightful kingship—a Hamlet too good for Denmark—a Hamlet who nevertheless knew everybody in the world worth knowing—a Hamlet who finally turned the tables on science, the only knowledge worth having. Adams's last superlative myth is a world that in the twelfth century stood still to worship the Virgin but in the twentieth is racing madly, whirling into outer space in its lust to satisfy Emerson's "immeasurable mind"—intellectual power.

SELF-HELP, SALVATION, AND SELF-RENEWAL

Henry James in his autobiographical prefaces to his collected works and in that staggering personal reverie over what the New World has become, *The American Scene,* showed what mastership over the visible world the literary American self could attain. William James in the personal testimony that is among the most valuable sections of that Emersonian manual in spiritual self-help, *The Varieties of Religious Experience,* showed—in the classic pattern of Protestant autobiography from *Pilgrim's Progress* to John Woolman's *Journal*—that a basic function of such writing is to cure oneself of guilt and self-division. . . .

Hemingway was to say that the only psychiatrist *he* needed was a Smith-Corona [typewriter]. But Hemingway, like Saul Bellow in our day, used his own experience obsessively in the form of fiction. So Hemingway kept up the pose to the end that he was invulnerable, famous for "grace under pressure," until the gun in his mouth made it too late for him to admit that his public pose was one great fiction. For the nonfiction writer, as I can testify, personal history is directly an effort to find salvation, to make one's own experience come out right. This is as true of Edmund Wilson in his many autobiographical essays and notebooks as it is of James Baldwin, Malcolm X, Claude Brown. It is even true of straight autobiography by fiction writers. Hemingway's account of his apprenticeship to letters in Paris, *A Moveable Feast,* is an effort to save himself by recovering an idyllic past. Fiction is never simply autobiography—not when it is written by a genuine novelist. The autobiographical impulse in fiction takes the form of satire, burlesque, grandiose mythology, as in *Moby-Dick*. It often mocks the hero and the novel form itself; it generally becomes something altogether different from autobiography by introducing so many other leading characters.

Even the most lasting autobiographies—St. Augustine, [Jean Jacques] Rousseau, Henry Adams—tend to be more case histories limited to the self, as its own history to begin with, than the self as the history of a particular moment and crisis in human history. Saul Bellow has written only one novel, *The Victim,* in which he has not sat for a leading character. [Fiction characters] Sammler and Charles Citrine, Herzog, and even Henderson represent Bellow in various stages of his life, different moods, different wives. But there are so many other people and points of interest in his novels, like the frolicsome portrait of the poet Delmore Schwartz in *Humboldt's Gift,* that it is clear that what makes the human comedy balance out right is the creative process for this self-renewing novelist, not Bellow's own history.

THE SELF AS LIVING HISTORY

Still, wholly personal documents like Whitman's *Specimen Days,* Adams's *Education,* Conrad Aiken's *Ushant,* Malcolm X's *Autobiography,* can be more lasting than many a novel. What preserves such books is the news they bring us of history in a new form. In every notable case of this form, from Franklin's *Autobiography* to Richard Wright's *Black Boy* and Frederick Exley's *A Fan's Notes,* we have the epic of personal struggle, a situation rather than a plot. The writer turns himself into a representative sinner or Christian or black or Jew—in Exley's case a comically incurable drunk.

This person, we say to ourselves as we encounter Franklin arriving in Philadelphia, has *lived* history. . . .

Walt Whitman is another great example of the self living history—first as a mere spectator; then as our common fate, history as the ultimate explanation of our individual fortunes in life. In *Song of Myself* Whitman wrote of the historical visions he painted of America at mid-century—"*I am the man, I suffer'd, I was there.*" In his great diary of the Civil War, *Specimen Days,* Whitman describes himself going down to Washington to look for his brother George, wounded in the second battle of Bull Run. What Whitman does not say is that he was at his lowest ebb as poet and man. *Leaves of Grass* had failed, he really had nothing to occupy himself with at the moment, and he must have had an instinct that the war would be one of those historical tragedies in which the rejected of history find their souls again, in which the epics of the race are reborn.

Early in *Specimen Days* Walt Whitman describes the beaten Federal soldiers in retreat lying along the streets of Washington. Only Whitman would have caught the peculiar poignance of the contrast between the marble Capitol and the helpless, often neglected suffering in what was now a very confused capital. The most splendid instance of Whitman's eye picking out such historical ironies is the description of the wounded soldiers lying in the Patent Office:

> A few weeks ago the vast area of the second story of that noblest of Washington buildings was crowded close with rows of sick, badly wounded and dying soldiers. They were placed in three very large apartments. I went there many times. It was strange, solemn, and with all its features of suffering and death, a sort of fascinating sight. . . . Two of the immense apartments are filled with high and ponderous glass cases, crowded with models in miniature of every kind of utensil, machine, or invention it ever entered into the mind of man to conceive; and with curiosities and foreign presents. . . . It was indeed a curious scene, especially at night when lit up. The glass cases, the beds, the forms lying there, the gallery above, and the marble pavement underfoot. . . .

Whitman does not neglect to tell us at the end of this description of the Patent Office that the wounded soldiers have now been all removed. There *was* an historical moment; he was there. Just in time to record fully the typical American contrast between our technical genius and what war does. Whitman was not a soldier, not even a real nurse. History may well wonder if he gave as much to the soldiers as they gave him. They made possible his great poems and prose of the war. But there is present in *Specimen Days* and in the cycle of war poems, *Drum-Taps,* a kind of historical light or atmosphere that is extraordinary. It is a quality one finds only in the greatest books—from the *Iliad* to *War and Peace*—that show history itself as a character. A certain light plays on all the characters, the light of what we call history. And what is history in this ancient sense but the commemoration of our common experience, the unconscious solidarity

of a people celebrated in the moments of greatest stress, as
the Bible celebrates over and again history as the common
experience of the race, from creation to redemption? . . .

PERSONAL VERSUS COMMUNAL HISTORY

The real problem for "personal history" now is how to ren-
der this excess of outer experience as personal but not private experience. This is the feminine tradition, and women
writers know better than men how to turn the glib age of incessant reportage back into personal literature. But there is
at the same time so clamorous a cry of personal weakness,
so much confessional poetry and fiction, that I ask myself, as
a "personal historian," what the spell is on all of us—not
least our readers. For of course [American confessional po-
ets] Plath, Lowell, Berryman, Rich, Olsen, Duncan, Gins-
berg, Sexton, Wakoski would not have written such texts,
would not be the stars of the classroom nowadays if there
were not so many readers who seem to read no poetry and
prose that is not confessional, who demand that literature be
about the confessional self—an invitation to become confessional themselves.

Does this mean that the theme I began with, the autobiographer as a triumph over his own life, has changed into
the self-proclaimed disaster? Of course not. Confession is
possible, even popular. We live in a society whose standards
of personal conduct have been mocked by all our recent
presidents, to say nothing of our leading corporation execu-
tives. The open lust for political advantage over human
rights and belief in our American superpowers have made
breakdown and confession, Vietnam, Watergate and investi-
gation a pattern of our time.

Erik Erikson says that all confession is an effort to throw
off a curse. Guilt seems more endemic than it ever did. It is
certainly more popular. Why? No doubt it makes possible a
confessional literature that is self-dramatizing in the absence of moral authority. At the same time the dramatization
of the self in American literature goes back to a very old
theme. How well have *I* made out? What am I to think of *my*
life, all things considered? Could it have been any different?
Let us not deceive ourselves: Each person, especially in this
historically still most hopeful of countries, is constantly
making up the progress report of his life, and knows that in

this respect everyone we know, love, and hate, everyone to whom we have ever been tied, shares our interests exactly— this life, my life, this time. . . .

So the anxious but somehow thrivingly preoccupied self, in a culture where personal fortune and happiness are more real than God has become even to many believers, cannot help connecting himself with people like himself in this period, with a history that betrays the most intimate passions. Once gods of the earth, presidents now seem all too much like ourselves. More and more the sexes are compelled to admit that men and women—alas!—are more alike than we had dreamed, egotists before anything else. Everywhere we turn we seem to be within the same bedroom walls, under pressure from the same authorities. Hence, not equality but *identity* becomes the condition of life.

The Many Masks of Benjamin Franklin

Robert F. Sayre

Robert F. Sayre, author of a pioneering study of American autobiography, *The Examined Self* (1964), traces three distinct personalities projected by Benjamin Franklin in his autobiography. According to Sayre the different personalities correspond to three major periods in Franklin's life when he worked on his autobiography—at age sixty-five, seventy-eight, and eighty-two. Of particular interest is the first part of his autobiography, containing maximum tension and timespan between the innocent self in the story and the experienced self telling it. Furthermore, the major theme of this first part (which covers Franklin's life up to the age of twenty-four) is the playing of numerous roles and his experimentation with various identities.

Now it might be argued that Franklin's *Autobiography* lacks literary form simply because it is in four parts. It is also unfinished, and scholars cannot be sure to what extent the surviving versions represent even the corrected second draft. Franklin wrote the first part in August 1771, while staying at the home of his friend Bishop Shipley near Twyford in Hampshire. He did not write the second part until 1784 at his home in Passy, outside Paris, after the conclusion of the Revolution and the signing of the treaty with England. He returned to America in the summer of 1785, but with the excitement of his homecoming, his duties as President of the Executive Council of Pennsylvania, and his work at the Federal Convention, he did not sit down to the third part until August 1788. The brief fourth installment was apparently written only shortly before his death, April 17, 1790. The first section treats the years in Boston, the early work in Philadelphia, his adventures in London, and his marriage to Debbie

Read in 1730. Franklin did not have this part with him when
he wrote the second part at Passy. He did have his outline,
however, and he picks up almost exactly where he left off
and proceeds to describe his advancement of the subscrip-
tion library project and the famous effort to arrive at moral
perfection. In the third part he resumes the record of his life
in the early 1730s and carries on with an account of his activity and reflection down to his arrival in England as agent
for the Pennsylvania Assembly in July 1757. Part four is a
memoir of his dealings with the Proprietaries in London. . . .

FOLLOWING THE OUTLINE OF HIS LIFE

Chronologically the parts fit together like beads on a string,
and . . . the incidents within the parts succeed one another
in the same clear, chronological order. It is almost as wrong
to believe, uncritically, that it lacks form because it was written at four separate times. Franklin endeavored to keep the
story perfectly coherent. He drew up an outline before starting to write in 1771, and he followed it carefully. His American friend Abel James enclosed a copy of it in the letter to
Franklin which, along with Benjamin Vaughan's letter, is in-
serted between parts one and two of the Temple Franklin
text. He used this outline, then, in 1784 and again in
Philadelphia in 1788.

The interesting feature of this outline, which is frequently
pointed out to young readers as evidence of the exemplary
Franklin's good preparation and orderly memory, is that it is
absolutely shapeless. It is not an *outline* at all; it is a mere
list. Everything, big and little, comes up in an order only
chronological:

> . . . Affection of my Brother. His Death, and leaving me his
> Son. Art of Virtue. Occasion. City Watch. amended. Post Of-
> fice. Spotswood. Bradfords Behaviour. Clerk of Assembly.
> Lose one of my Sons. Project of subordinate Junto's. Write oc-
> casionally in the papers. Success in Business. Fire Companys.
> Engines. Go again to Boston in 1743.

It indicates no intention to weight the events, to frame and
compare them, or to design chapters. The writer of the outline had no certain picture of himself; he was but secretary
to his own history, putting it all down in a sequence as near
to the way it actually occurred as he could remember. So it
is incorrect to attribute the formlessness of Franklin's *Autobiography* to the absence of a finished manuscript or to the

hiatuses in the writing of it. There are no conspicuous hiatuses in the narrative. Had Franklin held a more fixed and permanent notion of the story he wished to tell and of the character he wished to present, he could presumably have written a more modeled outline. This too he could have worked on at widely spaced intervals. But when he started and when he started again and recommenced, he had only a sense of order, no sense of form.

FORM DESPITE CHANGE AND DISCONTINUITY

But the exception to this rule is that each of the three major parts does have a form. The fragmentary fourth part is too short to consider, but the first three are outstanding in American literature as three separate explorations in self-discovery and self-advertisement. Franklin never, like Augustine, found one form and identity which could be made to stand for the whole life; he never even gives the appearance of having discovered one form and then written in it. He composed like the scientist rather than the saint. He assembled the materials and then worked with them and arrived at their intelligence. The life, as so starkly represented in the outline, was the raw material. The three bouts of writing were the investigations of it which produced three forms and identities. The image of himself, so variable that it grew as he wrote, altered materially between writings. Such is the hazard and the advantage of self-teaching. Had he written the whole work at one time, in 1788, for example, the picture might have been steadier, but it would not be the fascinating multiple exposure it is.

The problem Franklin unconsciously illustrated was the problem of the man whose life and character was one of change and discontinuity. He was, as he delighted in telling, the Philadelphia printer who had dined with kings. There are certain fundamentals of his character which were always the same, but they are by no means as prominent as the fundamental facts about Augustine's character, though his life had witnessed many revolutions and turnings about, too. With his paramount knowledge of himself as a new Christian, Augustine had a unifying and organizing identity. The chaos out of which he described himself as having emerged was a planned one; it was developed for the purpose of representing the disorder which he had already overcome. The Saint's pilgrimage had concluded in conversion, and the writer had undertaken the task not of completing the quest but of telling and explaining it. The scientist's life is in disorder right up to the time at which it is written. The pilgrimage is not complete. The writing of it becomes a kind of tentative completion, and the informing identity is discovered on the way. But Franklin's three parts of his *Autobiography* (in a sense three autobiographies in one) not only show that a man may write differently at ages 65, 78, and 82, but also that reproducing at any age one's portrait at another is extremely difficult. Between the first and second parts of the *Autobiography*, for example, is a parallel change in the picture of the youthful Franklin. . . .

A Different Person at Different Stages

Each of the three parts of Franklin's *Autobiography* reflects the time and circumstances of its composition. When Franklin wrote the first portion while visiting the Shipleys in Hampshire, he liked England. He was enjoying a welcome period of relief from his official duties, and he assumed the role of a retired country gentleman giving a private account of his unusual and adventurous history. This is certainly the character taken in the opening.

> Dear Son,
> I have ever had a Pleasure in obtaining any little Anecdotes of my Ancestors. You may remember the Enquiries I made among the Remains of my Relations when you were with me in England; and the Journey I took for that purpose. Now imagining it may be equally agreeable to you to know the Circumstances of *my* Life, many of which you are yet unacquainted with; and expecting a Weeks uninterrupted Leisure in my present Country Retirement, I sit down to write them for you.

As Franklin wrote, this piece began to take the shape of a short picaresque novel. It has the young Benjamin Franklin as a hero; and the themes are his ambition to be in business for himself, his education in writing, his inner struggle over religious questions, and his uneven progress toward marriage. He is a bright youth, but a proud one, and his pride and impatience to succeed make him incompatible with his older brother and vulnerable to the praise and promises of other men. . . .

There is a distinct juxtaposition of youth and age in this part of the *Autobiography*, symbolized by the device of writing it as a letter to his son William Franklin. One is led to believe that William was about the age of the young Benjamin, somewhere in his teens or twenties; yet in 1771 he was about forty years old and Governor of New Jersey! The piece was certainly intended for publication, although probably not until after death, and the signs of a letter are literary devices by which the author established his particular relationship to his material. In a sense Franklin was writing to himself as well as about himself, developing correspondences between the past and the present. It is the changes, the lack of coherence which another sensibility might have found alarming, which Franklin works upon to find dramatic and striking. The famous arrival in Philadelphia, "eating my Roll," is recognized to have enormous emblematic value, and the elder Franklin does all he can to bring out the contrast, "that you may in your Mind compare such unlikely Beginnings with the Figure I have since made there." The writer gives the exact itinerary of the boy's walk through the town, the people he met, the things he did, the places he stopped, and the "Meeting House of the Quakers near the Market . . . the first House I was in or slept in, in Philadelphia." Franklin was not quite the penniless waif he made himself out to be. He had arrived tired from the boat journey down the Delaware River, he had spent his last pocket money, and he had no change of clothes. But his luggage was coming around from New York by ship. He exaggerated the "unlikely Beginnings" in order to set them off against the adult Franklin. The penniless waif is built up as the opposite yet the origin of the gentleman "expecting a Weeks uninterrupted Leisure in my present Country Retirement."

SELF-DISCOVERY IN AUTOBIOGRAPHY

Continuity between these extremes exists because Franklin discovered it. It is customary to assert that the *Autobiography*, especially this first part of it, owes its structure to [John] Bunyan and [Daniel] Defoe and is a sort of "American Pilgrim's Progress" or American *Robinson Crusoe*. . . . The suggestive feature about the supposed debt to these writers lies in the assumption behind it that Franklin's life was a plastic and unformed substance that could be pushed and prodded into whatever mold he chose to put it. This is a rough but valid assumption. It tallies with Franklin's emphasis on the individual's large range of freedom in his own destiny and also with his method of writing about that life— to gather up the materials and see what forms appear. The distant structural approximations of *Crusoe* and *Pilgrim's Progress*, though, are discovered rather than imposed.

The question next arises, how were they discovered? The explanation lies in Franklin's talent for posing and for imagining roles for himself, an aspect of his character that has already been touched upon in his description of his arrival in Philadelphia. It is obvious that the waif was seized and carefully developed after it had once shown itself as a striking illustration of "unlikely Beginnings." It and the other role of the retired gentleman are held together by the professed purpose of writing an imitable tale for the instruction of posterity. . . .

The narrative becomes an adventure in living over the various provisional identities he found for himself until he unwinds, in the natural course of history, with the modest and ever so flexible one he used from 1728 until the end of his life, "B. Franklin, Printer."

TRYING ON MANY HATS

It is one demonstration of the number of his provisional identities just to list the various occupations he at some time or another entertained for himself: clergyman, seaman, tallow chandler and soap boiler, printer, poet, swimming instructor, and merchant. It is sententious to call the first part of the *Autobiography* a bourgeois adaptation of spiritual autobiography, with Franklin's progress in trade taking the place of knowledge of God, conversion and baptism. Poor Richard's pithy sayings were never so magisterial as that! It is better to think of Franklin merely trying on hats until he found that the printer's fit. And even when work as a printer expressed some of his talents very well (his playfulness, his love of attention, his spirit of adventure and eagerness for public good), he by no means thought of it as an end of his endeavor but as a base around which to build further images of himself: scientist, politician, diplomat.

A nice picture of the freedom Franklin had in the choice of his occupation appears in his recollection of his father's taking "me to walk with him, and see Joiners, Bricklayers, Turners, Braziers, &c. at their Work, that he might observe my Inclination, & endeavor to fix it on some Trade or other on Land." (Franklin's father did not approve of his going to sea.) The similar freedom he felt he had in the development of his habits and personality is demonstrated in his readiness to take up any idea he met in a book and give it a try. Happening "to meet with a Book, written by one Tryon, recommending a Vegetable Diet," he gave up meat and became a vegetarian. After reading some poems and ballads, he composed two broadside ballads for his brother's press. And what is most revealing, when he discovered the Socratic method in Greenwood's *English Grammar* and Xenophon's *Memorable Things of Socrates,* he "was charm'd with it, adopted it, dropt my abrupt Contradiction, and positive Argumentation, and *put on* the humble Enquirer & Doubter" (italics mine). The poses and masks which Franklin came

Two of Franklin's chosen roles, both illustrated above, were humble printer and public-spirited Philadelphian.

across in his reading—not only in Bysshe's eighteenth-century translation of Xenophon, but in Addison, Swift, Defoe, Arbuthnot, Gay, Dryden, Pope, and other [British] Augustan satirists—were more than literary ones to be assumed in his scores of hoaxes and pieces of satiric journalism; they were "real" ones to be tried out in life as well. This is evident in Franklin's tireless affection for pranks, for practical jokes, and disguises. Franklin readily slipped into poses in the *Autobiography* because he had lived in a fluid world. His day-to-day identities approached poses.

If no strict and dogmatic religion exactly defined man's role in respect to Heaven and no rigid social structure exactly defined his role on earth, then man's role could be whatever he chose to make it. Franklin was scrupulous in his religious convictions and he was not selfish or single-mindedly accumulative in his worldly activity. The point is that he arrived at both his religious and social philosophies by his own experimentation and intelligence. He recognized his freedom and realized that whatever actions he took were in a dramatic sense, "acts," roles to some degree thrust upon him but also consciously selected and therefore open to whatever interpretations he wished to make of them. The fact that he conducted such a large amount of his business by writing—letters, reports, scientific papers, pamphlets, proposals, propaganda pieces—is interesting in this respect because the printed page was obviously the medium through which he learned many of the gestures and postures of his multiple lives. Still, several lessons from "real life" (as handed on in the *Autobiography)* are to be noticed. . . .

Carl Becker observed that Franklin was never thoroughly submerged in anything he undertook. Everything he did he gave his best to, and most everything he did he did well, but behind the gestures and routines of his participation was always a reserve, a certain ironic sense which took amusement as well as satisfaction from the experience. This was the actor in him; one might almost say the dead-pan comedian in him, and it owed much to the fact that each participation was easily and freely chosen. The man behind the actor was always bigger than the single part. This is a most important fact about Franklin's personality, and it operated in all his achievements on all his many stages. The first section of the *Autobiography* is the story of Franklin's building of his roles—sampling sundry occupations, hoaxes, disguises, and literary masks—and of fitting himself out in the "plain dress" of his first and most lasting public character, flexible and adaptable as it was always to be for him, "Benjamin Franklin of Philadelphia, Printer.". . .

EIGHTEENTH-CENTURY PROJECT MANAGER

Franklin finds his identity in the first part of the *Autobiography* by reassessing all the provisional roles he played as a young man. The final character of Benjamin Franklin, Printer, is a satisfactory conclusion because it holds within itself both the retired gentleman of Twyford and the penniless waif of "unlikely Beginnings." The work is an amalgam of the man writing and the man written about. The same generalization applies to the two later parts composed at Passy in 1784 and in Philadelphia in 1788. What Franklin wrote in France is a most delicate manipulation of his youthful experience to the purposes of the public character he played at Versailles, in the salons of Mmes. Helvetius and Brillon, and in the French press. What he wrote back in Pennsylvania emphasizes his achievements as civic leader and American patriot.

We can begin by noting, however, that the two later parts have one important thing in common: both are accounts of projects. The Passy piece begins where Franklin had left off thirteen years before with the scheme of the Philadelphia Library Company; then, after a few pages on his domestic affairs and church attendance, it launches into the famous "bold and arduous Project of arriving at moral Perfection." The longer Philadelphia memoir is for the most part a chronology of Franklin's many local and colonial projects for a school, hospital, cleaner streets, a better city watch, fire department, militia, and supplies for General Braddock's army. Franklin was fond of conceiving of himself as a projector, and this fondness is one of the most markedly eighteenth-century aspects of his personality. . . . The important point to realize is that the projector is always wearing a mask. . . . The mask Franklin wears in describing the "Project of arriving at moral Perfection" is his French one of the *naïf* "Philosophical Quaker," a role both thrust upon him by the acclaim given him on his arrival in France and also cultivated by him in his diplomatic mission, his bagatelles, and even in the modest and ingenuous ways in which he showed his amusement with the role and attempted to deny it. . . .

The disarming quality of the attempt to reach moral perfection was the logic of it. Of the pretentiousness and vanity of such an aim, the young Franklin was sublimely unaware.

> I wish'd to live without committing any Fault at any time; I would conquer all that either Natural Inclination, Custom, or Company might lead me into.

In the next breath the elder Franklin means to disarm the reader as well.

> As I knew, or thought I knew, what was right and wrong, I did not see why I might not *always* do the one and avoid the other.

The young man was innocently reasonable, so reasonable that reason deceived him. "But soon I found," it is announced with inimitable understatement, "I had undertaken a Task of more Difficulty that I had imagined." Always doing the right and avoiding the wrong was really rather hard. "While my *Attention was taken up* in guarding against one Fault, I was often surpriz'd by another." Yet reality became a challenge to his diligence instead of a reminder to his modesty; so, adding diligence to his reasonableness, he devised his "Method" for concentrating his attention on one virtue at a time. By maintaining constant watch and subjecting his behavior to minute study, he would still persevere in this most charming madness.

Moral Algebra

The method was the famous list of thirteen virtues, the little maxims subjoined to each, and the book in which he kept the record of his moral progress. To accept the program didactically as an exemplary exercise in self-improvement or to look upon it cynically as a bumbling tradesman's petty commandments is to miss Franklin's *naïveté*, his cultivated "infantine simplicity." Only Franklin could have conceived it. By comparison, Robinson Crusoe's balance sheet of "Evil" and "Good" in being castaway on his island is primitive, mere arithmetic. Franklin's "moral algebra" is complete with lines in red ink, columns, mottos, dots, abbreviations, headlines. Yet with all these contrivances (or possibly because of them), the method retains its reasonableness and innocence. The intricacy of "arriving at moral Perfection" makes it the most artful of games. Children are absorbed by it.

> I made a little Book in which I allotted a Page for each of the Virtues. I rul'd each Page with red Ink, so as to have seven Columns, one for each Day of the Week, marking each Col-

umn with a Letter for the Day. I cross'd these Columns with
thirteen red Lines, marking the Beginning of each Line with
the first Letter of one of the Virtues, on which Line & in its
proper Column I might mark by a little black Spot every Fault
I found upon Examination to have been committed respect-
ing that Virtue upon that Day.

A sample page is included in the text. Franklin's proce-
dure was "to give a Week's strict Attention to each of the
Virtues successively," at the same time keeping account of
his performance regarding the others as well.

Thus if in the first Week I could keep my first Line marked T
[Temperance] clear of Spots, I suppos'd the Habit of that Virtue
so much strengthen'd and its opposite weaken'd, that I might
venture extending my Attention to include the next [Silence],
and for the following Week keep both Lines clear of Spots.

Proceeding in this way, the young Franklin could go through
a complete course in thirteen weeks, or four courses in a

FRANKLIN: WAYWARD BOY AND SUCCESSFUL MAN

William C. Spengemann, in The Forms of Autobiography:
Episodes in the History of a Literary Genre, *points out a
conflict within Franklin in his depiction of his own youth.*

[Franklin's] didactic purpose prompts him to explain how the
unreasonable, idiosyncratic youth became a reasonable, exemplary adult by overcoming the selfishness that alienates
him for society and by aligning his self-interest with the
larger, public interest. On the other hand, Franklin's evident
feeling that this wayward boy was father to the successful
man, coupled with his expressed desire to relive in the autobiography the life that has turned out so well, makes the highly
particularized boy a far more memorable, more completely
realized figure than the rather bland and featureless adult he
becomes as he sheds his distinctive, alienating traits. At the
same time, the reader cannot help but feel that the supposedly
peculiar boy, compelling though he is as a fictional character,
is really a quite typical figure, a prodigal son, and that the ostensibly representative adult is in fact a highly unusual and
inimitable man. Had the *Autobiography* been true to
Franklin's remarkable career, we feel, it would have failed in
its attempt to set an example for posterity. But, in pursuing
that aim, it had to suppress both the facts of the life and
Franklin's own nonetheless evident pride in his unusual accomplishments.

William C. Spengemann, *The Forms of Autobiography: Episodes in the History of
a Literary Genre.* New Haven, CT: Yale University Press, 1980, pp. 56–57.

year. The beginning of the book was given over to bolstering mottos and prayers; the end contained the "Scheme of Employment for the Twenty-four Hours of a natural Day," which was necessitated by the "Precept of Order." It is a further instance of his naïveté that as time went by he "was surpriz'd to find myself so much fuller of Faults than I had imagined." He found, in fact, that the wear and tear of erasing the spots of "old Faults to make room for new Ones in a new Course" was puncturing the pages of his book with holes, so he transferred his tables "to the Ivory Leaves of a Memorandum Book," from which the marks could be wiped away with a wet sponge.

Franklin the writer never breaks character in his story of this project or lifts his mask to expose the man beneath. Instead he even accentuates his innocent reasonableness from time to time. "Something that pretended to be Reason was every now and then suggesting to me, that such extream Nicety as I exacted of my self might be a kind of Foppery in Morals, which if it were known would make me ridiculous." He is so reasonable, as well as so diligent, that he does not let this "pretended" voice stop him. He dwells on the great difficulty he confronted with the virtue of "Order," leaving one to wonder that he should have reached "Justice" or "Moderation" more easily. He goes on and attributes to the effect of the "Project" his wealth and well-being and says it had once been his intention to write a great book to be called the *Art of Virtue.* He even shifts briefly into the third person, stating that "my Posterity should be informed, that to this little Artifice, with the Blessing of God, their Ancestor ow'd the constant Felicity of his Life down to his 79th Year in which this is written." Beginning in the rhetoric of understatement, he thus works up to the full-blown language of the *naïf* who has mastered his task and then been mastered by it. He becomes exhortative, rotundly pedagogic. The only way out is by coming back to the subject of "Humility," the last of the thirteen virtues. He says he never succeeded in "acquiring the *Reality* of this Virtue; but I had a good deal with regard to the *Appearance* of it." The concluding paragraph is on pride and humility.

> In reality there is perhaps no one of our natural Passions so hard to subdue as *Pride.* Disguise it, struggle with it, beat it down, stifle it, mortify it as much as one pleases, it is still alive, and will every now and then peep out and show itself.

You will see it perhaps often in this History. For even if I could conceive that I had compleatly overcome it, I should probably be proud of my Humility.

Thus Franklin collapses his philosopher's hubris in his "Quaker" simplicity. The two tendencies are beautifully reconciled, the frankly *naïf* young Franklin commencing the project with his scheme to become perfect, the famous elder Franklin carrying the idea along as a worthy endeavor that all men should be interested in, and the sophisticated, consciously *naïf* "Philosophical Quaker" finishing it in a discourse on pride and humility. The experience of fifty years before is thereby examined and recast in the mold of the present. The character of the young man is brought into line with the pose of the older man. His role as rustic philosopher demanded that he should at an early stage in life have entered upon a "bold and arduous Project of arriving at moral Perfection." Naturally, it failed, but the story of that failure was an opportunity to create a plain, reasonable, somewhat comical origin for the sage whose worldliness expressed itself in simplicity.

SENIOR CITIZEN AND POST-REVOLUTION AMERICAN

Franklin's identity in the third part of the *Autobiography* as patriot and civic projector gives it the form of a series of lessons in "doing good." As a series rather than a single story it does not have the interlocking structure of the first section or the roundness of the main part of the second. Perhaps this more literary order was not so available within the material itself. Perhaps the eighty-two-year-old Franklin did not have the artistic control he once had. Yet it is also true that this continued series of experiences does express the multiplicity of his interests and reflect the variety of lives he was leading at the time he wrote it. It bursts with things: fire ladders, dirty streets, smoky lamps, stoves, bags and buckets, wagons, munitions, whiskey, schools, pigs and chickens, bonds and subscriptions, forts. . . .

Back in the midst of Philadelphia, back in the whirl of civic and national contentions, Franklin reinterpreted his earlier undertakings in terms of their present applications. Of all parts of the *Autobiography,* this one is most like a memoir and of most value to the descendants of early American democracy. Franklin's projects strike the modern reader as entirely in the public interest; personal vanities should not have mattered. He became attentive, however, not only to how people *should* feel and respond but also to how they *do*. He allowed others to save their face instead of worrying always about his own. He helped them to go on living by their convictions. . . .

When Franklin wrote this part of his *Autobiography* in 1788, the Country was rebuilding from the destruction of the Revolution and in need of new ideas and energies and men with the social and political skill to employ them. Franklin is seeing himself not as the retired gentleman of the first portion of the *Autobiography* or the naïve philosopher of the second, but as the busy Philadelphian. It might be added that this is the only part of the book in which Franklin seems something of an Anglophobe. In the account of General Braddock's campaign, in the offhand remarks about working hours in London, in implications that the Royal Society scorned his scientific experiments, and in criticism of Lord Louden for delaying the ship on which he sailed to England in 1757—in all these places we know that the Revolution has come between the events and the reminiscences. But this section is most strongly American for its emphasis on *doing* and upon self-realization in public life. It does not present the whole Franklin; it does not present the whole American. But it presents the American Franklin as the writer saw himself at that time. The life has once again been made over in a discovery of the present by means of re-discovering the past.

Emerson, Thoreau, and Whitman: Seeking the Infinite Self

Brian Harding

Brian Harding, who teaches American literature at the University of Birmingham, argues that early American philosopher Ralph Waldo Emerson was developing his focus on self-cultivation while still a young minister. He demonstrates that the "self" for Emerson is a spiritual core of being that is above all fluid, dynamic, and constantly changing. When Emerson left the ministry, still a young man at twenty-nine, this spiritual concept of the transcendent self became all the more important—and it crucially influenced his followers Henry David Thoreau and Walt Whitman. This Emersonian self is the protagonist of both Thoreau's *Walden* and Whitman's "Song of Myself."

In 1827 Ralph Waldo Emerson noted in his journal that the age in which he lived was 'the age of the first person singular'. Three years later he preached, for the first time, a sermon which he was to deliver nine times in the next nine years; its title was 'Self-Culture'. In it he argued that the spirit of Christianity diverts man's attention from the outer world and directs him to look inward. The introspective character of the age could, therefore, be understood as a result of the Christian Revelation. In December 1830 Emerson first preached on the theme 'Trust Yourself'. In this sermon he stated that Scripture teaches us to value our own souls and to dare to be nonconformists. Religion, he claimed, produces greater self respect than is common among those without faith in God, because religion awakens man to a sense of the 'infinite spiritual estate' he possesses in his own soul. In 'Self and Others', a sermon first preached in January 1831, Emerson reminded his listeners that the spirit of God dwells in man and that 'an Eternal Voice' speaks through the individual soul.

THE CONCERN WITH SELF

Behind Emerson's belief that the Christian conception of the soul inspired self-concern and self-analysis lay, of course, a long foreground of Puritan preoccupation with the inner life. Behind his emphasis on the infinitude of the soul and the presence of God in man lay, more immediately, the liberal Christian concern with man's 'likeness to God'. Yet, when Emerson resigned from the Unitarian ministry in 1832, his concern with self-culture in no way lost its religious intensity. He had argued, in 'Self-Culture', that an unceasing effort to cultivate the self was a duty, for in calling on men to make themselves 'living sacrifices' St. Paul had implied nothing less than an obligation to develop the self to its full potential. In 'The Individual', a lecture delivered at the Masonic Temple, Boston, early in 1837, Emerson spoke as the champion of the 'individual heart', the 'sanctuary and citadel of freedom and goodness'. To look steadily and deeply into one's own being, he stated, is to become aware of the immortality of the soul; to feel the 'perfection of the universal' within the 'imperfect private life'. In fact, the continuity in Emerson's thought concerning the self is such that many of his early lectures might well have been sermons, though the 'God' of the Unitarian minister was replaced by the 'infinite essence' of the lecturer on 'Being and Seeming' and by the 'universal mind' of the lecturer who introduced a series on Human Culture at Boston in the winter of 1837–38. In an address on education he gave in June 1837, Emerson justified self-exploration as the goal of human life by reference to the 'Universal Soul dwelling within the souls of all particular men'.

As far as the young writers influenced by Emerson were concerned, the age was to be the age of the 'first person singular' quite literally. In the seven lines of the opening paragraph of *Walden* (1854), the first person pronoun occurs five times. In the first five lines of the first poem of *Leaves of Grass* (1855), the first person pronoun is used four times. Whitman's 'I celebrate myself' was to provide the more dramatic advertisement for the self, yet that 'I' was to remain anonymous until line 499 of the untitled poem that opened the first edition of *Leaves*. Only in what would become Section 24 of the poem did 'Walt Whitman' announce himself as 'One of the roughs, a kosmos'. Thoreau, in contrast, did put his name on the title page of *Walden*. He also devoted the second paragraph of that work to a spirited defence of his 'egotism', reminding his readers that 'it is, after all, always the first person that is speaking.'. . .

AN EMPHASIS ON SPIRITUAL GROWTH

Emerson's early journal comment on the introspective character of his age and its use of the first person singular was followed, after a very short interval, by lengthy reflections on the theme of change, decay and death: on the theme of mutability, in fact. 'We are the changing inhabitants of a changing world', he wrote, and went on to say 'The ground we stand on is passing away under our feet.' Self-consciousness often leads to intense awareness of the ephemerality of the self, in Emerson's thought, but his most daring and distinctive imaginative act was to transform 'mutability' into what he called 'metamorphosis'. The metamorphosis 'excites in the beholder an emotion of joy', as Emerson would argue in 'The Poet', because it liberates him from subjection to forms and allows him to participate in spiritual reality. The major statements of this idea would be published in his two volumes of *Essays* (1841 and 1844) but in 'The Protest', a lecture given in 1839, Emerson already made movement itself the attribute that distinguished the soul from the sensual or material life. 'Sense pauses: the soul pauses not' he wrote. 'In its world is incessant movement.' In the same lecture, he called for a spontaneity that was, he believed, only possible if men would free themselves from their memory and live 'extempore'. Here Emerson described 'the young soul' (and the source in the journals makes it clear that he was thinking of Henry Thoreau) as never satisfied and as seeking, determinedly, for 'the perfect, the illimitable'. In rejecting the bonds of the finite, this exemplary young soul is, plainly, not to be satisfied with any state of the self.

Two years earlier, in 'The Present Age', Emerson had made one of the most emphatic statements of a major theme of his lectures, and of the essays that were to follow them: the need for incessant growth of the soul and the danger of spiritual death that would result from any sense of satisfaction with goals already achieved. The life of the spirit, he maintained, depends on continuous action (even conflict) within the self. Man's godlike quality is his capacity for endless growth, it cannot be found in any of his attainments. In the words of the lecture, 'man was made for conflict, not for rest. In action is his power. Not in his goals but in his transition man is great.' Since 'the truest state of mind rested in, becomes false', there could be no achieved self, only the continuous process of becoming a self.

The thematic symbol of 'Circles' (1841) is in itself proof that Emerson could not have seriously engaged with an autobiographical project, for the 'self-evolving circle' rushing 'on all sides outwards to new and larger circles, and that without end' is incompatible with any attempt to construct a 'completely formed' life in letters. Believing that 'the only sin is limitation' and that a man ceases to be interesting the moment we discover his limitations, Emerson could not be interested in an autobiography that was not open on the side of the future. . . .

Not only was the Emersonian self a process rather than a state of being; it was also—at epiphanic moments of intense self-consciousness—a 'diffusion' of selfhood into the 'all-absorbing totality'. Expounding his paradoxical theory of the poetic self in 'The Poet', Emerson claimed that true artists, whether painters, composers, orators or poets, shared one desire, 'namely to express themselves symmetrically and abundantly, not dwarfishly and fragmentarily'. Dante, he claimed, was the poet who deserved admiration for his daring to write his autobiography 'in colossal cipher, or into universality'.

WHITMAN: UNIVERSAL AND PROPHETIC AUTOBIOGRAPHY

There can be no doubt that Whitman wanted his *Leaves of Grass* to be a 'universal' autobiography of the sort Emerson had credited Dante with writing. In a letter to William O' Connor, written on 6 January 1865, he expressed himself satisfied that his book had achieved what he intended:

> namely, to express by sharp-cut self assertion, *One's-Self*, and also, or may be still more, to map out, to throw together for American use, a gigantic embryo or skeleton of Personality, fit for the West, for native models.

'A Backward Glance O'er Travel'd Roads' reaffirmed Whitman's conception of his purpose. It was, he said, 'to articulate and faithfully express in literary or poetic form, and uncompromisingly, my own physical, emotional, moral, intellectual, and aesthetic Personality' and to 'exploit' it for purposes beyond those of his individual life. The poet's Personality was to 'tally' the spirit of its age and of America. Whitman, it is clear, set out to write what has recently been called 'auto-American-biography'.

'Song of Myself' can also be read as part of a 'prophetic autobiography' in which the distinction between literal and symbolic truth is dissolved. Certainly, as [critic] G. Thomas Couser points out, it is almost without verifiable facts of the individual life of the speaker. It is, in fact, at the same time an intensely personal and a remarkably impersonal poem. The 'voice'—the 'valved voice'—that the speaker 'loves' is the voice of his own soul, or rather it *is* his soul when the self attains to a mystic union with God (in Section 5), but the voice of the 'Song' becomes the voice of the whole American people in the course of the poem. Paradoxically, in the very section where the speaker-singer identifies himself by announcing his own name (Section 24) he also claims that 'voices of the interminable generations of slaves' speak through him. The 'diversity' which the speaker says is his 'own' and which he cannot 'resist' (Section 16) makes him '*of* old and young, *of* the foolish as much as the wise' (emphasis added). It also makes a self of the vast and varied life 'voiced' in the poem's catalogues.

Having celebrated his physical being by worshipping his own body in words that blend the self with the natural world—'Mixed tussled hay of head and beard and brawn it shall be you,/ Trickling sap of maple, fibre of manly wheat, it shall be you'—the speaker-singer in 'Song' returns, in a later section, to 'the puzzle of puzzles,/ And that we call Being' (Section 26). After all the affirmation the question comes again: 'To be in any form, what is that?' (Section 27). The answers are as diverse as the 'selves' of the poem. To be, for the speaker, is to be the culmination of all previous existence. Aeons have contributed towards him—towards the realization of his selfhood: 'All forces have been steadily employed to complete and delight me,/ Now I stand on this spot with my soul' (Section 44). Yet 'to be' in this poem is to be forever unwilling to accept the limitations of the self and to be forever dissatisfied with any 'being' attained:

> This day before dawn I ascended a hill and looked at the
>   crowded heaven,

> And I said to my spirit, When we become the enfolders of
> those orbs and the pleasure and knowledge of every
> thing in them, shall we be filled and satisfied then?
> And my spirit said No, we level that lift to pass and
> continue beyond. (Section 46)

Tramping his perpetual journey, the 'endless seeker' of 'Song of Myself' acknowledges his 'fugaciousness' in the concluding sections of the poem. Departing 'as air', he is uncertain that future readers will know 'who I am or what I mean'. Thus, 'Song of Myself' does not fit the archetypal myth of the American autobiography, as described by W.C. Spengemann and L.R. Lundquist. It does not take us on a pilgrimage with the speaker from imperfection to perfection, or from alienation to union with nature. It does give us moments of ecstatic union with God and moments of intense celebration of the self, but it enacts one of Whitman's intensest beliefs as recorded in his notes: 'If I have any principle & lesson', he wrote, 'it is that . . . of continual development, of arriving at any one result or degree only to start on further results and degrees.' In another prose statement, Whitman argues that the greatness of humanity is 'that it never at any time or under any circumstances arrives at its finality—never is able to say: "Now I stand fixed forever."' The insistence on incessant movement here—'Always changing, advancing, retreating, enlarging, condensing'—is unmistakably Emersonian, as is Whitman's programmatic subordination of the singer to the song. . . .

THOREAU: THE EXPERIMENT OF LIVING

Compared to Whitman's ambitious project for his own 'Personality' in *Leaves of Grass,* Thoreau's 'egotism' in *Walden* seems modest in scope. The 'I' of Thoreau's narrative does not 'incorporate gneiss and coal and long-threaded moss' nor are his words 'omnivorous'. The speaker in *Walden* does not 'become' John Field, John Farmer, Therien, or any of the people he encounters or describes. On the contrary, the speaker maintains an unambiguous and unblurred individuality. The 'Life in the Woods' of the book's subtitle is a particular life lived in a particular woods; it is not generalized. Time and place are specified. On 4 July 1845, the narrator 'took up [his] abode . . . by the shore of a small pond, about a mile and a half south of the village of Concord'. His personal past—even his infancy—is relevant to his narrative, it seems, for he considers it appropriate to mention that he was brought 'through these very woods and this field, to the pond' when he was 4 years old. Consequently, we are told, Walden Pond is 'one of the oldest scenes' stamped on his memory. Later memories are also mentioned by the speaker, who recalls hours spent drifting on the pond in his boat when he was younger. Personal experience also helps to explain the particular attraction of the Hollowell Farm, for recollections from his earliest voyages up the river Concord are adduced when the narrator tells of his imaginative experiment in buying a farm.

Walden, then, invites discussion as an autobiography, for it tells the story of part, at least, of one man's life. . . . The structuring that condenses two years' residence and almost nine years' experience into a narrative with a seasonal rhythm gives to the work a clarity of definition appropriate to autobiography. Yet, for all its insistent use of the first person pronoun, and for all its dependence on the writer's personal experience—'Where *I* Lived and What *I* Lived For'—*Walden* is obviously much more than the record and interpretation of an individual's life. The 'exemplary' quality of the life lived at the pond and the 'exemplary' nature of the egotism displayed by the narrator is implicit even in the brashest advertisement for the self. On the title page, beneath the picture of the house in the woods, words from the second chapter of the book are given as epigraph: 'I do not propose to write an ode to dejection, but to brag as lustily as chanticleer in the morning, standing on his roost, if only to wake my neighbours up.' In the 'Economy' chapter, the speaker tells us that if he seems to boast when he explains how little money he spent on his house, his excuse is that he brags 'for humanity' rather than for himself. He has merely demonstrated what can be done if there is the will to do it and the self-reliance necessary to break with conventional notions (of house-building, of indispensable comfort, or of propriety). Chanticleer is only one of the speaker's changes of garments, for he later sees himself ranging the woods as a half-starved hound. In almost buying the Hollowell Farm he almost becomes Atlas, bearing the world on his shoulders. In 'The Bean-Field' he does become a Greek hero as he levels a 'lusty crest-waving Hector' of a weed to the dust. In 'The Village' he becomes Orpheus, drowning the voices of the sirens who would lure him onto the domestic rocks. In

'Brute Neighbours' he appears in the form of the 'Hermit' and engages in repartee with the 'Poet'. So Protean a self cannot, evidently, be equated with the actual Henry David Thoreau who lived at the pond. Obviously, as many have noticed, the 'self' of *Walden* is [in the words of critic Joseph J. Moldenhauer] a 'deliberately created verbal personality'.

In 'Where I Lived and What I Lived For', the speaker makes it plain that his life at the pond is to be understood as an 'experiment' in finding an actual site for a house that conforms to the needs of his imagination. Having bought various farms, or considered buying them, in his imagination, he has now taken possession of a particular spot and has decided to make that the scene of an experiment in living. Beginning with a critique of the lives that his contemporary New Englanders 'are said' to live, the narrator adopts the rôle of the *Eiron* to disturb the complacency of the believer in common-sense notions of business and enterprise and adopts the rôle of the hero who acts out the possibilities of a nobler life. That life climaxes in the revelation of the 'Spring' chapter, when the metamorphosis of the thawing sand and clay into organic forms convinces the narrator that there is nothing inorganic in creation, that the earth is living poetry.

Yet the revelation does not bring the book to an end, nor does it provide the final fulfilment of the self, for, having vividly evoked the renewal of life in the spring and having perceived the thawing of the pond as a Christ-like resurrection ('Walden was dead and is alive again'), the narrator tells us that he left the woods finally on 6 September 1847. The apparently baffling statement (in 'Conclusion')—'I left the woods for as good a reason as I went there'—must be taken as an assertion of self-reliance. The speaker's reasons have to do with intuition rather than common sense. Having 'several more lives to live', he clearly cannot allow himself to remain within even the magic circle of Walden. Appropriately, the 'Spring' chapter is followed by a 'Conclusion' whose theme is breaking out of bounds or limits and exploring unknown realms of the self. The 'village life' that would stagnate 'if it were not for the unexplored forests and meadows which surround it' represents all life that is content to stand still. The wildness needed as a 'tonic' for our lives causes us to 'transgress' the limits of our known selves.

The story of *Walden* can be read as the story of the narrator's recognition of the true nature of the soul. In the Hindu fable recounted in the second chapter of the book, the soul mistakes its identity and assumes an unworthy character until a holy teacher reveals its higher nature 'and then it knows itself to be *Brahme.*' The narrator in *Walden*, like the singer in 'Song of Myself', is both a 'holy teacher' and the one who learns. . . . Certainly, the Transcendentalists' conception of the self was posited upon the belief in a changeless 'real self' beneath or beyond the ever-changing forms of selfhood, but—as Emerson went on to say in 'Circles'—the 'central life' with which that fixture or stability is equated is unable 'to create a life and thought as large and excellent as itself' in the world. Instead, it 'forever labors' to do so, and any story of the self must be the account of those labours rather than of the stability.

The Education of Henry Adams: Neglected Masterpiece

James M. Cox

James M. Cox is an English professor at Dartmouth College and the author of *Recovering Literature's Lost Ground*, a collection of essays on American autobiography. He laments the absence from the curriculum of *The Education of Henry Adams* but notes that the time may be right for greater inclusion of this masterwork. To outline Adams' broad themes and his interdisciplinary vision, Cox places the *Education* in its own proper context—as a companion-piece to another Adams book, *Mont Saint Michel and Chartres*—and he places Adams himself in the context of his presidential family.

The Education of Henry Adams remains a neglected book in American literature. It has always attracted attention of the highest quality. The books and essays on Henry Adams are nearly always good. . . . Ernest Samuels' edition of the *Education*, available in paperback, should be in the library of every educated citizen.

Yet the *Education* continues to be relatively unknown to students of literature—and even to students of American literature. Think of the students who know more than one work of Hawthorne, Melville, Henry James, Hemingway, or Faulkner, yet who have never read Adams. Of course all those writers are novelists, and everyone knows how completely the novel has come to dominate the literary curriculum. . . . Yet even in the realm of nonfiction, Adams remains much more obscure than Franklin, Emerson, or Thoreau. Other prose writers have suffered decline. [British autobiographers] Mill, Newman, Macaulay, and Carlyle have almost disappeared from the curriculum in the face of the novel's

Excerpted from James M. Cox, "Learning Through Ignorance: *The Education of Henry Adams*," *Sewanee Review*, vol. 88, no. 2, Spring 1980. Copyright © 1980 James M. Cox. Reprinted with permission from the editor and author.

onslaught. But Adams is different. The *Education* was never in the curriculum. In period anthologies it was represented by the invariable choice of "The Dynamo and the Virgin"; there Adams ended.

WHY THE *EDUCATION* IS OVERLOOKED

The neglect is not the result of a plot—or if it is, Adams himself may have been the first conspirator. Not only did he efface himself in his book, but he published the book privately in his own lifetime; when it was published after his death, he had taken pains to write a depreciative and deprecatory preface bearing the signature of his friend and former student Henry Cabot Lodge. The response to that 1918 publication of the *Education,* far from being negative, was sensitively and intelligently positive. The book was recognized for what it was—a remarkable achievement. If it has not penetrated the literary curriculum, it has nonetheless taken its place as an American classic in the minds of all who know it. If those minds are not legion, they have possessed enough force to keep it alive for the educated if not for education. Only in the schools can it be said to have failed.

Possibly the schools may take it up at last. It is, after all, an American book. . . . More important is the current rage for interdisciplinary courses, and if ever there existed a genuinely interdisciplinary book, it is the *Education.* Finally there are signs that recent literary criticism . . . may succeed in weakening the novel's stronghold upon literary study. . . . [A]utobiography has become a focal point for widely varying contemporary approaches: for critics seeking literature of sociological, psychological, and historical reference; for critics pursuing a more democratized definition of literature; and for critics contending for the ultimate absence or presence of linguistic signification. . . . [A]utobiography provides the literary model for much contemporary critical theory.

The Education of Henry Adams should thrive in this changed educational and critical scene. For those readers truly interested in interdisciplinary subjects, it affords a vision in which science, history, art, and literature are brilliantly integrated. At the same time, it challenges the most acute literary theorist with its literary form. All this does not assure it a place in either an interdisciplinary or a literary curriculum. The *Education* is a long, demanding work, and what follows is but an introductory hint of its identity and vision.

BOTH AUTOBIOGRAPHY AND HISTORY

First of all, *The Education of Henry Adams* is written by Henry Adams, which means that a reader—an American reader—is thrust simultaneously outward into the reality of American history and inward to the issue of autobiographical reference. Henry Steele Commager, writing on Adams as an American historian, contends that the most important fact about Adams as historian is that he was an Adams—was in fact the great descendant of one of the founding fathers and was therefore a cardinal embodiment of American history. He *was* history even as he wrote history. His nine-volume history of the United States in the administrations of Jefferson and Madison is by almost all counts the finest history written by an American. In method and focus it signals the triumph of history as science; in manner and theme it bears comparison with Gibbon's *Decline and Fall* and thus exemplifies history as art.

Yet, if the most remarkable thing about Henry Adams as historian is that he was an Adams, it is even more remarkable that Adams as an artist was an Adams. John Adams, consumed with his wartime duties as minister to Paris, had written home:

> I could fill volumes with descriptions of temples and palaces, paintings, sculptures, tapestry, porcelain, etc., etc., etc.; if I could have time; but I could not do this without neglecting my duty. The science of government is my duty to study, more than all the other sciences; the arts of legislation and administration and negotiation ought to take the place of, indeed to exclude, all other arts. I must study politics and war that my sons may have liberty to study mathematics and philosophy. My sons ought to study mathematics and philosophy, geography, natural history and naval architecture in order to give their children a right to study painting, poetry, music, architecture, statuary, tapestry, and porcelain.

AUTOBIOGRAPHER AS ARTIST

Although John Adams turned out to be wrong by one generation in his prophetic aim, his great-grandson nonetheless made the aim a prophecy. He not only was a student of all the items in his great-grandfather's list, but was himself an artist of the highest order in his two great books, *Mont Saint Michel and Chartres* and *The Education of Henry Adams.* He had been an artist in his long history of the United States, but the history had dominated and finally enthralled him until it had ended his life as historian. Approaching seventy, he set about once more not to leave history but to end it—and not merely the history he had inherited but all history, his own included—in art. The work he envisioned would not and could not be art for art's sake and thus an end in itself; it would not and could not be the precious luxury that John Adams' official duties forced him to defer. It would, and had to be, an end of himself in art, which would in turn be the education of future generations. To make one's art a life study for others meant that Adams had to convert himself into a student; to make an end of himself in history, he had to complete his life; and to make an end of himself in art meant that he had to convert himself into form and thus become a still life—which is to say a silent life, a fixed life, and yet a life still—not merely a life of motion but one in motion. If that was not the task Adams as autobiographer set himself, it was nonetheless the life he accomplished as an artist.

The task Adams actually set himself as a writer is plainly set forth in Chapter 29 of the *Education:*

> Eight or ten years of study had led Adams to think he might use the century 1150-1250, expressed in Amiens Cathedral and the works of Thomas Aquinas, as the unit from which he might measure motion down to his own time, without assuming anything as true or untrue, except relation. The movement might be studied at once in philosophy and mechanics. Setting himself to the task, he began a volume which he mentally knew as "Mont Saint Michel and Chartres: A Study of Thirteenth Century Unity." From that point he proposed to fix a position for himself, which he could label: "The Education of Henry Adams: A Study of Twentieth-Century Multiplicity." With the help of these two points of relation, he hoped to project his lines forward and backward indefinitely, subject to correction from anyone who should know better. Thereupon, he sailed for home.

UNITY AND MULTIPLICITY

There in a nutshell is the conception of Adams' still life of himself. It significantly ends the chapter entitled "The Abyss of Ignorance."

This is the conception of Adams' autobiography, not the order of his life. As Ernest Samuels points out in the third volume of his biography of Adams and again in his notes to his edition of the *Education,* there is no evidence that Adams actually planned the two works in such a fashion. When he wrote these words, he had already completed *Mont Saint Michel and Chartres.* But what would be distortion from the biographical point of view is the very essence of truth in the autobiographical act of consciousness. For even as Adams asserts his *conception* late in the book . . . he immediately casts his consciousness outside the *Education,* putting it between two books—one devoted to unity, the other to multiplicity. Thus, *relation,* which would move chronologically in a narrative of one's life, is made dynamic alternation, as the lines run forward and backward from one book to the other.

Although Adams' dynamic conception of education moves the two books away from chronological relation and into an instantaneous gravitational field of relation, the fact that the lines of force move forward and backward rather than from side to side indicates that temporal sequence is not lost. Unity is clearly the first term in the sequence both in order of time and in order of text, yet it just as clearly eventuates in multiplicity. Adams had put the issue clearly in the first chapter of the *Education:*

> From cradle to grave this problem of running order through chaos, direction through space, discipline through freedom, unity through multiplicity, has always been, and must always be, the task of education, as it is the moral of religion, philosophy, science, art, politics, and economy; but a boy's will is his life, and he dies when it is broken, as the colt dies in harness, taking a new nature in becoming tame.

The child begins in unity. . . . He is one with the will of nature, and the education that breaks his will, causing him to take on a new nature, is the working out of the very multiplicity of natures to find a new unity. At another point Adams puts the matter precisely:

> Truly the animal that is to be trained to unity must be caught young. Unity is vision; it must have been part of the process of learning to see. The older the mind, the older its complexities, and the further it looks, the more it sees, until even the stars resolve themselves into multiples; yet the child will always see but one. . . .

An account of *Mont Saint Michel and Chartres* throws light upon Adams' autobiographical enterprise. . . . Adams the historian went back to fix a point of unity in history that could be placed in relation to the multiplicity of his own time. . . . [H]e portrayed himself as a tourist uncle taking nieces into the medieval world through the art that had survived. . . .

[T]he tourist uncle with his nieces is . . . an American historian who emerges from the portals of his cathedrals not with unity but with multiplicity.

He has two churches—Mont Saint Michel, the masculine church, and Chartres, the church of the Virgin. . . . [H]e had set out to discover the precarious equilibrium between the old tower of the Virgin and the new tower, which he associates with St. Thomas Aquinas. For all his interest in the immediacy of art, it is the immediacy of history that Adams seeks. The immediacy of art is in the resistant stones and glass and structure of the cathedral; the immediacy of history is in the space between the old and new towers. . . .

In Adams' tourist feeling, the Virgin is the unity toward which and in which her petitioners and pilgrims aspired. . . . [A]nd then [there was] the second tower, taller than the first and beautiful, too, but this time masculine, as Adams' consciousness discovering itself in the space between the towers begins to generate the historical sequence between old and new tower. If the old tower belongs to the Virgin, the new one belongs to Aquinas, whose *Summa* was the external buttressing required by the vaulting imagination of the broken arch. . . .

In the relation between the books the sequence of force discloses itself. Seen through the *Education, Mont Saint Michel* becomes Adams' act of entering the past through the portal of art. He goes in as a tourist . . . and emerges as a historian of force. Thus, his romance with the Virgin ends with an account of St. Thomas' masculine and logical triumph over the church of the Virgin. The new tower thus stands taller than the old; it is the reassertion of masculine logic and judgment over feminine love and grace. . . .

THE OLD AND THE NEW HENRY ADAMS

Seen in this light, the image of the two towers of Chartres has sufficient meaning to generate a metaphor for *The Education of Henry Adams* and *Mont Saint Michel and Chartres.* The two books are analogous to the two towers: they are the artistic structure Adams leaves behind him. *Mont Saint Michel* is, of course, the old tower—simpler in its exterior structure, romantic and poetic in its tone, dominantly feminine in both its subject and its sensibility. The *Education* is the later larger structure—elaborate in style and logic, masculine in subject and aim. It is about Henry Adams, and its avowed purpose is "to fit young men, in universities or elsewhere, to be men of the world, equipped for any emergency.". . .

His task in *Mont Saint Michel* had been to convert the enduring art of the cathedral into historical force; his task in the *Education* was to convert the history of his own life and times into art. Both of his "towers" would be history, just as the towers of Chartres "were" religion. He knew that the primary barrier separating him from the world of Chartres was the force that had overcome or "converted" God into science and revelation into secular history. . . . Adams' historical research and writing had already led him to see that America was to be the scientific nation, and in the *Education* he made unmistakably clear how the United States was, by the end of the nineteenth century, overtaking England in the production of coal.

Adams realizes that at the beginning of the twentieth century he is confronted by a transitional moment possessing the magnitude of that which evoked Chartres cathedral. Then the attraction of woman drew man's imagination into the radiant generation of a cathedral and in effect converted the masculine God of judgment and thought into a God of love and mercy. Although Aquinas' theological synthesis regained masculine dominion, it started the process by which God was brought down toward nature. Adams saw his own time of conceiving and writing the *Education* (1905–1907) as the moment when the matter of nature, which had become the mass of the mechanical era, was being fully and finally converted into the electrical energy of the twentieth century. He knew that the process had been accelerating throughout the nineteenth century, as mechanical power was steadily and relentlessly converted into electrical power. Thus, [inventor] Faraday's primitive dynamo of 1831 had, by the end of the century, become the means of converting steam power into the electric power and light to run subways, lift elevators (and thus raise skyscrapers), and illuminate whole cities. Watching the dynamo at the Paris Exposition in 1900, Adams felt its power grasp his imagination.

> As he grew accustomed to the great gallery of machines, he began to feel the forty-foot dynamos as a moral force, much as the early Christians felt the Cross. . . . Before the end, one began to pray to [the dynamo]; inherited instinct taught the natural expression of man before silent and infinite force. . . .
>
> Between the dynamo in the gallery of machines and the engine-house outside, the break of continuity amounted to abysmal fracture for a historian's objects. No more relation could he discover between the steam and the electric current than between

the Cross and the cathedral. The forces were interchangeable if not reversible, but he could see only an absolute *fiat* in electricity as in faith.

He senses in this enormous electromotive and electromagnetic force the attraction upon his mind of a force equal to the Virgin of Chartres. She had actually come between God and man to generate the cathedral of the Gothic transition. . . .

AMERICA AND ADAMS—IN TRANSITION

Looking at his own time, Adams knows that it is the dynamo that has the power: it is the attraction as well as the attractive force. Moreover, as he sees history, the dynamo is literally attracting Russia and the East from what he sees as their racial inertia into the Western orbit of science and technology. Even more important, it is attracting woman from her orbit of reproduction and the family into equality with the male. Adams sees this dynamic breakdown of racial and sexual inertia as a part of the vast acceleration concentrated in and represented by America. The Declaration of Independence, the very sum and crystallization of Enlightenment political theory, had asserted by creative fiat the equality of all men, and in so doing it had opened up a new magnetic field of force. In such a field the individual, who had been mere matter, gained political power at the same time he faced infinite replication into political *mass*. Adams, looking back on the intrusion of America into the history of nations, could see not only how this political field was related to the religious, scientific, and sexual fields but also how inevitably America was to dominate the twentieth century. . . .

Adams was determined to define and chart the direction of the force that he felt had excluded him from occupying the office held by his great-grandfather and grandfather. . . .

Adams sought to survey, measure, volatilize, and even direct the force and motion of the history that had cast him aside and left him behind.

Norman Mailer: The Novelist as Public Citizen

Albert E. Stone

Albert E. Stone, University of Iowa English professor
and chairman of American studies, is the author of
Autobiographical Occasions and Original Acts, a
major work on American autobiography. Stone traces
in Norman Mailer's *The Armies of the Night* the evolution of Mailer's inner selves and self-awareness—
from an egotistical performer to a modest man—over
the course of several action-filled days in 1967.
During this time Mailer participated, along with
other public figures, in anti-government, anti-war
demonstrations in which many, including Mailer,
were arrested. Mailer's ability to make himself representative of the country allows him to write both history and autobiography simultaneously.

In *The Armies of the Night,* Mailer places himself squarely in
the Adams–Du Bois lineage of those proclaiming the public
self in the social arena as the proper subject for memoir.
Hence "History" takes precedence over "The Novel" in the
subtitle: "History as a Novel; The Novel as History." This priority prevails throughout, despite the novelistic devices and
literary theories later employed. All personal experience and
one's identity, he asserts, are fundamentally conditioned by
external circumstances, epitomized for him by the Vietnam
War and the institution of the Pentagon. In 1967, Washington
becomes the locus for a symbolic struggle between these po-
tent forces and the dissenting individual citizen. Despite its
manifest absurdities, the Peace March of that year demonstrates an indisputably historical fact—America was then
(and may well remain) a deeply divided culture and polity.
Mailer first defines and then embraces the occasion's polar-

ities: hawks vs. doves; urban hippies vs. small-town straight Americans; the mass vs. the single self; social involvement vs. passivity; technology vs. mystery. As representative Ego caught in cultural crisis, he feels himself similarly divided: he is both member of the march and the writer who stands outside in order to comment accurately and honestly upon its multiple meanings.

Author as Participant and Observer

The most immediately palpable of these is that American public life is a vast arena for egotistical display and histrionics, an insight equally well exemplified by the demonstrators, government officials, and Mailer himself. Throughout the first book he displays himself comically and mercilessly as the most outrageous of American swellheads. His theatrical manners annoy and sometimes offend even his closest friends and admirers. Slowly, however, another side emerges. Mailer the gross and drunken egomaniac—as many readers find him—is also a modest son and the scion of hallowed ancestors. The show-off claims descent from culture-heroes like [Walt] Whitman, [Ernest] Hemingway, and Henry Adams. These presences—and others equally august—hover in the atmosphere of his allusive prose. Yet this appropriated elite heritage never gentles the barroom Mailer, who offers himself, with all his accumulated contradictions and pretensions on display, as a proper guide through the "crazy house of history." Since he has found the Peace March a supremely ambiguous experience, Mailer cheerfully nominates himself as historian with special qualifications: some "ambiguous in his own proportions, a comic hero" with an imagination already trained "to recapture the precise feel of the ambiguity of the event and its monumental disproportions." In short, a Novelist offers himself in service to History.

His dual role as participant and observer sensitizes Mailer to both the substance of public action and the style of official utterance. Thus though the prime target of his personal polemics is American imperialist technology and its ideology, equally deadly enemies are the writers and photographers of the mass media. Their accounts of the march, like the press's coverage of Vietnam, provoke this corrective account, which opens with the promise, "Now we may leave *Time* in order to find out what happened." Against the professional prevaricators of Madison Avenue he pits his own historical memory and artistic vision. "One could not communicate the horror to anyone who did not write well," he remarks with some smugness about these other clumsy, meretricious journalists. Unlike theirs, his story will be authenticated not only by an appropriate idiom but also by imaginative penetration into the secret recesses of history; he will go where mere journalists dare not go. This movement within events by way of the self establishes the principal autobiographical dimension of *The Armies of the Night*, which as a mixed narrative—part history, part testament, part confession—recalls similar American books with very different subject matters: books like [Thoreau's] *Walden*, [W.E.B Du Bois'] *The Souls of Black Folk*, and [James Agee's] *Let Us Now Praise Famous Men*. Mailer, too, aims to write a prose classic. . . .

Because he genuinely desires to fill the shoes of Thoreau and Agee, Mailer cannot play the literary role of the detached and omniscient author, any more than he can or will imitate the newspaperman whose daily duty is to mask the self. Thus New Journalists like John Hersey and [Truman] Capote—creators of modest, relatively impersonal prose in *Hiroshima* and *In Cold Blood*—are no fit models for Mailer. The American military behemoth of the 1960s presents a threat which Mailer believes is so malign, self-satisfied, and ultimately so "obscene" that it can only be described and defied by an equally assertive individual voice. Ego has become, he declares, a national disease; ego endowed with moral sensibility must be the social cure. This is the plain—yet plainly ambiguous—rationale for the book. The writer feels acutely the obligation to put his self on the line (literally and figuratively) as neither Hersey nor Capote were impelled to do by their violent subjects.

AUTHOR AS GENERATIONAL SPOKESMAN

Furthermore, Mailer's own past makes authorial reticence impossible as it renders passive conformity unthinkable in the realm of action. For more than two decades, this narrative keeps reminding us, Mailer has collected within himself the most explosively creative forces in contemporary culture manifesting them forth as personal energy, imagination, experimentation, passion, *chutzpah*. Brooklyn, Harvard College, and the army during World War II ushered him into a career organized around the claim to be the representative spokesman of his generation. . . . That in actuality he has earned more notoriety than true fame is a fact he wryly admits, for Mailer knows and plays off the fact that he is the average American reader's archetypal male and aggressive Jew as Intellectual, Activist, Innovator, Iconoclast. . . . [H]e is a bull in his culture's china shop, smashing old forms and challenging accepted beliefs, just as, in his latest novel *Why Are We in Viet Nam?* he has deliberately "kicked goodbye . . . to the old literary corset of good taste." One "civility" long since discarded is authorial detachment, for in Mailer's previous works he has usually identified intimately with his creatures and their fantasies. Furthermore, Mailer's long-standing ambition to write the Great American Novel is another dimension of his historic and histrionic career about which, like Franklin in his plan for moral perfection, he is ironic and serious.

These reminders of a personal past and stake in the present reach the reader through many direct and indirect references. Each contributes to the picture of a powerful authorial identity with a usable past who is managing this literary performance and playing the leading role. Even more immediately significant than his past, however, is Mailer's present mood and situation as participant and author. Mailer begins by acknowledging himself at a crossroads in his private life. Confessing to the suspicion "that he was getting a little soft, a hint curdles, perhaps an almost invisible rim of corruption was growing around the edges," Mailer carries to Washington some middle-aged doubts about "career, his legend, his idea of himself." These too are soon employed to characterize the corrupt culture symbolically revealed on the steps of the Pentagon.

EXPERIMENTAL THIRD-PERSON AUTOBIOGRAPHY

Personal doubts never undermine Mailer's conviction that he is prepared by his total past for this symbolic showdown between two parts of America's collective ego, typified by the soldiery and the peaceniks. As this public confrontation takes place, an inner confrontation also occurs between Mailer and an alter ego encountered in Washington. This split authorial self is perhaps prophesied in Mailer's choice—a surprising one to many readers—of third-person narrative. Instead of the intimate and insistent "I," he employs other terms—"your protagonist," "Mailer," "the Historian," "the Novelist," "the Participant.". . .

One side of the self is displayed at the crucial opening episode at the Ambassador Theatre, where Mailer reinvents himself as the Wild Man who first performs an "unscheduled scatological solo" in the men's room and then happily broadcasts the fact in a drunkenly obscene speech to the assembled marchers. As a demonstration of a New Journalist's inventiveness, the scene is a *tour de force*. It ushers the reader into Mailer's "Theatre of Ideas" while also announcing a major metaphor of self in this experimental autobiography. For the Ambassador Theatre, with its pitch-black men's room, brilliantly lit stage, cast of mildly disapproving supporting characters, and divided audience out front, is offered as a convincing image of Normal Mailer himself. As the story unfolds, the theater neatly contrasts with the other symbolic building, the Pentagon, that "blind, five-sided eye of a subtle oppression," "undifferentiated as a jellyfish or a cluster of barnacles; . . . anonymous, monotonous, massive, interchangeable." Through these two edifices, at once actual and symbolic, *The Armies of the Night* asserts its claim as personal and public history.

Mailer's unsparingly comic display of his uncouth self at the Ambassador also serves to introduce the book's central issues and moral values. The drunken master of ceremonies acts out, however ironically, his passionate belief in ego moving spontaneously in the grace of the existential moment. Yet he knows afterward he has made a fool of himself, and this sense of shame escalates into an assertion later that a strong sense of guilt is essential to one's sharpest social insights. Also part of a familiar Mailerian ideology is the old conviction about the social value of obscenity in language. "There was no villainy in obscenity for him," he declares, "just— paradoxically, characteristically—his love for America. . . ." So Mailer never felt more like an American than when he was naturally obscene—"all the gifts of the American language came out in the happy play of obscenity upon concept, which enabled one to go back to concept again. What was magnificent about the word shit is that it enabled you to use the word noble. . . ."

Scatological fireworks do work effectively to illustrate Mailer's ideology and exhibit an inner (and somewhat different) self. That *The Armies of the Night* is apology as well as memoir and confession is seen in Mailer's unspoken rejoinder to Robert Lowell, whose "one withering glance" backstage bespeaks that patrician poet's distaste for Mailer's public manners:

> You, Lowell, beloved poet of many, what do you know of the dirt and the dark deliveries of the necessary? What do you know of dignity hard-achieved, and dignity lost through innocence, and dignity lost by sacrifice for a cause one cannot name? What do you know about getting fat against your will, and turning into a clown of an arriviste baron when you would rather be an eagle or a count, or rarest of all, some natural aristocrat from these damned democratic states. No, the only subject we share, you and I, is that species of perception which shows that if we are not very loyal to our unendurable and most exigent inner light, then some day we may burn.

What makes this soliloquy at once sincere, flatulent, and genuinely moving is not its self-pitying opening but the sudden intimation at the close of the ideal from which Mailer knows he is diverging in this very performance.

With many of his well-known eccentricities underlined (if not explained), Mailer carries the reader dramatically back into the recent past. At the same time that he shows up the foolish, obscene, brilliant, honest adult, he drops a few well-chosen hints about the younger man and boy who is also Norman Mailer. Childhood and youth are, however, gingerly handled by this author who otherwise prides himself on the range of his imagination. . . . He prefers the present because his aim is not reminiscence but seizing the "feel of the phenomenon," finding words for the grace and shame of the immediate moment. Though written almost entirely in the past tense as befits its claim to History, *The Armies of the Night* strives insistently to dramatize perceptions, ideas, and memories as if they were as immediate as scenes in Anaïs Nin's *Diary.* Both conscious and preconscious processes are served by this preference. "Consciousness, that blunt tool," he explains, "bucks in the general direction of the truth: instinct plucks the feather. Cheers!" But what is most significant about Mailer's consciousness (History) and instinct (Novel) is their availability only to the *mature* man. Childhood provides no reservoir of significant truths to be tapped. Maturity—*manhood* in his case—is paramount, for "you earned manhood provided you were good enough, bold enough." In the present social crisis only a fully mature person can see and act.

Fidelity to historical and psychic imperatives, then, led Mailer to turn his back on childhood with its lesser virtues, innocence and modesty. Yet this decision contains a paradox, one Mailer acknowledges when he watches a group of young protesters turn in their draft cards at the Justice Department. Standing there, nursing his hangover,

> a deep gloom began to work on Mailer, because a deep modesty was on its way to him, he could feel himself becoming more and more of a modest man . . . and he hated this because modesty was an old family relative, he had been born to a modest family, had been a modest boy, a modest young man, and he hated that, he loved the pride and the arrogance and the confidence and the egocentricity he had acquired over the years, that was his force and his luxury and the iron in his greed, the richest sugar of his pleasure, the strength of his competitive force. . . .

Though less dramatic than the earlier scene in the theater, this is an equally meaningful autobiographical moment. In the immediate "feel" of the experience Mailer is struck by how different he is from his own youthful self and how far he stands from the true modesty of these young men. Last night's showboating at the Ambassador was, for all its excess, a man's act with social implications to be winnowed from the waste by mature reflection. If it was also boyish exhibition, now is the time to repudiate that dimension of his identity. Standing on the sidewalk and looking at these young men who are *not* playing games, he experiences a flash of genuine self-recognition.

> As if some final cherished rare innocence of childhood still preserved intact in him was brought finally to the surface and there expired, so he lost at that instant the last secret delight he retained in life as a game where finally you never got hurt if you played the game well enough.

Nevertheless, many readers will find it hard to accept the fact Mailer has suddenly become an adult in this epiphanic moment at the Justice Department. Rather, the autobiographical truth is that he genuinely wishes us to honor his boyish need to deny his boyishness.

A GRADUAL EVOLUTION

However, after this ambiguous confession Mailer begins to relate to others with a somewhat different mixture of his usual strident competitiveness and sensitive empathy. Feeling like "a damn Quaker" gentles and sharpens him and permits the modest man he's so ambivalent about to reap-

pear in book 2. Thus in the very act of repudiating innocence
and modesty Mailer renews and repossesses them. Even in
book 1 there are several fleeting views of the rejected youthful Mailer. One occurs in "The Armies of the Dead," a brief
gem of cinematographic description of the marchers "pranc-
ing" past the reflecting pool toward the Lincoln Memorial.

> Going to battle! He realized that he had not taken in precisely
> this thin high sensuous breath of pleasure in close to twenty-
> four years, not since the first time he had gone into combat, and
> found to his surprise that the walk toward the fire fight was one
> of the more agreeable—if stricken—moments of his life.

The youthful marchers "streaming to battle" wear weird
and comic costumes. They are like actors from a movie-set
America, illustrating its past (Daniel Boone, Wyatt Earp,
Confederate gray) and present (Sgt. Pepper's Band, Martians
and Moon-men); "the aesthetic at last was in the politics—the
dress ball was going to battle." Yet despite his own acknowl-
edged weakness for theatricality, Mailer perceives a grim
reality behind the gay parade: "the history of the past was
being exploded right into the present." He perceives that
these middle-class "Crusaders" possess only a fractured
sense of the cultural past their costumes are meant to evoke,
for the "tissue" connecting them to an earlier America has
been torn—literally and figuratively bombed away by Eni-
wetok, Hiroshima, Nagasaki, and Vietnam. War is not the
only explosive; LSD too has helped destroy many personal
and collective pasts. Mailer thus matches two "villains"
against each other at the Pentagon: militarism and counter-
culture self-indulgence. His insight emerges from the sym-
pathetic double-consciousness of the middle-aged reporter
who secretly cherishes, as he formally denies, the boy
within.

Temperament and technique, personal presence and the
ironic absence of the past are, then, inextricably connected
aspects of reality brought to a pitch of intensity and symbolic
resonance in the book's later chapters. Even as this height-
ening takes place, the author springs his surprise of the
cameraman who has all along been recording The Participant for British television. This mild shock is immediately
converted into significant self-revelation. Mailer contrasts
the image of his present self with an earlier record also
made for television. "Watching himself talk on camera for
this earlier documentary," he notes,

He was not pleased with himself as a subject. For a warrior, presumptive general, ex-political candidate, embattled aging enfant terrible of the literary world, wise father of six children, radical intellectual, existential philosopher, hardworking author, champion of obscenity, husband of four battling sweet wives, amiable bar drinker, and much exaggerated street fighter, party giver, hostess insulter—he had on screen in this first documentary a faint taint, a last remaining speck of the one personality he found absolutely insupportable—the nice Jewish boy from Brooklyn. Something in his adenoids gave it away—he had the softness of a man early accustomed to mother-love.

From the ironic perspective of his present public identity, this youthful, anonymous self is indeed an "insupportable" role. Nonetheless, Mailer reminds us in several oblique ways of the son of Mrs. I.B. Mailer and the grandson of modest immigrants. First, there is his ambiguous yet genuine patriotism. . . . Another legacy is his empathy and understanding for others as ordinary and undistinguished as his once-adenoidal self. Still another reminder of the "nice Jewish boy from Brooklyn" is the running game of emulation with his fellow marchers, particularly with [highbrow protesters and public figures] Lowell, Macdonald, Coffin, Nichols, and the other liberals whose eyes always glint with "that old-fashioned Wasp integrity." These embodiments of "everything principled and austere in the American character" are treated with more respect and less irony than any other social group. There is wistfulness in Mailer's description of Lowell marching as if at

a damn Ivy League convocation . . . ; he looked for the moment like one Harvard dean talking to another, that same genteel confidential gracious hunch of the shoulder toward each other. No dean at Harvard ever talked to *him* that way, Mailer now decided bitterly.

"Mailer is a Jew." This abrupt and not irrelevant explanation occurs at the end of a *Washington Post* account of Mailer's speech upon his release from Occoquan jail. It underlines another of the paradoxical autobiographical features of *The Armies of the Night.* The sentence is a newspaperman's ironic addendum to Mailer's widely quoted remark: "Today is Sunday . . . and while I am not a Christian, I happen to be married to one. And there are times when I think the loveliest thing about my dear wife is her unspoken love for Jesus Christ." Mailer turns a journalist's jibe at his contradictions and rhetorical excesses into a major cultural statement. . . .

EMPATHIZING WITH QUAKERS

Faithful to his promise, the novelist-historian transforms himself into the Modest Man whose shadowy presence appears in book 1. The experimental narrative abandons overt celebration of self (though personal judgments and opinions continue to abound) in order to simulate a kind of documentary film, with Mailer as cameraman but no longer chief actor. His prose-camera focuses both on behavior and inner emotional states as the seated demonstrators are threatened and brutally treated by the equally threatened soldiers and marshals. The book's pervasive metaphors of theater and costume return, ironically united and completed in the aftermath of this dramatic climax, when Mailer's impassioned imagination penetrates the last mystery of the historic event: the Quaker pacifists who, stripped of their clothing, lie naked in the Hole of the D.C. Jail. In a peroration worthy of [Walt Whitman's] *Specimen Days* (and far more eloquent than the actual peroration, "The Metaphor Delivered," which closes the book), Mailer crystallizes the spiritual vision at the core of his story. Of these naked protestors, he reports, "For many days they did not eat nor drink water. Dehydration brought them near to madness."

> Here was the last of the rite of passage, "the chinook salmon . . . nosing up the impossible stone," here was the thin source of the stream—these naked Quakers on the cold floor of a dark isolation cell in D.C. jail, wandering down the hours in the fever of dehydration, the cells of the brain contracting to the crystals of their thought, essence of one thought so close to the essence of another—all separations of water gone—that madness is near, madness can now be no more than the acceleration of thought.

> Did they pray, these Quakers, for forgiveness of the nation? Did they pray with tears in their eyes in those blind cells with visions of a long column of Vietnamese dead, Vietnamese walking a column of flame. . . .

> The prayers are as Catholic as they are Quaker, and no one will know if they were ever made, for the men who might have made them were perhaps too far out on fever and shivering and thirst to recollect, and there are places no history can reach.

On this egoless and mysterious note *The Armies of the Night* ends its highly personal exploration of the American Ego.

CHAPTER 3

Ethnic American Autobiographies

 Autobiography

Autobiographical Conventions and Ethnic American Experience

James Craig Holte

James Craig Holte, author of *The Ethnic I,* reviews
some of the conventions of autobiography—
confession, memoir, autobiographical fiction—and
applies them to the many autobiographies of ethnic
Americans. Holte places the ethnic autobiographies
in the context of the Anglo mainstream and its cen-
terpiece, the *Autobiography of Benjamin Franklin.*
For some of the ethnic American autobiographers,
their experience is a drama of democratic inclusion,
a triumphant enactment of the American dream; but
for others, it is an ironic or bitter story of disillusionment with mainstream American culture.

The American literary tradition is not a catalogue of isolated
masterpieces; it is an almost obsessive inquiry into what it
means to be an American. Every generation asks this question and comes up with its own answers, but the way the answers are discovered is influenced by literary perceptions as
well as individual concerns. Perceptions are influenced by
conventions; we often discover what we set out to find. For
some, the tradition of frontier millennial evangelicalism im-
bues every act with religious significance; others see every
event as part of a class struggle or mythic pattern; and others
view their life stories as part of a process of assimilation or
rejection. To be aware of the literary conventions that influence us is to be aware of both our perceptions and our literary history. In answering the question of what it means to be
an American, our writers, in a relatively fluid society, have
put little emphasis on class or manners. [James Fenimore]

Cooper, [Nathaniel] Hawthorne, and [Henry] James, among others, have noted that this society lacks a cultural tradition. Thus our writers have had to look to themselves and their own experiences as the primary source of value and meaning, and as a result we are constantly attempting to define who and what we are.

AUTOBIOGRAPHICAL FORMS

To understand how writers have answered the question of identity, we must understand some of the conventions of the autobiography. From the reports of the earliest explorers to the writings of Maxine Hong Kingston, Jerre Mangione, and Theodore White, there exists a continuity of conventions and concerns as well as radical differences in the social contexts from which the literature emerged.

Critical and popular attitudes toward a literary genre can reveal significant cultural attitudes. Every genre exists within a specific framework of textual forms, functions, materials, authorial intentions, and reader expectations. The development and popularity of a literary form are of more than academic interest; they have wider cultural implications. The popularity of such "nontraditional forms" as the occasional essay, the novel and the sermon in the seventeenth century, and the western and the proletarian novel in our more recent past reveals not only the interests of those who produced this literature but also the concerns of those who read it.

Understanding the conventions of a genre is essential for a writer as well. This knowledge enables writers to draw on a wide range of forms and structures. . . .

Autobiography is a complex literary form. At first glance it would appear simple, since in its most basic structure it is a record of a person's life, and because all of us have some kind of life it would seem that the autobiography would be accessible to all. And the sheer number of autobiographies is overwhelming. Lewis Kaplin, in *A Bibliography of American Autobiographies* (Madison: University of Wisconsin Press, 1961), lists over 6,000 published American autobiographies.

In creating an autobiography, however, a writer transforms the complex interaction of self and society into a literary form. Raw experience must be shaped. The question of whether this imposition of form on experience takes place during the actual activity or is an act of literary imposition that occurs during the construction of a narrative may be unanswerable, but there is evidence that many writers use the autobiography as a means of imposing order on experiences that are disruptive and confusing. *The Autobiography of Malcolm X* and Maxine Hong Kingston's *The Woman Warrior,* for example, are excellent examples of literary form imposing order on chaos.

Two fundamental questions are raised by all autobiographers: Who am I and how did I become what I am? In addressing themselves to these questions, writers can choose among a variety of autobiographical forms to organize their experiences. Some of the forms are relatively simple. Exploits and memoirs, for example, are related objective forms in which the autobiographer chronicles his life and records famous events witnessed and famous people encountered. In this kind of autobiographical writing chronology is the primary organizing principle; little attempt is made to examine the motivations and thoughts of characters, and as a result these kinds of narratives often reveal more about an autobiographer's time than about the autobiographer. Sections of the autobiographies of Andrew Carnegie and Carl Schurz, men who accomplished much in their lifetimes, conform to this pattern.

Other forms are more complex. In the defense, the confession, and the conversion narrative, for example, a single significant experience or an overriding idea controls the entire narrative, dictating what is included and what is emphasized. The autobiography of Nicky Cruz, *Run, Baby, Run,* is a good example. Cruz writes a traditional religious conversion story, and as a result only those parts of his life that emphasize the conversion experience are included. Similarly, Carlos Bulosan's *America Is in the Heart* is essentially a defense of Filipino immigrants; Bulosan organizes his narrative around the struggle faced by Filipinos on the West Coast in the 1930s.

An even more subjective and complex form than these narratives is the developmental autobiography, a form discussed at length by Wayne Shumaker in his excellent study of the autobiography, *English Autobiography: Its Emergence, Materials, and Form* (Berkeley: University of California Press, 1954). In this form, which employs many of the techniques of fiction, the primary purpose is to show how the writer lived and thought, not just what he or she accomplished or observed. In writing this kind of personal narrative an autobiographer creates a complex character within a realistic social setting, and the narrative moves around a central, well-developed theme. Maxine Hong Kingston's *The Woman Warrior*, Piri Thomas' *Down These Mean Streets*, and Richard Wright's *Black Boy* are examples of successful developmental autobiographies. . . .

WRITING ABOUT AMERICAN EXPERIENCES

Autobiographies provide models for readers, and Franklin's "effacious advertisement" for himself and his country became the primary model for the growing commercial nation. It was adapted and transformed into hundreds of other versions, including the related homilies of Horatio Alger. Franklin's optimistic story of freedom and progress in a new land became one of the favorite American stories, and his secular conversion became a national obsession. Many immigrant and ethnic writers acknowledge a debt to him, and behind every narrative of success stands the figure of Benjamin Franklin. Mary Antin's *Promised Land*, for example, is one Jewish immigrant girl's version of Franklin's story, and Edward Bok's *Americanization of Edward Bok* tells a Dutch immigrant's version.

Franklin did more than define the proper transformation for Americans; he transferred the moral implications from private spirituality to public success and gave the ideas of progress and change a validity by describing them in the language of salvation. Progress, mobility, and change became American traditions, but in addition to denoting worth, they also created a sense of dislocation and dissatisfaction. . . .

The autobiography is one way of imposing order on change, and perhaps one reason for the popularity of this form in the United States is the feeling of rootlessness felt by so many Americans. It is no surprise to find that those Americans who have experienced this uprootedness most dramatically, immigrant and ethnic Americans, have produced a large body of autobiographical writing. Some, like Mary Antin, Andrew Carnegie, and Jacob Riis, have followed the tradition of assimilation, but others, like Piri Thomas, Malcolm X, and Black Elk, seeing themselves as outsiders, have used the autobiography, and often the conventions of the conversion narrative, as a way of pointing out the defects in Franklin's vision (which has become the official standard vision of the nation), which assumed the absence of class, racial, or sexual discrimination, the essential good will of all men, the ameliorative effects of public education, and the continued abundance of natural resources.

The very language used to describe ethnic and immigrant experience underscores the notion of change and conversion. The image of the melting pot, used as a symbol of adaptation and assimilation and popularized in 1908 by Israel Zangwell's play, *The Melting Pot*, is both complex and confusing. The ideology behind the image, whether used by the proponents of assimilation or those opposed, as well as the ideology of those who put forward the concept of cultural pluralism as the correct way to describe the ideal relationship among the various cultures in the United States, suggests some kind of transformation. While scholars have debated whether this transformation was to take place in the culture at large or just in the ethnic community, the idea of transformation or conversion on the part of someone has been central to the debate. Ethnic writers themselves have taken both sides of the issue. Edward Bok and Richard Rodriguez argue that the throwing off of ethnic behaviors and the assumption of white, middle-class values are beneficial for ethnic Americans, while Maya Angelou and Maxine Hong Kingston assert that ethnic diversity enriches American culture. Along with the language chosen to describe the experience—language that not only describes the experience but prescribes the perception of it—there was, of course, the actual unsettling experience of migration. In her dissertation on immigrant personal narratives, "The Foreign-Born View America" (New York University, 1962), Cecyle Neidle notes that the autobiographical impulse arose among immigrants because of the shock and disillusionment occasioned by a prolonged state of crisis that they experienced upon their arrival in the United States.

> This reality is fully confirmed by people who differed in personality, background, and educational preparation. It can be asserted that the emotional impact of the experience was not dissipated though decades lay between the time of arrival and the writing of one's experience.

This echoes Oscar Handlin's observation in *The Uprooted* (Boston: Little, Brown, 1951) that this period of shock and resulting crisis came about as a consequence of the disorientation caused by the failure of American reality to match immigrant expectations. Even a brief survey of ethnic narratives would confirm this. A common element in almost all ethnic autobiographies, whether the writer ultimately comes to succeed in the United States or not, is a description of the disappointment and trials and tribulations faced when first confronting the reality of American social and economic structures. The autobiographies of such diverse writers as Emma Goldman, Jacob Riis, Monica Sone, and Mary Anderson all emphasize this point.

WRITING FOR ETHNIC COMMUNITIES

Ethnic writers often assume the role of outsiders when they write about their experiences in America. Ethnic writers and other ethnic Americans recognized the pluralistic nature of American society from daily experience, while official American ideology continued to proclaim the unitary nature of the culture. Facing the pressures of Americanization—pressures to abandon a language, a religion, a community, a tradition—many felt confusion and anger, while others accepted the need to adapt to a majority culture. The ethnic autobiography, the outsider's story, takes many forms, but two major approaches can be seen. Starting from outside the culture, some writers chronicle the transformation from outsider to insider, from immigrant to American. The narratives of Mary Antin, Edward Bok, Andrew Carnegie, and Frank Capra are excellent examples of this kind of success story. Some other writers, however, beginning at the same point, observe and record the opposite lesson; it is the dominant culture that keeps them out for reasons of race, sex, class, or language, and their narratives record the failures of a society as much as the inability of an individual to rise in the world. The autobiographies of Emma Goldman, Black Elk, and Malcolm X present this kind of analysis of American experience. Even in these narratives some of the conventions of the conversion story are employed, for in failing or electing not to enter "mainstream" culture, the writer is still transformed. One of the conventions of the conversion narrative is that the writer becomes a spokesperson for the community at the end of the story, and often in narratives where a writer rejects assimilation, the representative voice of the narrator is one of the major themes of the autobiography. The development of a self takes place in a community apart from middle-class America, and the writer becomes, in the narrative, the voice of that community.

Whether affirming their experiences in America or chronicling rejection, ethnic-American writers have left a large and diverse record of their observations. Some of the observations are famous. Andrew Carnegie's *Autobiography, The Autobiography of Malcolm X,* and Maxine Hong Kingston's *Woman Warrior* are all well-known and popular works. Some of the narratives are obscure. Few readers are familiar with Zora Neale Hurston's *Dust Tracks on a Road* or *The Autobiography of Mary Jane Hill Anderson.* The autobiographies, however, whether famous or forgotten, provide an overview of significant aspects of American culture from a unique perspective. Ethnic and immigrant writers saw America with new eyes. Beginning at the edges of American culture, these writers, whether they moved toward the cultural center or remained at the outside, perceived and recorded life in America as few native-born writers could. Jacob Riis' depictions of tenement life in nineteenth-century New York, Black Elk's story of prereservation life, and Emma Goldman's account of the anarchist movement in the ethnic community are just three examples of the important observations contained in these works. . . .

The autobiographies of Carl Schurz, Mary Jane Hill Anderson, and Andrew Carnegie . . . describe the experiences of immigrants who came to the United States prior to the mass migrations of the late nineteenth century, and as a result their stories are substantially different from the works of Mary Antin and Edward Corsi, who came at the height of immigration to the United States. Richard Rodriguez and Maya Angelou, on the other hand, document the complexities of ethnic life in contemporary American society.

These and other writers . . . have left a large body of literature that is just beginning to be studied. The work of ethnic-American writers demands further analysis—a task that is being undertaken by more and more scholars and students concerned with American ethnic cultural identity. Through such examinations we can continue to study the process of cultural evolution in the United States and gain additional insights into the question that lies at the heart of our literature: What does it mean to be an American?

The Power of Literacy in Frederick Douglass's *Narrative*

Valerie Smith

Valerie Smith, the author of *Self-Discovery and Authority in Afro-American Narrative*, views Frederick Douglass's autobiography as an attack on slavery. Douglass shows how slavery abuses family relations, and he refutes the idea that blacks are satisfied as slaves. Above all, by demonstrating his own courage, determination, and perseverance in the events described in the book, and his skillful rhetoric, symbolism, and structure in writing it, Douglass puts the lie to the racism that denies black humanity and justifies slavery. But according to Smith, Douglass's ability to triumph over slavery ironically diminishes the reader's appreciation of its destructive power.

Frederick Douglass's *Narrative* participates in one of the major ideological controversies of his day, the dispute over the question of Negro humanity and equality. Rarely before the 1830s did slavery's apologists articulate a case for the innate inferiority of blacks. They argued instead that slavery was necessary not only to support the agrarian economy but also to socialize blacks out of a condition degraded by the circumstances of their environment. Only after the rise of the abolitionist campaign did they develop a systematic theory of racial inferiority that justified the institution of slavery. For a slave simply to write the story of his or her own life represented an assault on this line of argument, since to make oneself the subject of a narrative presumes both the worth of that self and its interest for a reader. The structures of Douglass's *Narrative* may be seen to address subtly the apologists' arguments. By using various clusters of imagery

Excerpted from Valerie Smith, *Self-Discovery and Authority in Afro-American Narrative* (Cambridge, MA: Harvard University Press). Copyright © 1987 The President and Fellows of Harvard College. Reprinted with permission from the publisher.

and an overarching pattern to unify his account, he discloses a complex, symbolic meaning of his life that further evinces his humanity.

SYMBOLISM IN DOUGLASS'S *NARRATIVE*

Critics have discussed the ways in which images of animals, ships, and sails bestow thematic unity on the events in Douglass's *Narrative*. His use of blood as an image for the human spirit also binds various events to one another and connects him to the suffering of other slaves. Repeatedly Douglass asks the reader to visualize the blood that masters draw from their slaves. It is not enough to say that his Aunt Hester is beaten with a whip. Instead he writes that as a young child he watched his aunt being beaten with a "blood-clotted cowskin" where "the blood ran fastest," until she is "literally covered with blood." This experience marks Douglass's passage from the gate stained with his fellows' blood, from naiveté to understanding. Of Demby, a runaway slave shot by his own master, he writes: Demby's "mangled body sank out of sight and blood and brains marked the water where he had stood." To verify his assertion that self-professed Christians make the worst masters, he recalls an incident in which Captain Auld, his owner, whipped a lame young woman, "causing the warm red blood to drip." Passages such as these provide vivid symbols of the process of dehumanization that slaves underwent as their lifeblood was literally sapped. Significantly, after Douglass whips Covey and achieves the first stage of his ultimate emancipation, he underscores the fact that he himself lost not a drop of blood; on the contrary, he drew blood from the "nigger-breaker."

The primary figure for the meaning of Douglass's life is, however, a pattern that oscillates between slavehood and manhood. The rhetoric of the opening chapter demonstrates several of the ways in which the institution closes off the categories and relationships that ordinarily circumscribe human identity and thus dehumanizes slaves. Douglass, for example, does not know his age and can say little about his parentage. Son of a black woman and her master, he possesses origins that offer counterevidence of his humanity, for his very existence derives from the conflation of sexual and property rights that slavery endorsed. His account, like those of so many of his counterparts, reminds us that by raping their women slaves, masters simultaneously obtained sexual satisfaction and increased their store of human property. Douglass is, therefore, to his master-father nothing more than "chattel personal," with no particular right to either a birth date or parental affection.

During his earliest years Douglass lived with other slave children in his grandmother's cottage on the outskirts of the plantation. As a result he remained ignorant of the brutalities of slavery until he was old enough to work. He dates his initiation into the meaning of his status from the time he watched his aunt being beaten for daring to visit her lover. Plummer, her master, strips her to the waist, crosses and ties her hands, and hangs her from a hook in a joist. He then beats her until her blood runs. As he watches this scene, the young Douglass is forced to confront the physical and emotional horror of slavery: "[It] was the blood-stained gate, the entrance to the hell of slavery, through which [he] was about to pass." Paradoxically, this recognition also makes possible his ultimate escape to freedom, because it compels him to acknowledge the horrors of his condition. On a profound level it thus initiates the process by which the slave was first "made a man."

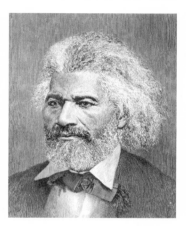

Frederick Douglass

A New Identity

Douglass's first stay in Baltimore is the culmination of this initial movement from slavehood to manhood, for in the city he learns to read and write. In this episode he creates what has become a prototypical situation for later Afro-American writers by linking the acquisition of literacy to both the act of rebellion and the achievement of freedom. As Albert E. Stone notes, Douglass sets up the journey in emblematic terms, foreshadowing its significance as a new stage in the development of his identity. Before leaving for Baltimore he spends "three days in the creek, washing off the plantation scurf and preparing [himself] for his departure." En route to the city, he rides in the bow of the sloop, literally and figuratively "looking ahead."

Douglass begins to learn to read because his naive, originally well-intentioned mistress, Mrs. Auld, does not realize that as a slave, he is to be treated differently from a white child. Just as she discourages his "crouching servility" in her presence, so does she begin to teach him upon discovering his illiteracy. More sophisticated in the ways of the slave system than his wife is, Mr. Auld puts an abrupt end to Douglass's education. But by revealing that literacy would "unfit him to be a slave," Auld kindles Douglass's nascent rebelliousness and yearning for freedom. Although the young slave does not yet understand the explicit connection between freedom and literacy, he is inspired to learn to read and write by any available means, precisely because his master denies him this privilege and associates these two forbidden fruits (that is, freedom and literacy) with each other. Douglass acknowledges that although he has lost his means of education, he has acquired an "invaluable instruction" about his condition from the very master who tries to keep him ignorant. As both Stone and Stephen Butterfield indicate, Douglass's use of antithesis in this section of the *Narrative* reveals his budding awareness of the disjunction between his oppressor's interests and his own: "What [Auld] most dreaded, that I most desired. What he most loved, that I most hated. That which to him was a great evil, to be carefully shunned, was to me a great good, to be diligently sought; and the argument which he so warmly urged, against my learning to read, only served to inspire me with a desire and determination to learn."

The acquisition of literacy facilitates Douglass's achievement of freedom in two ways. The act of reading provides the intellectual basis of his quest for liberation, introducing him to forbidden and unfamiliar ideas such as freedom and abolition. Indeed, his new skill apprises him of so many notions that he comes to consider literacy a mixed blessing:

> What I got from Sheridan was a bold denunciation of slavery, and a powerful vindication of human rights. *The reading of these documents* enabled me to utter my thoughts, and to meet the arguments brought forward to sustain slavery; but while they relieved me of one difficulty, they brought on another even more painful than the one of which I was relieved.
> . . . In moments of agony, I envied my fellow slaves for their stupidity. (emphasis mine)

WRITING HIS WAY TO FREEDOM

Learning to write, in contrast, enables him to manipulate the language of his superordinate to his own advantage. When he first attempts to escape, he writes passes or protections for himself and two fellow slaves. The narrative itself is, moreover, a symbolic, self-authored protection, for in the process of presenting and organizing his experiences, Douglass celebrates his achievement of autonomy.

After the independent-minded, newly literate Douglass returns to the plantation from Baltimore, his owner, Master Thomas, sends him to work for Covey, "the nigger-breaker." Because of Covey's persistent abuse, Douglass loses much of his independence of mind and slips back into the emotional lethargy he associates with mental and physical enslavement. But if the acquisition of literacy first enabled him to

WRITING AND FREEDOM IN DOUGLASS

Henry Louis Gates Jr., author of Figures in Black: Words, Signs, and the "Racial" Self, *gives Douglass credit for establishing the idea of a correlation between literacy and power as a major theme of African American autobiography.*

Long after the issues for which he struggled so ardently have become primarily the concern of the historian, Frederick Douglass will continue to be read and reread. And surely this must be the literary critic's final judgment of Frederick Douglass: that he was Representative Man because he was Rhetorical Man, black master of the verbal arts. Douglass is our clearest example of the will to power as the will to write. The act of writing for the slave constituted the act of creating a public, historical self, not only the self of the individual author but also the self, as it were, of the race. Indeed, in part because of Douglass's literary successes, blacks in general compensated . . . for the absence of a collective written history by writing a remarkable number of individual histories, which taken together begin to assume the features of a communal, collective tale. In literacy was power; . . . the slave who was the first to read and the first to write was the first slave to run away. . . . [T]he correlation of freedom with literacy not only became the central trope of the slave narratives, but it also formed a mythical matrix out of which subsequent black narrative forms developed.

Henry Louis Gates Jr., *Figures in Black: Words, Signs, and the "Racial" Self.* New York: Oxford University Press, 1987, p. 108.

feel free, the act of physical resistance precipitates his second and lasting period of liberation. Indeed, if the sight of his aunt's wrongful punishment initiated him into slavery, one might argue that he emancipates himself by revising that earlier episode and refusing to be beaten:

> This battle with Mr. Covey was the turning-point in my career as a slave. It rekindled the few expiring embers of freedom, and revived within me a sense of my own manhood. It recalled the departed self-confidence, and inspired me again with a determination to be free. . . . My long-crushed spirit rose, cowardice departed, bold defiance took its place; and now I resolved that, however long I might remain a slave in form, the day had passed when I could be a slave in fact. . . .
>
> From this time I was never again what might be called fairly whipped, though I remained a slave for four years afterwards. I had several fights but was never whipped.

Douglass's *Narrative* thus celebrates both explicitly and symbolically a slave's capacity to achieve humanity in a system that conspires to reduce him to nothing. In his ironies and diatribes alike, he exposes the fundamental contradictions of the slaveholding system that make a mockery of American principles and Christian mores. As I suggested earlier, he argues that the slavocracy potentially destroys the sanctity of family relations. Furthermore, his countless descriptions of the conditions under which slaves live rebut any theories that slaves love their assigned station or are humanized by the system. He discredits the apologists' evidence of the slaves' contentment by decoding the misery contained within their songs. And he reveals the misuses to which slaveholders put their religious beliefs. Indeed, in his description of the racism he confronts in New Bedford, he debunks even the myth of the North as the Promised Land.

By uncovering such systemic contradictions Douglass seems to call for a radical cultural transformation. . . . But Douglass's tone is sufficiently acerbic that even in his appendix, where he tries to clarify his position on Christianity, he fails to distinguish effectively his contempt for the slaveholder's religion from a general critique of religion.

DOUGLASS IN THE MAINSTREAM

And yet, as Houston A. Baker, Jr., and Annette Niemtzow have argued, Douglass is entrapped by the very rhetorical and ideological structures he seeks to undermine. Baker demonstrates that by associating freedom with a Christian context, Douglass displays his inability to imagine a self distinct from his superordinate's construction of identity. Similarly, Niemtzow argues that merely by writing about himself in the form of autobiography, Douglass defines himself according to the values of the mainstream culture. I would further suggest that the plot of the narrative offers a profound endorsement of the fundamental American plot, the myth of the self-made man. His broad-based indictments notwithstanding, by telling the story of one man's rise from slavery to the station of esteemed orator, writer, and statesman, he confirms the myth shared by generations of American men that inner resources alone can lead to success.

This myth ignores the role of historical forces in making some men more equal than others. By failing to acknowledge the impact of economic and political policy on individual circumstance, it denies the necessity of social reform to ensure genuine equality of opportunity. Douglass articulates numerous ways in which the slavocracy conspires against black achievement. Surely he believes that American society requires widespread transformation. But the story of his own success actually provides counterevidence for his platform of radical change; for by demonstrating that a slave can be a man in terms of all the qualities valued by his northern middle-class reader—physical power, perseverance, literacy— he lends credence to the patriarchal structure largely responsible for his oppression. . . .

Douglass . . . attempts to articulate a radical position using the discourse he shares with those against whom he speaks. What begins as an indictment of mainstream practice actually authenticates one of its fundamental assumptions.

The Testimonial and the Blues: Modes of African American Autobiography

Elizabeth Schultz

Elizabeth Schultz, an English professor at the University of Kansas, draws several specific contrasts between two styles of African American autobiography. While the testimonial mode tends to focus on political issues, the blues-oriented autobiographer writes to express himself as an individual, rather than to move an audience to political action or awareness. Appropriately, the blues style is more personal and idiosyncratic than the more formal testimonial style, but in a way that fulfills the autobiographer's African American identity instead of diminishing it.

In America in the eighteenth and nineteenth centuries, thousands of former slaves set down the history of their escape from bondage into freedom in writings which came to be called "slave narratives" and to be identified as an independent literary genre; the first of these was printed in 1705, and the last was Booker T. Washington's memorable *Up From Slavery* (1901). In the 1930s, however, the genre was further expanded by the addition of over 2,000 oral narratives: the interviews with former slaves which were conducted as part of the Federal Writers' Project of the Works Progress Administration and collected in over 10,000 pages in the Library of Congress. The written and the oral autobiographical narratives may be considered antecedents for two differing modes within the rich genre of black autobiography.... The emotional drive of the written narrative, as with traditional

Excerpted from Elizabeth Schultz, "To Be Black and Blue: The Blues Genre in Black American Autobiography," *Kansas Quarterly*, vol. 7, no. 3, Summer 1975. Reprinted with permission from *Arkansas Review*.

church testimonial, is toward the reader or listener, whereas the impact of the oral narrative, as with traditional blues, is first upon the individual writer or singer himself; the former assumes an external community, whereas the latter seeks to create a community through the sharing of psychic experiences in the process of their articulation. Black autobiography, then, has a testimonial as well as a blues mode.

"I" AND "WE" IN TESTIMONIALS AND BLUES

In both the written and the oral autobiographies, however, the individual discovers himself to be and describes himself as a member of the black community. Traditional autobiography . . . focuses emphatically upon the individual. . . . Characteristic of the black autobiography, however, is the fact that the individual and the community are not polarities; there is a community of fundamental identification between "I" and "We" within any single autobiography in spite of differences in autobiographical modes and in the autobiographers' visions. [In his introduction to Claude McKay's *A Long Way from Home: An Autobiography*] St. Clair Drake maintains:

> The genre [of Afro-American autobiography] is one in which more intimate aspects of the autobiographer's personal experience are subordinated to social commentary and reflections upon what it means to be a Negro in a world dominated by white men. There have been no black Marcel Prousts and André Gides. The traumatic effects of the black experience seem to have made confessional writing an intellectual luxury black writers cannot afford.

In its development, all black autobiography might be compared to the development of the blues; [in *Blues People*] LeRoi Jones, noting that traditional African songs deal "with the exploits of the social unit," points out that in America the African began to sing songs concerned with his own personal exploits:

> . . . the insistence of the blues verse on the life of the individual and his individual trials and successes on the earth is a manifestation of the whole Western concept of man's life, and it is a development that could only be found in an American black man's music. . . . The whole concept of the *solo*, of a man singing or playing by himself, was relatively unknown in West African music.

Black autobiography in general, however, like the blues, expands the solo; the voice of the single individual retains the tone of the tribe. Of Richard Wright's autobiography, *Black Boy* (1945), Ralph Ellison [in *Shadow and Act*] says that it is, like the blues, "an autobiographical chronicle of personal catastrophe expressed lyrically," but that "in it thousands of Negroes will for the first time see their destiny in public print."

The written slave narrative, however, and those autobiographies of the late nineteenth and twentieth centuries written in a similar mode seek explicitly to change the destiny of the community. As in a traditional church testimonial, the intention of the autobiographer's description of his experience of conversion and salvation in these works is to bring his audience to a like conversion and salvation; consequently the particular facts of personal experience are generalized through logic or exaggeration, so that listeners or readers may readily grasp their significance. The revelations of slave narratives and their autobiographical successors also have the tone of urgency typical of testimonials: Be Saved or Perish in Hell; Find Freedom or Die in Slavery. The apparent intention of the testimonial autobiography thus seems to be to make the experiences of a personal history felt with revolutionary impact upon the present and the future.

THE OVERRIDING THEME OF FREEDOM

The general theme of the written slave narratives, as Arna Bontemps explains [in "The Slave Narrative: An American Genre"], is "the fetters of mankind and the yearning of all living things for freedom." Their specific theme, however, is the abolition of slavery, and as a result, they were widely used in the nineteenth century in support of the Abolition Movement. Through eyewitness accounts or the accounts of firsthand experiences, through practical polemics or impassioned rhetoric, the autobiographers' conviction remains the same as that of former slave Gustavus Vassa who concluded his *Life* [of *Olaudah Equiano, or Gustavus Vassa, the African*] (1789) with the following very simple, very powerful words: "The abolition of slavery would be an universal good." At the outset of his autobiography, the testimonial writer is fully conscious of his conclusion, with each subsequent description or argument being used as evidence to contribute to the final irrefutability of his initial premise; the writer, in reflecting on his slave past, can view that past only from the perspective of his own freedom and therefore directs every word he writes to obtaining freedom for his brothers and sisters. Thus the horrors of slavery overshadow even Vassa's early memories of his beautiful African homeland and his gracious tribal life; in the testimonial autobiography, the end is truly in the beginning, for the tone of urgency must be sustained through the work and beyond.

Testimonial autobiographies of the late nineteenth and twentieth centuries have the same general theme as the written slave narratives, but their specific themes vary. Freedom, for example, in Washington's *Up From Slavery* is freedom to join the American middle class in things economic, whereas in Leslie Lacy's *Rise and Fall of a Proper Negro* (1970) it is freedom from hypocritical middle-class materialistic and aesthetic values; in W.E.B. Du Bois' *Autobiography* (1968), as in Angela Davis's *Autobiography* [1974], it is freedom from capitalistic oppression; in Malcolm X's *Autobiography* (1964) it is freedom from the illusion of white supremacy and toward the development of a powerful black community, and in Donald Reeves's *Notes of a Processed Brother* (1971) it is specifically freedom from a white supremacist educational system. In the autobiographies of Marshall W. "Major" Taylor, Lt. William J. Powell, Matthew A. Henson, W.C. Handy, and Mary Church Terrell, whom Rebecca Chalmers Barton in the first full-length study of black autobiography, *Witnesses for Freedom* [1948], calls "The Achievers," it is freedom to prove their individual worth.

Often in these testimonial autobiographies, the personal voice is subsumed by the writer's desire to minimize himself because of the urgency of his theme. Not only are intimate facts of personal history omitted, but lengthy documents or newspaper accounts are included to prove objectively the historicity of a specific theme. Thus W.E.B. Du Bois curtails a discussion of his personality to a single chapter entitled "My Character," but presents such historically valuable resolutions as those concerning the founding of the Niagara Movement or those concerning a program of race studies at black colleges in the South.

As with Vassa's *Life*, the beginning of the testimonial autobiography anticipates the conclusion. Malcolm X, therefore, opens his *Autobiography* with an account of the Ku Klux Klan terrorism of his family's home at the time he was in his mother's womb and of his father's early dedication to Garveyism; it seems, therefore, that he was destined even before birth to become an effective spokesman for the Black Muslims and for black consciousness. . . .

FOLKLORE, DETAILS, AND TRANSCENDENCE

The oral slave narratives as well as the late nineteenth- and twentieth-century autobiographies written in a similar mode, however, like the blues, do not seek to change their listeners' destiny. Although they testify to the marvel of the black American's capacity to survive the inequities and brutalities of racism and to survive with wit, imagination, exuberance, and grace, although they express a multitude of personal convictions, they do not expound abstractly. Taken together, the oral slave narratives are a compendium of the factual details of the day-to-day activities of plantation life, of the South during the Civil War, and of Reconstruction; of folklore generated in the black community; of vignettes of acquaintances and of family genealogies; as such they are an invaluable source of information for students of American history, as Eugene Genovese's *Roll, Jordan, Roll* (1974) amply exemplifies. The individual voice also sings out loudly in these narratives. . . .

If the testimonial autobiography is concerned with the objectification and development of a specific conviction, the blues autobiography is concerned with the process of discovering meaning, a process synonymous with the discovery of consciousness, with the reader implicitly being engaged in this process. [In *Metaphors of Self: The Meaning of Autobiography*] James Olney explains that an autobiography "intentionally or not [is] a monument of the self at the summary moment of composition." Ellison, in his essay on Wright's autobiography, associates it with the blues, for like the blues, it "is an impulse to keep the painful details and episodes of a brutal experience alive in one's aching consciousness, to finger its jagged grain, and to transcend it, not by the consolation of philosophy but by squeezing from it a near-tragic, near-comic lyricism."

The experiences related in the blues as in the blues autobiography are not unmitigatedly brutal; they are too staggeringly complex. The consciousness of the blues autobiographer, however, while not always aching, is always active and alert, always evolving. The blues singer or autobiographer, by articulating his experiences—by fingering them in his consciousness, by grasping to give them verbal or musical expression—makes them comprehensible to himself and to those who listen to him, and thereby he transcends them. In this sense they express what Ellison has said of both the blues and of Wright's autobiography, they reveal at once "the agony of life and the possibility of conquering it through sheer toughness of spirit.". . .

If, to use the key word from Ellison's autobiographical novel, *Invisible Man* (1952), they make themselves less invisible by discovering their consciousness in the process of writing their autobiographies, they also make the black community less invisible. Our ideas about both the black community and the white community are sharpened by reading a testimonial autobiography; but by reading a blues autobiography, our sense of the complex life of the black community and of human possibilities is deepened as the writer's life is so thoroughly permeated by his people's heritage.

Whether the autobiographer discusses his experiences in the human community around the world as do Langston Hughes, Claude McKay, James Weldon Johnson, and Chester Himes, or restricts himself to corners of the United States as do Anne Moody, Claude Brown, Richard Wright, or Maya Angelou, it is their experience in the black American community which shapes their vision. [In *Dust Tracks on a Road*] Zora Neale Hurston may seem to be tidying up her relationship with the black community by relegating her thoughts to a single chapter entitled "My People! My People!"; yet the first statement she makes about herself is, "I was born in a Negro town.". . .

The "tales of God, the Devil, animals and natural elements" which she heard in the community churches and on the front porch of the general store, besides introducing her to the dynamics of black society, aroused her imagination as a child and led to her extensive research later into black folklore. It led to the throbbing evocation in her autobiography of the spirit of

> Polk County. After dark, the jooks. Songs are born out of feelings with an old beat-up piano, or a guitar for a mid-wife. Love made and unmade. Who put out dat lie, it was supposed to last forever? Love is when it is. No more here? Plenty more down the road. . . .

CONFRONTING THEIR OPPRESSORS

The first confrontation with whites is, for several blues autobiographers, an emotionally jarring experience as well as the experience which catapults them into an awareness of particular ethnic groups as well as the possibility of a single human group. . . .

For Richard Wright [in *Black Boy*], an awareness of white oppression seems to begin in his subconscious when he is a child; his early fears and guilt become embodied in a dream-image of "huge wobbly white bags, like the full udders of cows, suspended from the ceiling above me." Of his adolescence, he says,

> Nothing challenged the totality of my personality so much as this pressure of hate and threat that stemmed from the invisible whites. . . . Tension would set in at the mere mention of whites and a vast complex of emotions, involving the whole of my personality, would be aroused. It was as though I was continuously reacting to the threat of some natural force whose hostile behavior could not be predicted. I had never in my life been abused by whites, but I had already become as conditioned to their existence as though I had been the victim of a thousand lynchings.

Yet Wright triumphs in his struggle to keep the forces of fear and anxiety from stripping him of his imagination or reducing him to the status of the white man's "nigger":

> The white South said that it knew "niggers," and I was what the white South called a "nigger." Well, the white South had never known me—never known what I thought, what I felt. . . . No word that I had ever heard fall from the lips of southern white men had ever made me really doubt the worth of my own humanity.

As he flees the South, he imagines a wider community of mankind, one in which all peoples "might win some redeeming meaning for . . . having struggled and suffered here beneath the stars.". . .

DIFFERENCES IN STYLE

The style of the blues autobiography, unlike that of the testimonial autobiography, also seems a blending of the single voice with the group voice. In the blues autobiography, as in the oral slave narratives, the individual's idiosyncrasies of speech merge with the cadences and idioms of black American speech. As blues singers Mississippi Fred McDowell or Mississippi John Hurt, Lonnie Johnson, or Robert Johnson have distinctive singing styles and yet retain the inflections and rhythms recognizably belonging only to black American song, so are blues autobiographies both individualistic and ethnic in their style. By contrast the style of the testimonial autobiography is often that of the well-written editorial, its tone controlled by a reliance upon abstract generalizations and logic; the testimonial, written in the clear objective style of good journalism, would seem, therefore, easily translatable. Whereas the whole of Iceberg Slim's *Pimp: The Story of My Life* (1969) and Taylor Gordon's autobiography are written in dialect, demanding a glossary at the conclusion, Malcolm X, who spent years in Harlem as a hustler, gives only an isolated example of the hustler's cant along with his translation to illuminate a particular point in his argument, rendering the whole of his autobiography in the clear tones of impersonal history. The style of the blues autobiography may require special translation, and yet, ironically, like the oral slave narratives, the effect of their reliance upon language as it is spoken is to create a sense of dialogue and hence a sense of community with the reader.

Zora Neale Hurston's prose, for example, rings with the rhythms, the natural metaphors, and the anthropomorphisms of the black sermon, even as she exposes her very personal feelings to us. Of her mother's death and its effect upon her, she writes:

> Just then, Death finished his prowling through the house on his padded feet and entered the room. He bowed to Mama in his way, and she made her manners and left us to act out our ceremonies over unimportant things. . . . But life picked me up from the foot of Mama's bed, grief, self-despisement and all, and set my feet in strange ways.

In summing up her life, she says, fusing secular and sacred images: "I can look back and see sharp shadows, high lights, and smudgy inbetweens. I have been in Sorrow's kitchen and licked out all the pots. Then I have stood on the peaky mountain wrappen [*sic*] in rainbows, with a harp and a sword in my hands."

In [jazz musician Charles] Mingus's autobiography [*Beneath the Underdog,* 1971], the narrative sequences have the flow of uninterrupted speech, with his numerous re-created dialogues seemingly improvised against them; he seems therefore to be playing out a long jazz set in reverse, with the solo part doing the back-up work. His dependence upon the present tense, expletives, and the accretion of phrases and nouns also gives his prose the immediacy and vitality of a jazz composition. For example, in one short typical paragraph, his style involves the reader in the tension of a personal episode, an episode which the style also forces us to feel is typical of the history of black people in a racist society:

> Charlie Davis is playing a piano intro and just as Dan begins to sing Phil Moore's "Shoo Shoo Baby" Bo screams—"Oh God! That nigger's got a gun!" Shots ring through the room. The lighted juke box shatters. Glass spatters. People scramble under tables and rush toward exits. Before I know it my boy has calmly laid his bass down and is walking toward the gunman. "Man, you crazy?!" Bo shouts. "Get down! He shooting a gun!" The man is aiming right at him but looks frightened and as Mingus yells "I'll kill you! I'll kill you! This is *Bo's* place!" he fires a wild shot and runs for the door. In the confusion outside a voice calls "Halt in the name of the law!" RAT TAT TAT! All is quiet. And another nigger lies dead in front of Bewley's Black Rooster. But as usual it's the wrong man, it's just poor Half-Pint, the bootlegger who supplies whiskey to the after-hour joints.

The understatement of "as usual it's the wrong man, it's just poor Half-Pint" is characteristic of the "near-tragic, near-comic lyricism," "the agony of life and . . . sheer toughness of spirit" which Ellison considers essential to the blues; such understatement is characteristic of the ironic tone underlying both the blues and the blues autobiography which gives the singer and the writer the means to endure.

The Invisible Author of *The Autobiography of Malcolm X*

John Edgar Wideman

Novelist John Edgar Wideman, an English professor at the University of Massachusetts at Amherst, points out that when author Alex Haley appears for the first time at the close of *The Autobiography of Malcolm X*, many readers are surprised to discover that Haley has been there all along. Wideman admires Haley's accomplishment in making Malcolm's experience and thought accessible and compelling through a writing style so effectively neutral that readers, undistracted and totally focused, feel it is they who are in Malcolm's presence instead of Haley, and they who become one with Malcolm.

You are sitting in a room listening to a man talk and you wish to tell the story of the man's life, using as far as possible the words you are hearing to tell it. As writer you have multiple allegiances: to the man revealing himself to you; to the same man who will read and judge what you write; to an editor with an editor's agenda and maddening distance; to yourself, the demands of creating a text that meets your aesthetic standards, reflects your politics; to a potential publisher and reading public, etc., etc. You are serving many masters, and inevitably you are compromised. The man speaks and you listen but you also take notes, the first compromise and perhaps betrayal. Your notes are intended to capture the words you hear, but they are also designed to compress, select, filter, discard. A net, no matter how closely woven, holds some things and loses others. One crucial dimension lost, like water pouring through the finest seine, is

Excerpted from John Edgar Wideman, "Malcolm X: The Art of Autobiography," in *Malcolm X: In Our Own Image*, edited by Joe Wood. Copyright © 1992 John Edgar Wideman. Reprinted with permission from The Wylie Agency.

143

the flow in time of the man's speech, the sensuous environment of orality that at best is crudely approximated by written words.

You may attempt through various stylistic conventions and devices to reconstitute for the reader your experience of hearing face to face the man's words. The sound of the man's narration may be represented by vocabulary, syntax, imagery, graphic devices of various sorts—quotation marks, punctuation, line breaks, visual patterning of white space and black space, markers that encode print analogs to speech—vernacular interjections, parentheses, ellipses, asterisks, footnotes, italics, dashes. . . . The drama of the encounter between yourself and the man may be enhanced by "stage directions" that set the scene and cue the reader to the hows and whys of what's being said.

> Visiting the Muslim restaurant in Harlem, I asked how I could meet Minister Malcolm X, who was pointed out talking in a telephone booth right behind me. Soon he came out, a gangling, tall reddish-brownskinned fellow, at that time thirty-five years old; when my purpose was made known, he bristled, his eyes skewering me from behind horn-rimmed glasses. "You're another one of the white man's tools sent to spy!" he accused me sharply.

Imagine yourself in a hotel room late at night listening to a man whose life story you wish to write and perhaps you'll invent other means serving the end of representing the man's voice, his presence, ultimately his *meaning* on the page. Perhaps you'll begin to appreciate how intimately truth and technique are entangled.

THE INTERTWINING OF WRITER AND SUBJECT

What's striking about Alex Haley's *Autobiography of Malcolm X* is the peculiar absence of the sorts of narrative strategies listed above. Haley presents a "talking head," first-person narration recorded from the fixed perspective of a single video camera. With a few small and one very large exception to this rule—the Epilogue from which the quote above is drawn—what we get from first to last page of the *Autobiography* is one voice addressing us, an extended monologue, sermon rap, recollection in tranquility of the awesome variety and precipitous turnabouts of Malcolm's life. The enormous popular success of the autobiography (millions of copies sold and selling), the power and persistence of the image of Malcolm it achieves, makes it worth-

while to investigate how Haley does so much with so little
fuss, how an approach that appears rudimentary in fact con-
ceals sophisticated choices, quiet mastery of a medium.
First, what does the exception tell us about the rules?
Though the Epilogue was written after Malcolm's death and
focuses upon his assassination and its aftermath, it remains
a record of life as much as death, a concrete manifestation of
how a spirit transcends the physical body's passing if the
spirit's force continues to touch those who loved it, or those
who didn't love but can't forget its impact, its continuing
presence. Appended to the *Autobiography*, the Epilogue in
many reader's minds blends with Malcolm's story, becomes
part of the "as told to," a further conversation between the
writer and Malcolm, Malcolm and the reader in spite of the
attempt of Malcolm's enemies to silence him.

Several new, important subjects are introduced in the
Epilogue: the writer of the *Autobiography*, the process of
constructing the book, the relationship between writer and
subject. Haley utilizes a variety of narrative modes and
devices in the Epilogue. He inserts himself into the story, describes how, where, and why Malcolm is speaking, Malcolm's appearance, state of mind. Haley quotes, summarizes,
cites other sources for points of view on Malcolm, ventures
his own analysis and opinions explicitly in first person. This
mixed form of narrative exposition is handled quite adroitly.
The Epilogue becomes an eloquent extension of the *Autobiography*, a gripping, dramatically structured fugue that im-
pels the reader toward the climax of assassination, the
inevitable slow shock of recognition afterward as the world
assesses the loss of Malcolm. Nearly one-sixth of the *Autobiography* (74 pages out of 456—a 4-page comment by Ossie
Davis, a 6-page Introduction by M.S. Handler complete the
volume), the Epilogue is proof positive that Haley's choice of
a "talking head" for the body of his book was not chosen because he couldn't compose in another fashion.

"Nothing can be in this book's manuscript that I didn't
say, and nothing can be left out that I want in." Malcolm insisted this guarantee be part of the contract between Haley
and himself. In return Haley received a pledge from Malcolm to "give me a priority quota of his time for the planned
100,000 word 'as told to' book," and later Haley asked for and
tells us he received from Malcolm permission to write "comments of my own about him which would not be subject to

his review." How Malcolm's death affected this bargain, what kind of book his final cut of the manuscript might have produced, we can only guess. We could have posed this question to Haley, but now he's gone too. However, the nature of writing biography or autobiography or any kind of writing means that Haley's promise to Malcolm, his intent to be a "dispassionate chronicler," is a matter of disguising, not removing, his authorial presence.

AN INVISIBLE AUTHOR

Allowing Malcolm to speak for himself meant constructing a text that *seems* to have no author (in a first draft I slipped and wrote "*no other*"), that *seems* to speak for itself without mediation. I've encountered many readers who experienced the book in just such a fashion, who were surprised when reminded of Alex Haley's role. Calling the book an autobiography is of course an explicit denial of an authorial presence and encourages this reaction in readers. Yet as we should have learned from Afro-American folklore or from novelists such as James Joyce who confess the secrets of their craft, effacing the self is also a way of empowering, enabling the self. If you're skillful enough at the sleight-of-hand of storytelling (witness Charles Chesnut's "Uncle Julius"), you can disappear, charm your audience into forgetting you're there, behind and within the tale, manipulating your audience, silently paring your fingernails. Haley performs a double-dip, disappears twice. Once into Malcolm and again with Malcolm as Malcolm the monologist, oracular teacher/ preacher, the bardic bluesman who knows there because he goes there, Malcolm the storyteller collapses the distance between teller and tale, tale and audience.

In the *Autobiography* Malcolm's voice issues from no particular place, no particular body, no particular time. The locus of the voice is his mind, and of course the mind can routinely accomplish what the most sophisticated experiments in written narrative can only suggest and mimic: flashback, flashforward, a seamless flow/exchange between inner and outer worlds, great leaps from location to location, lightning switches between levels of diction and discourse, switches in verb tense, grammatical person, time-space elisions, characters bursting into a scene full blown, announcing, establishing their intricate histories, their physical appearance with a single word. So it's not exactly as if Haley has narrowed his options by situating and representing the *Autobiography* as the first-person flow of Malcolm's speech and thought. Haley grants Malcolm the tyrannical authority of an author, a disembodied speaker whose implied presence blends into the reader's imagining of the tale being told.

Physical descriptions the *Autobiography*'s speaker offers of himself are "time capsules" scattered through the narrative, snapshots of how he appeared at various periods of his life, the boy with "reddish brown mariny color" of skin and hair, the conked teenager in zoot suit and knobby-toed shoes. The voice presently speaking is as generic as the business suits Malcolm X wore as a minister delivering the Honorable Elijah Muhammad's message. Yet the voice also gains a larger-than-life status as it gradually usurps our attention. We make up a body to match the deeds being described, a body substantiated by our participation, identification. No actor could ever match the image of the Lone Ranger I conjured as a kid listening to the masked man's adventures on the radio (who knows, part of the attraction, part of me may have been seeing part of him as black) so I never cared much for the disappointing version of the masked rider that eventually appeared in a TV series.

Haley's disappearance into Malcolm's voice permits readers to accomplish an analogous disappearing act. We open the boundaries of our identities, we're suspended, taken up to the higher ground of Malcolm's voice as a congregation is drawn into the crystal-clear parables and anecdotes of a righteous sermon. We recognize ourselves in what's being said. We amen it. Speaking for us as well as to us, the voice attains the godlike veracity and authority conventionally attributed to the third-person omniscient mode of history texts. The story becomes our story; we manufacture a presence to fill the space Haley seems to have left undefined, unoccupied. Of course some readers, fewer and fewer now, would bring living memories of Malcolm to their reading, and many would have seen photos or films, but these fragments don't alter the rhetorical design of the book and may even enhance it because the *Autobiography*'s omnipresence, its compelling version of its subject, continues to influence images of Malcolm preserved in other media.

MALCOLM'S "VOICE"

Haley's choice of standard English for Malcolm's voice sustains the identification, the exchange between speaker and audience. Vernacular expressions, idiomatic, traditional formulas of African-American speech, occur infrequently in the *Autobiography,* and usually appear within quotes, italics, marked explicitly to indicate that the speaker is abandoning his chosen register. Conservative as the device of a talking head, the strategy of mainstreaming Malcolm's voice is just as quietly effective. The blandness of the language of the *Autobiography* invites the reader not to perform it, but ignore it. The choice of a particular black vernacular would have raised questions of class, as well as race, potentially divisive issues. Would Malcolm be speaking only *for* and *to* those people who speak like him? Would a publisher try to sell to predominantly white readers a book in which one black man addresses other black people in terms only partially comprehensible to the white audience? (How gender is implicated raises further issues that won't be addressed here.) Haley finesses potential problems by sticking to transparent, colorless dialect. Words in the *Autobiography* are cloaked in the same sort of invisibility as its author. Haley signals us to read the text as the events of a life, directly told to us by the person who lived it. Someone is talking to us. When we listen, the writing, like the narrator, disappears into the seemingly unmediated report. Haley's genius is to convince us to hear, not read.

Another advantage Haley gains by his choice of the standard English of TV announcers, textbooks, cereal boxes, and most best-sellers is the conspicuous absence of all but the

The compelling voice of Malcolm X (pictured) is heard in his autobiography through author Alex Haley's role in writing it.

most commonplace, inert, rudimentary figurative language. Attention is drawn to action, to what's being represented, not how it's represented (unless you stubbornly, peevishly insist on asking the latter, often very relevant question). The "personality" of the narrative voice is minimalized, its role as camera eye, objective chronicler, window on reality is enhanced. (Consider the reverse of this process, TV stations juicing up the inert "facts" of weather by foregrounding the "personality" of the weatherperson.) The narrator becomes an unintrusive "voice-over" in the movie the audience constructs from his relation of incidents. If not exactly infallible, the voice Haley fashions for Malcolm has the authority of a courtroom witness, well dressed, articulate, educated, intelligent, one whose account of his experience is seductive, can't be easily discredited or ignored. Another way of saying this is that particular registers of language contain very distinct shorthands or versions of reality, and what's being activated, confirmed when a speaker skillfully manipulates a given register is the world, the assumptions that consenting adults have agreed in advance constitute what's real. Tit for tat the speaker becomes real as he or she verifies the unspoken compact.

Finally, Haley's choice of a voice for Malcolm (himself), because it's designed to transparently reveal what actually happened, can neatly accommodate an audience whose first language may not be standard English. Most African-American readers, whatever registers of English they commonly speak, can amen the familiar people, places, and events of Malcolm's story, can identify with the content of Malcolm's experience, with someone who's been down and out, 'buked and scorned. Many would understand his immersion in the fast life, prison, his religious awakening, his outrage, his simmering frustration and anger toward the American way. The structure of Malcolm's discourse complements its content. The ideological core of the *Autobiography*, the interpretation and analysis of Malcolm's life, would be familiar and convincing to African Americans whose primary mode of communication is oral, not written because in the culture of sermons, blues, street-corner raps, the speaker offers his or her life (our life) as parable, illustration, example, reasoning concretely, directly from the personal to the archetypal, from common nuggets of experience to general principles. Speakers share experiences you share with them. His or her conclusions are seldom surprises. You're taken where you've been. But because nothing is ever exactly repeated, return is not simply repetition, but sometimes often revelation. That's me he's talking about, singing about, praying about, insulting. Yes. Yes. I was there. It happens just that way, every day. Tell the truth.

MALCOLM AS REPRESENTATIVE

Malcolm in the *Autobiography*, like Richard Wright before him in *Black Boy* or Frederick Douglass in the *Narrative*, becomes representative in all the complex, exciting self-reflexive senses of that word. Microcosm paralleling macrocosm, laws governing the molecules in my body replicated in the movements of galaxies, ontogeny reproducing phylogeny, Picasso's art passing through stages that mirror the development of western art in the twentieth century, Du Bois embodying in *Souls of Black Folk* a multidisciplinary, multigenre, humanistic paradigm for African-American studies, a body dancing to the phases of the moon. Richard Wright was a black man born in rural Mississippi at the turn of the century who migrated to Chicago and learned the north was not the promised land. Wright's life reflects a people's passage from south to north, rural to urban, dependency to self-determination, illiteracy to literature, silence to assertion. The witness of Malcolm's life picks up and expands Wright's story, the terrible, destructive pressure of the industrial urban north on traditional black family life, the nearly inevitable adolescent rebellion and crime, imprisonment, the phoenix rise to consciousness, black consciousness, and political activity, discovery of spirituality in forms other than Christianity, the growing awareness of a larger context in which the oppression of African Americans is symptomatic of a global struggle, the struggle of the formerly enslaved, the colonized, the outcast, the dispossessed to seize responsibility, to forge personal identity and communal consciousness that will reverse centuries of subjugation, self-hate, a consciousness capable of opening doors through which healing, healthy people might walk unbowed. Richard Wright and El-Hajj Malik El-Shabazz, representative men whose lives recapitulate the general experience. Malcolm center stage at the podium, in charge of his story, proclaiming "I remember . . . I did thus and so . . . nothing is lost." A Malcolm created and re-created in the space Alex Haley has vacated so the reader may step in, identify, become.

N. Scott Momaday: Native American Autobiographer

H. David Brumble III

H. David Brumble III, the author of American Indian Autobiography, shows how the organization and texture of N. Scott Momaday's autobiographies, The Way to Rainy Mountain and The Names, are derived from the conventions of Native American oral storytelling. One such convention is having many short, separate stories that freely shuttle back and forth between three frames of reference—the personal, the tribal, and the mythic. While Momaday's autobiographies are in fact written, they cultivate and celebrate the older oral style in a way that represents the major Native American theme of nostalgia for a past, golden age.

The Indian autobiographers differ in interesting ways from the black autobiographers. Black autobiographers characteristically write about their attempts to enter into the promised land, a land flowing with milk and honey and freedom, a land peopled with new Canaanites determined to forbid them the fords of the Jordan. Indian autobiography looks back to Eden. Like the Ghost Dancers, most Indian autobiographers want to return. Two Legging's sense of himself has entirely to do with the stories that keep his past vital. White Bull has taught himself to glory in later deeds as though they were coups. Sanapia, Beetus, Maxidiwiac, Black Elk, Benjamin Calf Robe, and many others want to pass on their knowledge of the old ways to a younger generation, so that the old ways might flourish again, or that at least the old ways might not utterly pass away. Beverly Hungry Wolf's autobiography records her attempt to leave "civilization" and return in the most literal sense to the "ways of her grandmothers."

Some Indian progressives, like Thomas Wildcat Alford and the early Charles Eastman, speak with conviction about the superiority of new ways to old. But Alford and Eastman, and even the most devout Christian Indian autobiographers seem never to be far from a sense of loss. Sometimes this rises bitterly to the surface, as it does in the case of Gertrude Bonnin, Jimmie Durham, Jim Barnes, Thrasher, and Bobbi Lee. Sometimes we sense it despite the autobiographers' own assertions that all is well, as in the case of Blowsnake and Hensley. Often it is an ache at the back of the throat, nostalgia fused sometimes with conviction, sometimes with despair. The editors, of course, played their part in all this, but in some way, in some sense most Indian autobiographers seek to return—if only by the workings of the memory, if only by mounting a memorial in words.

THE ORAL TRADITION ON PAPER

N. Scott Momaday certainly participates in this tradition. But for Momaday this notion of a return to the old ways is more than a subject, more than an organizing principle; it has determined the form of his autobiographical books. The choice of archaizing forms was quite self-conscious on Momaday's part, for when Momaday set out upon his autobiographical project, he had a much wider awareness of autobiographical forms and traditions than . . . other autobiographers. . . . This autobiographer occasionally teaches a course in autobiography at the University of Arizona. He has his students read such books as Isak Denisen's *Out of Africa*, Robert Graves's *Goodbye to All That*, and Nabokov's *Speak, Memory*. The reading list reflects the range one might expect of a man who earned his Ph.D. from Stanford. . . . But he chose none of these moderns for his model. In his two published volumes of autobiography, *The Way to Rainy Mountain* (1969) and *The Names* (1976), he chose to write autobiography after the fashion of the nonliterate, oral Indian storytellers: "In general," Momaday wrote on the first page of *The Names*,

> my narrative is an autobiographical account. Specifically, it is an act of the imagination. . . . When Pohd-lohk told a story he began by being quiet. Then he said *Ah-keah-de*, "They were camping," and he said it every time. I have tried to write in the same way, in the same spirit. Imagine: They were camping.

Momaday, then, will *write* autobiography after the fashion of an *oral* storyteller. This was to attempt something quite new. His method produces something that in many ways is like what we have found in White Bull's *Personal Narrative* and like what we can see through Wildschut's editorial veil in *Two Leggings*. In neither *The Way to Rainy Mountain* nor *The Names*, for example, do we find continuous, chronologically ordered narrative. *The Way to Rainy Mountain* contains twenty-four sections. Each section is three pages long and consists of three related accounts, one from Kiowa myth or folklore, one from Kiowa recorded history, and one from Momaday's personal or family history—"the mythical, the historical, and the immediate," as Momaday put it in his own commentary on *The Way to Rainy Mountain*. There are drawings, images, throughout. None of these sections is longer than about three hundred words. Momaday tells the story of the twins and the giant in just two hundred words; the story of the arrow maker and his enemy in about the same space; he tells about the image of *tai-me*, central to the Kiowa Sun Dance, in about a hundred and fifty words.

Momaday has called this "staccato-like narrative," one brief story after another. He wrote with such studied compression in order to convey in writing a sense of oral storytelling (interview, 1985). Oral narratives can, of course, achieve epic length. But Momaday's autobiographical narratives are meant to recall the kinds of stories he himself heard as a child. It is for this reason too that Momaday only rarely makes explicit connections between one story and the next— just as no explicit connections would have been made for the boy Momaday when his grandmother would tell him a story about the emergence of the Kiowas from a hollow log, and then the next night, before bedtime, tell him a story about his grandfather—just as there is no explicit connection when I tell my own children the story of Jack and the beanstalk one night, and a story about one of my schoolyard triumphs the next. Clearly, Momaday wanted his readers to experience something like his own experience of listening to his mother and father and his Kiowa relatives telling stories.

In *The Names* Momaday's plan remained essentially the same. He writes in short units (although not as short as in *The Way to Rainy Mountain*), and very few explicit connections are made between this story and that. Again, there are images, family photographs this time.

That Momaday is attempting to write after the fashion of oral storytellers explains, too, why *The Names* and *The Way to Rainy Mountain* lack literary allusions. In his 1966 novel, *House Made of Dawn,* by contrast, an Indian named *Abel* kills an evil man, who is an albino. Most readers have recognized in Abel a reference to the story in Genesis and in the albino an allusion to Melville's whale and to Melville's reasons for painting evil white (and Momaday has himself confirmed this reading). But he wrote nothing like this in either of his autobiographical works. Again, in these books Momaday is writing in a way as nearly like that of the old oral storytellers as possible. And so he writes without literary allusions.

THE SELF AND THE TRIBE IN NATIVE AMERICAN AUTOBIOGRAPHY

No literary allusions and brief, unconnected narrative: such features of preliterate storytelling are relatively easy to imitate. It is rather more difficult to imagine how such a man as Pohd-lohk, who could have been acquainted with no tradition of modern, written autobiography, might have gone about the task of describing his self and its development. I think Momaday responded to this problem by including tribal and personal history and myth in his autobiographical books.

Certainly just such a mix is one of the striking features of many of the Indian autobiographies. Geronimo's autobiography, for example, includes the following:

> In the beginning the world was covered with darkness. There was no sun, no day. The perpetual night had no moon or stars.

> There were, however, all manner of beasts and birds. Among the beasts were many hideous, nameless monsters. . . . Mankind could not prosper under such conditions, for the beasts and serpents destroyed all human offspring.

And Geronimo also spoke of the history of the tribe:

> The Apache Indians are divided into six subtribes. To one of these, the Be-don-ko-he, I belong. Our tribe inhabited that region of mountainous country which lies west from the line of Arizona, and south from the headwaters of the Gila River.

Of course, he also tells about his own life. Myth, tribal, and personal history—"the mythical, the historical, and the immediate," in Momaday's phrase. *Black Elk Speaks* includes these same three components of identity. The boundaries between the three are not as sharply drawn in *Black Elk Speaks;* but myth, tribal history, and personal history are at least as important here as in *Geronimo.* Early in the first chapter, for example, we read Black Elk's story of how the holy pipe came to the Oglalas. A sacred woman came to the Oglalas:

And after a while she came, very beautiful and singing, and as she went into the tepee this is what she sang:
"With visible breath I am walking.
A voice I am sending as I walk.
In a sacred manner I am walking.
With visible tracks I am walking.
In a sacred manner I walk"
... Then she gave something to the chief, and it was a pipe with a bison calf carved on one side. . . . "Behold!" she said. "With this you shall multiply and be a good nation." (3–4)

As to tribal history, Black Elk's narrative is never far from this; almost everything that he tells us about himself is explicitly or implicitly related to the history of the tribe. Black Elk tells about how things were for his tribe before the coming of the white man, about the great herds of buffalo before the railroad cut the herd in two. Even the Great Vision, which dominates the book just as it dominated Black Elk's life, has to do with Black Elk's relation to the tribe and its well-being. . . .

Given his academic training and his work in Indian Studies programs, and given the number of Indian autobiographers that combine tribal with personal history, one might assume that Momaday went to work as he did because of his reading. In fact, however, Momaday had read virtually none of these narratives when he was at work on his own autobiographies: "Until quite recently I really knew very little about Indian autobiography as such," Momaday said in 1985. "I came very late to *Sun Chief* and *Black Elk Speaks* and other such books":

I was working pretty much with oral tradition exclusively when I wrote *The Names*. . . . I loved hearing people talk about their experiences—my father especially, to whom I was very close. And he told me stories from the first time I could first deal with language. And I loved just to be around when he was recalling something from his childhood. And I think that it was that kind of immediacy, that kind of personal involvement. I wasn't thinking about Indian biography as a classification; I was simply thinking of it as a recounting of experience, very personal.

Momaday combined tribal and personal history, then, largely because of his own childhood immersion in oral narrative traditions, traditions that were not far removed from those which guided Two Leggings, Geronimo, Patencio, and many other unacculturated Indians in their autobiographical labors. . . .

The guiding principle of Momaday's autobiographical writing, then, is that his sense of himself is determined not only by his own remembrances but also by all that his tribe (and his family, Kiowa *and* Anglo) remembers in its myths and its history. This is how he imagined he might write autobiography after the fashion of nonliterate Kiowas. Insofar as we have seen White Bull and Geronimo and other Indians include tribal history and myth along with the recounting of their own deeds, we may see that Momaday's solution is traditional. Indeed, when Momaday tells us in *The Way to Rainy Mountain* and in *The Names* that his sense of himself is intimately related to the movement of his Kiowa ancestors down out of the Rocky Mountain forests onto the Plains, that he is who he is because of his mother's people's relation to

MOMADAY AND THE COMMUNAL SELF

Hertha Dawn Wong, in Sending My Heart Back Across the Years: Tradition and Innovation in Native American Autobiography, *asserts that Momaday's* The Way to Rainy Mountain *is as much a history of the Kiowa tribe as it is a personal autobiography.*

Finally, we have to ask what is autobiographical about *The Way to Rainy Mountain.* It could be simply an exquisitely written history of the Kiowa tribe, rather than an artfully shaped personal history of a Kiowa individual. Momaday's point, however, is that these are one and the same. He attempts to reclaim the communal sense of self, the land-based sense of identity, and the cosmic-related sense of being of his ancestors. The only way that is possible for him, with his twentieth-century, Stanford-educated literary sensibility, is through an impassioned act of the imagination realized in language. Although he refutes the comparison, Momaday may be likened to a Native American Emerson espousing an Indian oversoul. He wants . . . to see no distinction between the mythical and the historical, between the individual and the racial experience. But more than that is his decidedly twentieth-century Western obsession to remake himself anew through the power of the word.

Hertha Dawn Wong, S*ending My Heart Back Across the Years: Tradition and Innovation in Native American Autobiography.* New York: Oxford University Press, 1992, pp. 173–74.

the hills of Kentucky, that his sense of self is shaped by the Kiowa's genesis, their coming forth out of a log—in all of this and in the very form of his autobiographies, Momaday encourages us to see in his personal development the analogue of the effects of oral transmission on preliterate societies. I quote the philosopher/anthropologist Robin Horton:

> In considering oral transmission, we must stress that its most distinctive effects depend upon the use of human memory as a storage device. On the one hand, memory tends to remould the past in the image of the present, and hence to minimize the amount of change that has taken place down through the ages. On the other hand, memory tends, over the generations, to ascribe all innovations, whether sociocultural or intellectual, to an initial "time of the beginnings." Oral transmission, therefore, encourages a view of the past which sees the main outlines of one's society as having been shaped long ago and as having undergone little essential change since then.

This, then, is Momaday's solution. The ancients did not write autobiography; neither did they conceive of themselves in a way that would have led them to compose autobiography-as-self-discovery even if they had been literate. But, says Momaday, their idea of themselves was a product or a creation of the free interplay of imagination and three kinds of memory: the mythical, the historical, and the immediate. For Momaday, "an Indian is an idea which a given man has of himself." An unlettered, traditional Indian such as Pohd-lohk may never have given explicit utterance to any such single idea of the self, but the constituents of the idea were there nonetheless. And so Momaday can write autobiography after the fashion of the ancients by setting down all the fragments that make up the unuttered whole. . . .

TOWARD A WRITTEN TRADITION

Of course, other influences also worked on Momaday. He would not, for example, have worked as he did with limited point of view, nor would he have asked his readers to piece together his stories on their own had he not read Faulkner and Joyce. But, still, I think it may be said that Momaday set for himself the task of writing autobiography according to the conventions of an autobiographical tradition that had never before been considered to be a tradition. . . .

Momaday's work, then, may be seen as a kind of embodiment of a particular moment in the history of American Indian autobiography. He is also a force in this transition from oral to written traditions. And Momaday is quite self-conscious about this. His plan here is in keeping with his sense of the history of literature in the largest sense. In 1970 Momaday wrote that he had for "three or four years" been interested "in the matter of 'oral tradition'":

> Specifically, I began to wonder about the way in which myths, legends, and lore evolve into that mature condition of expression which we call "literature." For indeed literature is, I believe, the end-product of an evolutionary process, and the so-called "oral tradition" is primarily a stage within that process, a stage that is indispensable and perhaps original as well.

Momaday is speaking in general of the transformation of oral literature into a written literature. But I think that Momaday's aims here are particularly important to the history and development of American Indian autobiography. Before Momaday, these narratives were regarded as a miscellaneous if fascinating assortment of anthropological, historical, psychological, and literary documents. Momaday's self-conscious attempt to write autobiography after the fashion of the oral storytellers has done much to make this miscellany into a literary tradition. No Indian autobiographer before Momaday, I think, tried to imagine the literate equivalent of preliterate autobiography.

CHAPTER 4

Women's Autobiographies

 Autobiography

Women's Autobiography and the Male Tradition

Estelle C. Jelinek

Estelle C. Jelinek, the author of *The Tradition of Women's Autobiography* (1986), describes the broad characteristics of women's autobiographies as antithetical to men's in that women are usually much less confident than men in presenting their lives, but also more honest. The idyllic childhood and the heroic adulthood are male conventions and therefore rarely appear in women's autobiographies. In addition, the writing styles women use tend to be more indirect and understated than men's, and the form more fragmentary and anecdotal.

Even if we ignore the subjective biases of critics of autobiography, we find that most of their objective theories are not applicable to women's life studies. For example, James Cox argues that the history of America and the history of autobiography have developed together and that the periods of greatest productivity in autobiography correspond to important events in American history. By meticulously calculating the number of diaries and autobiographies listed in various bibliographies according to historical periods, one finds contrary evidence for women. The periods of increased diary writing by men, for example, during the Revolution and the Gold Rush, are periods of decreased productivity by women. During the Civil War period, there was an increase in autobiographies by military men, but women's autobiographies did not begin to be published in significant numbers until the end of the nineteenth century. Female diaries and autobiographies increased as literacy and educational opportunities for women improved. The peak periods of autobiographical productivity for women have been during the

Progressive Era—1890 to the First World War, an era of unprecedented public service by women—and during the late 1960s and 1970s. The periods of greatest productivity for women's autobiographies have not been during revolutionary (male) times but during the high points of women's history. In *The Female Experience* (1977), historian Gerda Lerner notes:

> The periods in which basic changes occur in society and which historians commonly regard as turning points are not necessarily the same for men and women. This is not surprising when we consider that the traditional time frame in history has been derived from political history. For example, neither during or after the American Revolution nor in the age of Jackson did women share in the broadening out of opportunities and in the political democratization experienced by men. On the contrary, women in both periods experienced status loss and a restriction of their choices as to education or vocation, and had new restraints imposed upon their sexuality, at least by prescription. Thus, the traditional political and military chronology is largely irrelevant to the history of women.

EVALUATING WOMEN'S AUTOBIOGRAPHY

More significant are discrepancies between the critical canon and women's autobiographies on matters relating to their form and content. Despite the fact that women's life studies are excluded from the evidence from which the characteristics of the genre are drawn, it is assumed that they will either conform to them or else be disqualified as autobiographies. One may reasonably question whether including women's autobiographies in critical studies might force modifications in their definitions and theories. Or we might find that different criteria are needed to evaluate women's autobiographies, which may constitute, if not a subgenre, then an autobiographical tradition different from the male tradition.

Since "autobiography" is etymologically and in practice the story of a person's life, we shall first compare the content of women's and men's life studies before contrasting their stylistic differences. While not every autobiography may conform to the conclusions we have drawn here and readers will no doubt be able to cite examples to disprove every one of them, nonetheless, the patterns that emerge cannot be wholly ignored.

One such distinguishing pattern is related to the restrictive male view of history. The consensus among critics is that a good autobiography not only focuses on its author but also reveals his connectedness to the rest of society; it is representative of his times, a mirror of his era. This criterion is adequately supported by the many male autobiographies which concentrate on chronicling the progress of their authors' professional or intellectual lives, usually in the affairs of the world, and their life studies are for the most part success stories. Augustine's *Confessions* (400), an essential philosophical document of his time, traces the vicissitudes of his spiritual progress until his successful conversion. [Jean Jacques] Rousseau's *Confessions* (1781), [Edward] Gibbon's *Autobiography* (1793), and [Johann Wolfgang von] Goethe's *Poetry and Truth* (1812-31), though personal in some respects, are also success stories and can be read as histories of their eras. [Jon Stuart] Mill shapes his *Autobiography* (1873) around the theme of his intellectual development, by means of which he traces the social and economic history of his century. In America the theme of progress or success in the affairs of the world is continued in [Benjamin] Franklin's *Autobiography* (1791), a history of the stages of his rise to the career of international diplomat. [Henry] Adams adheres so closely to this theme that he excludes twenty of his mature years as husband and professor in order to detail the conflict of his age between eighteenth- and nineteenth-century sensibilities. Others of such radically dissimilar origins as *Black Elk Speaks* (1932), *The Autobiography of Malcolm X* (1965), Willie Morris' *North Toward Home* (1967), and most obviously Norman Podhoretz' *Making It* (1967) stress their authors' successful professional life and concomitantly its relationship to their times, with little or a much smaller percentage allotted to their personal lives.

CONTENT OF WOMEN'S WRITING

On the other hand, women's autobiographies rarely mirror the establishment history of their times. They emphasize to a much lesser extent the public aspects of their lives, the affairs of the world, or even their careers, and concentrate instead on their personal lives—domestic details, family difficulties, close friends, and especially people who influenced them. Agrippina's *Memoirs* from the first century A.D. depart radically from earlier autobiographical reminiscences by stressing her family members rather than the political affairs of state. In *The Book of Margery Kempe* (1436) the emphasis is on both the hostile and friendly people Kempe met on her pilgrimages rather than on her religious progress. Teresa's *Life* (1562–65) is addressed to other nuns, to convince them to persist in their faith in their visions as she had done for twenty years until she found a confessor who believed in their authenticity. In both English and American religious narratives and personal diaries of the seventeenth and eighteenth centuries, it is domestic details that comprise the larger proportion of their accounts. We recall the "lasting service" done autobiography by those eighteenth-century *vies scandaleuses* and their affective descriptions of people of the court and the men they loved. In Lucy Larcom's *A New England Girlhood* (1889) we learn little about her work in the Lawrence factory but much about her relationships with her friends and about their efforts to find personal diversions to their work. Later when she travels to the frontier to teach school, we get only glimpses of her classroom activities but detailed descriptions of the cultured people she met, to her surprise, in the supposedly barren Midwest. Even missionaries rarely write about the work in which they were engaged but emphasize the people they encountered and the hardships of frontier life. Most frontier autobiographies share this characteristic, as do the narratives of Indian captives, ex-slaves, and pioneers, which concentrate on efforts to be reconciled with their families, to acquire food, to build homes, to endure childbirth, and to survive emotionally and physically in the wilderness—all "domestic" details that . . . were not the province of autobiography.

Even in the autobiographies by women whose professional work is their claim to fame, we find them omitting their work life, referring obliquely to their careers, or camouflaging them behind the personal aspects of their lives. Elizabeth Cady Stanton states in her preface to *Eighty Years and More:*

> The story of my private life as the wife of an earnest reformer, as an enthusiastic housekeeper, proud of my skill in every department of domestic economy, and as the mother of seven children, may amuse and benefit the reader.

> The incidents of my public career as a leader in the most momentous reform yet launched upon the world—the emancipation of woman—will be found in "The History of Woman Suffrage."

Though we do learn much about the history of the American woman's suffrage movement and Stanton's major role in it, she softens her political message to the predominantly female audience she is addressing with humorous and distracting anecdotes about her arduous travel adventures as a lyceum lecturer, with advice to young mothers about caring for their children, and with sketches of the many socially prominent and unsung pioneer women whom she met in America and abroad.

[Gertrude] Stein goes to great lengths to place her concern for her work in the background by camouflaging it behind humorous anecdotes about others. Interspersed among her entertaining stories are some allusions to her actual writing, to [Alice B.] Toklas' typing of her manuscripts, and to her failures and successes at publishing them, but the reader must struggle to piece together the progression of her literary output and to see it as a separate and important subject, which like an antiphonally recurring theme does persist until it emerges into fuller view in the last chapter.

Neither Edith Wharton's *A Backward Glance* (1934) nor Ellen Glasgow's *The Woman Within* (1954) tells us about the writing of their successful novels or of the recognition that resulted from them. *The Living of Charlotte Perkins Gilman* (1935) focuses on Gilman's struggles to overcome the severe emotional handicaps that plagued her work life in the reform movement. [Lillian] Hellman concentrates on portraits of friends in her three autobiographical works, and in the one chapter on the theater in *Pentimento* (1973), she tells us amusing stories about eccentric producers, directors, and actors but nothing about her writing. [Sally] Carrighar is a frequently published naturalist, but she devotes her autobiography almost entirely to her depressing emotional life up to her mid-thirties, *before* her professional work began. (She wrote *Home to the Wilderness* [1973] in her late sixties.) What [anthropologist Margaret] Mead relates about her early field trips in *Blackberry Winter* (1972) is for the purpose of explaining the development of her interest in the maturation of children; she, like [Henry] Adams, skips twenty years of her life, but they are her most active professional years—the time between the birth of her daughter and granddaughter— because her autobiographical intention is to outline the proper training of children. Even so historical an autobiography as Emma Goldman's *Living My Life* (1930) dilutes the political activities of the anarchists with portraits of their personal lives and details of her own relationship with Alexander Berkman and other close friends.

This emphasis by women on the personal, especially on other people, rather than on their work life, their professional success, or their connectedness to current political or intellectual history clearly contradicts the established criterion about the content of autobiography. . . .

CHILDHOOD AS SUBJECT: MEN'S VIEWS

Because most autobiographers of both sexes describe their childhoods, which are usually recalled as unhappy times, we can most easily see this difference in the way they handle their early years, but it also pervades the accounts of their adult lives as well, whether they stress careers or personal subjects. Men tend to idealize their lives or to cast them into heroic molds to project their universal import. They may exaggerate, mythologize, or monumentalize their boyhood and their entire lives. Perhaps for fear of appearing sentimental, they often desist from revealing crises in their childhood but are more likely to relate adult crises, usually turning points in their professional lives.

[St.] Augustine's narrative dramatizes his sinful youth and culminating conversion at the onset of middle age. Franklin idealizes his rise from poor boy to international statesman and exalts himself as the first American. He seems to see no necessity to dwell on the cutting short of his education or of his inclination for the sea by his father's forcing him to work at the age of ten; instead, the difficulties he encounters are political ones as a career diplomat. . . . Booker T. Washington skips over his deprived youth to document his role as the father of his race. Foreseeing his destiny when his fortunes begin to change, he assumes the surname of the father of his country. The turning point of his life occurs at the kiln firing of the first bricks for his revolutionary Tuskegee Institute. Adams casts himself as a symbol for American history, split between eighteenth- and nineteenth-century sensibilities and incapable of dealing with the twentieth—another crisis that comes in middle age. . . .We cannot be certain how Malcolm X would have written the *Autobiography* himself, but under Alex Haley's shaping, we read a heroic narrative of Malcolm's rise to fame, from a childhood of extreme poverty and violence, and his catastrophic demise. Richard Wright converts a childhood of hunger and alcoholism, emotional suffocation, and racial trauma into a miracle of survival and salvation through literature.

This view of their childhoods as idylls of innocence and redemption and of their lives as heroic seems to be a male literary tradition. The proclivity of men toward embellishing their autobiographies results in the projection of a self-image of confidence, no matter what difficulties they may have encountered. This is contrary to the self-image projected in women's autobiographies. What their life stories reveal is a self-consciousness and a need to sift through their lives for explanation and understanding. The autobiographical intention is often powered by the motive to convince readers of their self-worth, to clarify, to affirm, and to authenticate their self-image. Thus, the idealization or aggrandizement found in male autobiographies is not typical of the female mode.

CHILDHOOD AS SUBJECT: WOMEN'S VIEWS

Women's self-image is projected by the very means used to distance or detach themselves from intimacy in their life stories—a variety of forms of understatement. In place of glowing narratives, women tend to write in a straightforward and objective manner about both their girlhood and adult experiences. They also write obliquely, elliptically, or humorously in order to camouflage their feelings, the same techniques used to play down their professional lives. Even when they risk themselves by relating crises, usually in girlhood, it lacks that nostalgia men seem to experience (perhaps because, as Ellen Moers has noted of female fiction [in *Literary Women*, 1975], it is more usually the "brutishness of childhood" and the "savagery of girlhood" that are most remembered). Instead, the accounts of girlhood crises, while conveying their authors' awareness of their importance in shaping their later lives, are distanced by this understated treatment.

Stanton wrote her autobiography to sway her readers to the cause of women's suffrage, and she dates her career as a fighter for women's rights from her traumatic experience at the age of eleven when she learned that her adored father valued only boys. Yet she recounts this incident objectively in the same reportorial style that informs all the trials of her fifty years of petitioning, lecturing, and herculean traveling on the lyceum circuit in her fifties and sixties, a narrative both relieved and distanced by her many humorous anecdotes.

Stanton's style could be attributed to her restrictive nineteenth-century upbringing were it not for the fact that this same kind of detachment continues among autobiographers in the twentieth century. All eight essays in Mary McCarthy's *Memories of a Catholic Girlhood* (1957) are directed toward examining the complex childhood influences that shaped her adult personality, and though each one reveals a crucial turning point in every formative area of her girlhood—family, character development, intellectual growth, and sexuality—she skillfully detaches herself from these events by utilizing an abstract and intellectual style, as well as by choosing to analyze each essay in a critical epilogue. In *I Know Why the Caged Bird Sings* (1969), [Maya] Angelou consistently understates her girlhood experiences, like her first shocking encounters with racism and her rape at the age of eight, as well as her adolescent struggles to gain self-reliance and to attain womanhood. [Sally] Carrighar, whose autobiography documents her successful resolution of the many traumas of her childhood persecution by her mother, also understates her experiences, as in the accounts of her mother's attempt on her life and of her command to "lose" a cherished dog. Hellman camouflages the trials of her childhood behind humorous anecdotes, especially in *An Unfinished Woman* (1969), like the nose-breaking incident, which diverts us from her school frustrations and loneliness, and her running away from home, which sidetracks us (for a time) from her budding sexuality. In *Pentimento* she relies heavily on an elliptical style and especially on oblique dialogue, both of which distance her and her readers from her uncomfortable childhood and adult memories. While Stanton and Hellman use humor on occasion to detract readers from their feelings, Stein relies almost entirely on this means of detachment in the many anecdotes about her expatriate life. In her case, it is an ironic and mocking humor, wholly untypical of the serious genre of self-portraiture.

UNITY VERSUS FRAGMENTATION

A final autobiographical feature upon which critics agree is that autobiographers consciously shape the events of their life into a coherent whole. By means of a chronological, linear narrative, they unify their work by concentrating on one period of their life, one theme, or one characteristic of their personality. It is not surprising that with men socially conditioned to pursue the single goal of a successful career, we find such harmony and orderliness in their autobiographies. Such unity betokens a faith in the continuity of the world and their own self-images. The unidirectionality of men's lives *is* appropriately cast into such progressive narratives.

On the other hand, irregularity rather than orderliness informs the self-portraits by women. The narratives of their lives are often not chronological and progressive but disconnected, fragmentary, or organized into self-sustained units rather than connecting chapters. The multidimensionality of women's socially conditioned roles seems to have established a pattern of diffusion and diversity when they write their autobiographies as well, and so by established critical standards, their life studies are excluded from the genre and cast into the "non-artistic" categories of memoir, reminiscence, and other disjunctive forms.

Our earliest male autobiographer, Augustine, narrates his life story progressively up to the time of his conversion and then crowns it with three chapters of brilliant intellectual analysis. Rousseau's confessions, however excessively detailed, are persistently chronological and progressive. Franklin wrote his autobiography during several sittings over a period of eighteen years, yet he resumed the narrative each time where he had left off. Goethe's autobiography, also written over a number of years, is methodically chronological. Washington, Mill . . . Wright . . . and Malcolm X all proceed linearly with no miscellaneous forms to disrupt the orderly time sequence or the style. Though Adams omits twenty years of his life, the hiatus causes no break in the continuity of his theme, whatever curiosity readers may have about those hidden years.

But as early as the fifteenth century, we find Kempe constantly interrupting her narrative with long apostrophes to God and with descriptions of her many weeping fits. Teresa's life story is broken with a long dissertation on prayer and with sporadic descriptions of her raptures. In Mary Rowlandson's account of her captivity by Indians (1682), frequent quotations from the Bible halt the narrative, and an exhortation on improved means for combating the Indians increases our suspense only sentences before her eventual release. Pioneer narratives and accounts by women disguised as soldiers and sailors in order to experience lives denied them as women describe their adventures and trials episodically and fragmentedly. Stanton's history is interrupted by anecdotes, portraits of people, and quoted letters and articles of her own and by others. In the twentieth century, we find the situation unchanged.

Stein's anecdotes of the famous artists and writers whose friendships legitimized her before she received public recognition are well known; so is her method of accreting details of her tales, and arranging many of her chapters, in nonchronological order. McCarthy's *Memories* are a collection of eight previously published essays. Hellman's *Unfinished Woman* starts off chronologically, but shortly becomes a pastiche of diary notes from her trips to Spain and Russia and concludes with studies of her closest adult friends. By the time she came to write *Pentimento,* subtitled *A Book of Portraits,* she had recognized that her forte in autobiography was the same dramatic character development that informed her playwrighting, and each chapter in her second work is a self-contained unit. Had she forced an orderly and linear narrative on the events and persons that affected the development of her personality and values, she would have destroyed the achievement of a cumulative, three-dimensional portrait of herself. Angelou's *Caged Bird* proceeds somewhat chronologically, but most chapters or groups of chapters are self-sustaining vignettes or short stories. Almost half of [Hannah] Tilich's *From Time to Time* (1973) consists of poems, playlets, dreams, dramatic allegories, diary extracts, and character sketches distributed throughout a narrative organized around the various towns and cities she inhabited as a child and adult. The controlled chaos of [Kate] Millett's autobiography, with its mixed chronology, flashbacks within flashbacks, sometimes three times removed, and its stream-of-consciousness and associative narrative, clearly reflects the fragmentation she experiences in her multiple roles as writer, teacher, filmmaker, critic, sculptor, political activist, bisexual, and feminist.

A CONTINUALLY CHANGING GENRE

Surveying quite a number of bibliographies from various countries and periods, one is struck by the number of women writing diaries, journals, and notebooks, in contrast to the many more men writing autobiographies proper. From earliest times, these discontinuous forms have been important to women because they are analogous to the fragmented, interrupted, and formless nature of their lives. But they also attest to a continuous female tradition of discontinuity in women's autobiographical writing to the present day. Fragmented narratives are not unknown among men's autobiographies, nor are progressive narratives absent in women's, especially in life studies which include more about their work life than the norm. But even when they are basically linear, as are Stanton's, Gilman's, and Goldman's, they exhibit the same anecdotal and disruptive characteristic we find in other women's autobiographies.

Thus, the final criterion of orderliness, wholeness, or a harmonious shaping with which critics characterize autobiography is often not applicable to women's autobiographies. No such restrictions adhere in defining or evaluating fiction, to which critics long ago adapted their standards to accommodate fragmented and stream-of-consciousness narratives, however chaotic, that are integral to their content. The various forms in which women write their life studies are often appropriate for rendering the authors' intentions and/or personalities, and autobiographical critics do a disservice to these many fine works and to the genre itself when they saddle the autobiographical mode with their confining criteria.

Perhaps this situation will change. In the late twentieth century, the autobiographical mode has been undergoing considerable experimentation, which may prod critics into modifying their standard definitions and theories, modifications long overdue for judging women's autobiographies. While linear and detached autobiographies by people who concentrate on their professional lives still dominate, more men are writing in less regular forms and are including more personal subjects; Merle Miller's *On Being Different* (1971), Mark Vonnegut's *The Eden Express* (1975), Jerry Rubin's *Growing (Up) at 37* (1975), and Mark Harris' *Best Father Ever Invented* (1976). In addition, autobiography is no longer the sole province of older people looking backward reflectively and consciously on their past, for young people are recording their lives as they live them.

Whatever their ages or circumstances, contemporary autobiographers are having more difficulty making sense of the past than did their historical predecessors. The complexity of the atomic era has made a wholistic view of life difficult, and it has affected the form and content of autobiography as well. But however much the gradual collapse of traditional values has made women's values more acceptable to the present male culture, what may appear new is, in fact, for women the culmination of a long tradition.

Politics, Love, and Personal Integrity in Emma Goldman's *Living My Life*

Blanche H. Gelfant

Blanche H. Gelfant, an English professor at Dartmouth College and the author of *Women Writing in America*, analyzes the complex way early twentieth-century anarchist Emma Goldman revised her public image as the rabble-rousing "Red Emma" without compromising her principles or the truth in her autobiography, *Living My Life*. Goldman portrays her radicalism as part of a historical process and an American tradition going back to Ralph Waldo Emerson and Henry David Thoreau. Goldman describes her affairs with a succession of lovers in a way that is self-deprecatingly honest and literary in its language and references. In her book as in her life, Goldman makes being honest and outspoken the essence of her identity.

In 1928 . . . the fifty-eight-year-old Goldman . . . had been living in exile for almost ten years. She was disillusioned with Soviet Russia, a refuge she had by now rejected as she rejected all coercive states (and to her all states were coercive). She was tired of wandering. She wanted to return to the United States, the country she considered home. Since she had been deported because of ideas the government considered politically dangerous, she needed to place her anarchism within a context that would demystify it without attenuating its social and moral urgency. She would not deny her revolutionary past—she could not, since she considered fidelity to the "Ideal" of anarchism the essence of

Excerpted from Blanche H. Gelfant, "Speaking Her Own Piece: Emma Goldman and the Discursive Skeins of Autobiography," in *American Autobiography: Retrospect and Prospect*, edited by Paul John Eakin. Copyright © 1991 The Board of Regents of the University of Wisconsin System. Reprinted with permission from The University of Wisconsin Press.

her life. But she would try to dispel fears her anarchism aroused by contextualizing it within a historical process of conflict and change. Centering herself within this process, she described her actions as consistently furthering the cause of freedom. This was, she noted, a quintessentially American cause. It was also a universal dream, for all revolutionary ideas of liberty—including those of Thoreau and Emerson, whom she considered early American anarchists—flowed together, she believed, in a historic ideological stream coursing toward freedom.

RECOUNTING HER LIFE WITHOUT MISREPRESENTING IT

As Goldman faced the task of writing herself into history—while, conversely, personalizing history by writing it into her life-story—she had to resolve problems other than those usually attributed to women autobiographers (and to women writers in general). She did not have to overcome a fear of speaking in her own voice or displaying herself upon a public stage. She had not lived a private, silenced, and covertly rebellious life. On the contrary, like other radical women of her time—Mother Jones, Elizabeth Gurley Flynn, Charlotte Perkins Gilman, and Margaret Sanger, all of whom wrote autobiographies—Goldman shattered the stereotype of woman as private, selfless, and submissively conforming to social expectations she sought secretly to subvert. Goldman's rebellion was overt, her stage public, and her voice, heard by thousands, respected and feared. In 1917, when she was ordered by a United States Marshal not to speak in public, she had an audience stomping and screaming as she appeared on stage with a handkerchief stuffed in her mouth. Even gagged, she could not be silenced. Nor could she be domesticated. Her autobiography recounts her lifelong resistance to men who wanted her to marry, bear children, and stay at home as wife and mother. She defied her father, whose physical violence and emotional abuse blighted her young years; and she refused her lovers, who wanted her to relinquish her political ideals and public persona. Though autobiography, one might think, was generically different from propaganda, Goldman would not mute or mutate her political discourse because she would not misrepresent the woman it had taken her a lifetime to create. On the other hand, simply to restate her ideology would have been redundant and inexpedient. Autobiography permitted her to recontextualize her much-rehearsed social criticism within the personal story of a woman's life, while at the same time, it allowed her to reidentify the woman with her ideas. "E.G. the woman and her ideas are inseparable," she wrote.

RE-CREATING A PUBLIC IMAGE

Goldman realized that creating the autobiography implied an act of self-appropriation that placed her in a politically contentious position, for she was in effect challenging a public image of Red Emma, the notorious demagogue who could, presumably, persuade a naive listener to violence, even to assassination. Like other public women in American history, Elizabeth Cady Stanton and Charlotte Perkins Gilman, for instance, Goldman believed she had to confront a factitious image created by the public to serve interests often antithetical to her own. Like these women, she proposed to modify and correct, or erase, a portrait painted by admirers as well as adversaries. Autobiography would permit her to reclaim her image from the public and redefine herself. She defined also her own recuperative strategies, different from those of other radical women. Stanton, for example, tried to modify a public perception of her as an extraordinary person by emphasizing her ordinary daily activities; the story of her private life as wife, housekeeper, and mother, she wrote, might "amuse" and "benefit" her readers. Gilman, on the other hand, stressed her debilitation, calculating for her reader the productive years she might have enjoyed had she not been incapacitated by recurrent episodes of depression. At the same time that these women were disavowing their public images, they reiterated their ideological positions, so that their autobiographies reinscribed an impression that, ostensibly, they wished to revise. Even as they revealed their ordinariness or inadequacy (usually equated with conformity or debilitation), they emerged as extraordinary women, strong and contentious, and threatening to the established social order from which, for all their attempted reconciliations, they remained alienated. Goldman's need for an ideological reconciliation with her readers was more urgent than that of Stanton and Gilman because her situation was more critical. And her motives were more conflicted than theirs, her discursive modes more diverse and entangled. She wanted to assert her Americanism, but she could not resist advertising her alienating (and alienated) political views. Her complicated and perhaps duplicitous design was to persuade her readers that alienation itself was an American strain—an indigenous tension and ideological identification. As an unregenerate revolutionary, she could be an American and a prodigal American daughter returning home. Goldman's efforts to revise Red Emma's tabloid image tested her rhetorical powers as a writer. She knew she possessed the power of speech. Indeed, if she had been less persuasive as a speaker, less public and publicized and, of course, less sweepingly revolutionary, she might not have marshaled against her the full power of the United States government. Now she needed the power of the written word to create a self-portrait that would show everyone that E.G. and her ideas were benignly conceived and morally sound. As she knew, Red Emma personified two ideologies unacceptable to the American public: anarchism and radical feminism. Both were perceived, as she herself perceived them, as forces that would destroy society's founding institutions: marriage and the state. To Goldman, both were inherently oppressive. As a woman who had not only advocated but also acted out a woman's right to economic and sexual independence—and sought to subvert accepted views of family life, motherhood, and education—Goldman now faced formidable obstacles in creating a portrait of herself that would validate her politics and her person. . . .

As a woman, she may have been conflicted and complex—"woven of many skeins," she wrote. She knew she was elusive to others and, sometimes, to herself. But even when she admitted that she had "never been able to unearth" the "real" Emma Goldman, she was implicitly affirming the existence of a continuous and authentic identity. The problems she encountered in translating Emma Goldman or E.G. into an autobiographical "I" were rhetorical and emotional . . . and she resolved them by casting Goldman the writer in a variety of authorial roles. Writing as a revisionist historian, she interjected long expository descriptions of the background for her political actions, authenticating her accounts of the past with verifiable dates, places, and names. . . . Goldman devoted chapters to American labor history and, as the setting of her story changed, to the early years of the Russian revolution. In describing the Haymarket Affair that had converted her to anarchism, she recounted historical events she had heard reported; in writing about the Hempstead strike—which linked her destiny indissolubly with that of Alexander Berkman, the young anarchist she had met on her first day in New York— she revealed how her actions created history. . . . Goldman recalls her young, impressionable self listening to the socialist Johanna Greie tell of the 1886 riot in Haymarket Square.

FRACTURED CHRONOLOGY

In describing how the Haymarket Affair had converted her to anarchism, Goldman's narrative strategy was complexly involuted, as were her autobiographical designs—her intentions and her narrative form. Almost fifty years after the Haymarket riot, Goldman still wanted to assert the innocence of the convicted anarchists and to justify her commitment to their cause, a definitive, lifelong commitment that was to transform her from a young immigrant woman into the Red Emma of tabloid notoriety. Goldman recalls that Johanna Greie had beckoned the awed young Goldman to her and prophesied that some day she would make the Haymarket anarchists' cause her own. The prophecy, the speech, and the "cause" are framed as the memory of a memory. Goldman begins by remembering her first night in New York. She is excited and sleepless, having just heard a stirring "denunciation of American conditions" by the anarchist orator Johann Most. Then, as she tosses about, she once more "live[s] through the events of 1887"—events that had taken place in Rochester almost two years ago and that recapitulated still earlier events now [irrefutably] part of American history and Goldman's past. Thus Goldman links her past, as she is remembering herself remembering it, to the American scene, tracing her feelings as well as her future to a flashback of Johanna Greie's impassioned speech. This involuted chronology coalesces time and the historical times. It places historical events in the past, while it makes history immediate in the living narrator (Greie) present before Goldman; simultaneously, it foreshadows the future by prophesying the execution of the Haymarket anarchists and Goldman's conversion to their cause. As this framing suggests, Goldman was violating the chronology of events in order to rationalize her radicalism as a justifiable response to what she believed were acts of flagrant injustice. She was also giving her life an inherently dramatic structure by beginning her story at a climactic moment of conversion that decides her to set out for the city in quest of a new life. Then, through intermittent flashes of memory, she recovers her childhood and past. Unlike the autobiographies of activist women that begin with the moment of birth—"I was born in the city of Cork, Ireland," writes Mother Jones, and Elizabeth Gurley Flynn begins, "By birth I am a New Englander"— Goldman's autobiography opens with a memory of herself at the age of twenty hopefully arriving in New York, a strange "new world."

Goldman's fractured chronology allows her to present historical events like the Haymarket Affair as self-contained and didactic passages of exposition and as crucial moments of self-revelation that expose the genesis of desire. . . . Goldman's recapitulation of historical events provided an origin for the desire that Goldman said determined the course of her life. . . . Goldman would never realise her "great ideal," though it remained the only permanent element in her life. Thus, her story thematized an irrefragable contrast between aspiration and history, between the permanence of human desire and life's disappointing transitoriness. This contrast is reflected in Goldman's rhetorical vacillations as she moved from an inviolable and ideal "Cause" to the various causes into which she was thrust by the vicissitudes of history. While she depended upon the hard cogency of facts to assert the necessity behind these causes, she represented human aspiration through a romantically elusive image—that of humanity reaching for the stars. The image became muddled in its spatial designations when Goldman's aspiration signified sexual, rather than political, desire; then it described her "soaring high" (towards the stars) in a desire to experience the "depths" of passion. As in time the object of Goldman's sexual passion changed, each lover receded into the past to become part of her history, but her yearning for sexual fulfillment . . . never abated. Personal love began to seem as elusive to Goldman as her political ideals, and as enduringly desirable. However, though the end of one affair after another led her to question whether a woman's public life inevitably destroys private happiness, she never questioned or abandoned her ideals in order to keep her lovers. . . .

BOOKS AND LOVERS

A coalescence of literature with life is one of Goldman's rhetorical strategies of self-ratification. When she described moments of heightened emotions, she typically merged her character with those of fictional heroines and often spoke her piece in the clichéd language of sentimental or romantic novels. The effect was self-subverting, since she simultaneously enhanced and diminished an image of herself as an exemplary woman of her times—enhanced by imbuing herself with the emotional intensity of self-sacrificing and self-aggrandizing heroines . . . and diminished by equating her own reality with that of merely imagined or unreal women. She seemed untroubled by discrepancies between herself as a "real" person and literary characters, or between women characters created by writers whose ideologies were diametrically opposed. However, literary characters could create

Emma Goldman

trouble between her and her lovers. She tells, for example, how Ben Reitman, to whom she felt passionately enslaved, abruptly left her after reading D.H. Lawrence's novel, *Sons and Lovers;* like Lawrence's hero, Reitman was obsessed with his mother and he projected his emotional conflicts upon a character torn between sexual and maternal love. She lost another lover, Edward Brady, because of [German philosopher Friedrich] Nietzsche. Brady's denunciation of

Goldman's intellectual idol seemed to her more than a philosophical disagreement; it signified, she said, an intolerable violation of her freedom, "more precious to [her] than life." Following their quarrel over Nietzsche, she accused Brady of "binding" her "body" and her "spirit" and (in ascending order of insult) of trying to "tear" her away from "the movement," her "friends," and "the books I love."

Usually, however, a shared love of books mediated Goldman's relationship with men. *What Is To Be Done?* immediately established a rapport with Berkman, her lifelong companion. When Goldman first met the young anarchist, she confided to him her dream: "I wanted to have time for reading," she told him, "and later I hoped to realize my dream of a co-operative shop.". . . A brief quarrel ensued when Berkman could hardly believe that this young woman had read a prohibited Nihilist novel. Goldman resented having her word or independence of mind questioned: "I repeated angrily that I had read the forbidden book and other similar works . . . ," she said, citing her reading as proof of her political and personal liberation. The books she named created a bond between the two young anarchists. They also recalled scenes of violence Goldman had seen as a girl in Russia and the novels . . . that had articulated her inchoate feelings of sympathy for Nihilists executed by the Tsar—sympathies later conferred upon the Haymarket anarchists.

As the autobiography reveals, men who gave Goldman books became her political idols and her sexual partners, the list of her readings expanding with that of her lovers: Jacob Kershner, her feckless husband, whose "interest in books . . . had first attracted her"; the anarchist Johann Most, who supplied her "with a list of books" that grounded her in revolutionary theory; Edward Brady, who introduced her "to the great classics of English and French literature"; to [Jean Jacques] Rousseau, Voltaire, [Johann Wolfgang von] Goethe, and Shakespeare. . . . Ironically, prison offered Goldman the luxury of time to read; she always carried a book with her when she thought she might be arrested (she mentions, for example, [James Joyce's] *A Portrait of the Artist as a Young Man*). One of the prison reforms she effected was to win library privileges for women inmates.

PORTRAYAL OF A PASSIONATE HUMAN BEING

Among the books Goldman remembered reading as a schoolgirl were popular romances—especially those of the nineteenth-century German writer Eugenie Marlitt—that had made her "grow tearful over the unhappy heroines." These romances left an indelible impression. Years later she recalled their trite sentimental images as she wrote about her own love affairs, the "ecstasy" and unhappiness that, like their romantic heroines, she too experienced. Clearly, Goldman adjusted her discursive mode to her immediate subject, changing from the journalistic, or didactic, or caustic style that described historical events to a murkily melodramatic language for romance. From popular novels she appropriated the prose she considered suitable to sexual passions she believed herself politically obligated to reveal. As an anarchist and a feminist, she wanted to dramatize through her own life a woman's freedom to love as she desired. She advocated frankness as an ideological principle; and in her autobiography she would describe her erotic yearnings, her passionate responses, and her abjectness toward lovers she knew were not her equals, particularly Ben Reitman, with whom she had a ten-year liaison. After all, if she was going to humanize Red Emma, she needed to show that she had experienced weakness and humiliation, as well as fulfillment, in her relationship with men. She told how she endured Reitman's obsessive infidelities, his boorishness, desertions, demands, and even his dishonesties and betrayals—and she was honest enough to suggest ulterior motives. For as her manager, "travelling companion," and "helpmate," Reitman relieved her of the burdensome details of her lecture tours and significantly enlarged her audiences. As her "lover," he caught her in a "torrent of elemental passion" and she "responded shamelessly to its primitive call." Goldman knew that Berkman and other friends deplored her dependence upon a man inferior to her in intellect and conscience, but she turned to Reitman because, she wrote, he satisfied her "great hunger for someone who could love the woman in me and yet who would also be able to share my work. I had never had anyone who could do both." He fulfilled also her fantasy of experiencing in life the passions she had felt vicariously through literature. Indeed, as she described Reitman's "primitive" sexual appeal, she re-created him as the "savage" male considered generic to the naturalistic novel. The story of his chaotic life, as she recounts his telling it, drew her to him because he "came from a world so unlike mine": "I was enthralled by this living embodiment of the types I had only known through books, the types portrayed by Dostoyevsky and Gorki.". . .

Given Goldman's explicitness about her love affairs, one would think the issue of frankness irrelevant to her autobiography. Nevertheless, critics have raised it. . . . To ask, as modern critics do, what she was hiding is to assume a total congruence between the living woman and the autobiographical "I" (a naive assumption for contemporary theorists) and to overlook all that Goldman did reveal: an enslaving passion for Reitman inappropriate to her as an independent woman; desire for younger men that she could satisfy only by risking humiliating rejections; and (highly damaging to her image of herself as a feminist), constant need for support—moral and intellectual backing, money, and admiration—that she sought and received from men. She did not hide the fact that men bought her beautiful clothes and that . . . she wore them with pleasure.

REFUSING THE SAFETY OF SILENCE

More significantly, she did not hide her doubts about the psychological motives underlying her political commitments. She repeatedly stated her suspicions that work may have represented an escape from the emptiness of her life, as though her work and her life were discrete and not, as she also stated, interwoven. She did not hide her fear of nihilism. She referred recurrently to a sense of inner void she identified with her empty womb; and she wondered if her desire to care for humankind was a displaced expression of her desire for motherhood. Her equation of personal feelings with socially conditioned views of woman as biologically determined— as influenced in temperament and desire by her womb— subverted her feminist declarations of freedom. Nevertheless, she did not hide her sense of subservience to biological forces. Nor did she hide her periods of depression. She admitted her violent temper, her irascibility, her weaknesses, and her sexual wildness. Given her hope that the autobiography might present her favorably enough to allow her readmission into the United States, she was remarkably candid about her private life and admirably loyal to her anarchist beliefs. She never disavowed her social and political principles or attenuated her revolutionary purposes. She never hid opinions she knew would alienate her fellow revolutionists. Late in life, she paid dearly for her criticism of Soviet Russia, just as she had, years ago, for her expressions of sympathy for President McKinley's assassin. But she considered herself morally obligated to criticize a regime that she believed subverted the principles and purposes of social revolution. She might have hidden views she knew were unpopular with radical audiences she depended upon for support, but instead she insisted upon advertising them, and she devoted almost half of the second volume of *Living My Life* to a chronicle of disillusioning discoveries about the revolution that had been her visionary ideal. She might have tried to protect this ideal by hiding the facts as she knew them, but though her secrecy would have been undetected, since few at the time had the access to Russian life that she did, she refused the safety of silence.

Speaking out and speaking her own piece constituted her integrity and the identity Goldman created for herself in life and in her autobiography.... She ... insisted she would speak her own piece, and though she made her first public appearances as a disciple of the anarchist Johann Most, lecturing on subjects he had chosen in a style he rehearsed, she soon saw "the need of independent thought." In time, she condemned the "meaningless prattle" she had appropriated from Most: "I realized I was committing a crime against myself and the workers by serving as a parrot repeating Most's views."...

As such declarations attest, the issue in autobiographies of radical public women was not only women's claim to their own voice, but also their insistence upon self-possession: upon the "I" reiterated in their statements. . . . Their pronouns signified their opposition to others, women and men, who presented them with social scenarios, as though they were derivative speakers, merely actresses reciting someone else's piece.

The Matrilineal Bond in Margaret Mead's *Blackberry Winter*

Stephanie A. Demetrakopoulos

Stephanie A. Demetrakopoulos, an English professor at Western Michigan University and feminist critic, discusses Margaret Mead's autobiography, *Blackberry Winter*. She traces Mead's security in her womanhood and her professional success as a ground-breaking anthropologist back to the influence of her mother and especially her grandmother. From them Mead learned to appreciate her connection to nature, especially plants, as well as stability and inner strength. This matriarchal upbringing profoundly informed her identity as a woman and helped her to embrace motherhood, survive divorce, and pursue a distinguished professional career.

In the first chapters of *Blackberry Winter*, Mead presents her mother as an active, intellectual, loving, and strong woman. Her mother maintains an orderly matrix for the family, can instantly find things for her careless husband, and seems mainly to embody the Great Mother as the trustworthy manager of resources. She is an "anchor" for the father and uses this family position of centrality to force him to allow Margaret to go to college. She is so socially responsible that she tends to be "Spartan," unable to play; and her practicality sometimes dampens the family's spontaneity. But, on the whole, Margaret seems satisfied in a cool way with her mother.

"SHE SIMPLY COMMANDED RESPECT"

It is in her grandmother that Mead finds a more numinous image of primal and nurturing strength that extends the

Excerpted from Stephanie A. Demetrakopoulos, "The Metaphysics of Matrilinearism in Women's Autobiography: Studies of Mead's *Blackberry Winter*, Hellman's *Pentimento*, Angelou's *I Know Why the Caged Bird Sings*, and Kingston's *The Woman Warrior*," in *Women's Autobiography: Essays in Criticism*, edited by Estelle C. Jelinek. Copyright © 1980 Indiana University Press. Reprinted with permission from Estelle C. Jelinek.

more limited personage of her mother into a strong, developed, monumentally maternal matriarchate. There is a sense of bulk, of massiveness, of fortress-like centrality about the grandmother that is typical of this archetype. Mead devotes a whole chapter to her as the most "decisive influence in my life." Although her autobiography is journalistic in its stripped down, matter-of-fact, almost Protestant prose, Mead waxes lyrical and even symbolic about her grandmother:

> She sat at the center of our household. Her room—and my mother always saw to it that she had the best room, spacious and sunny, with a fireplace, if possible—was the place to which we immediately went when we came in from playing or home from school. There my father went when he arrived in the house. There we did our lessons on the cherry-wood table with which she had begun housekeeping and which, later, was my dining room table for twenty-five years. There, sitting by the fire, erect and intense, she listened to us and to all of Mother's friends and to our friends. In my early childhood she was also very active—cooking, preserving, growing flowers in the garden, and attentive to all the activities of the country and the farm. . . . Grandma was trustworthy in quite a different way [from Mother]. She meant exactly what she said, always. If you borrowed her scissors, you returned them. . . . She simply commanded respect and obedience by her complete expectation that she would be obeyed. And she never gave silly orders.

Helpful here is the Jungian[1] precept that rooms symbolize parts of the psyche. Notice Mead's development of this place as the most important, central, light-filled, and warm room. This is where their education and family interchanges took place. Everyone went there first upon return to the home. The connection with nature, especially plants, is developed more fully within this chapter and is important in evoking the Lady of the Plants archetype, one aspect of the Primal Good Mother. . . . The importance of this room to the family is underlined by her rhetorical use of the word "there," which she repeats three times. The loving though iron rule of this archetype is reflected in the grandmother's trustworthiness. Mead again emphasizes this stability and inner strength later, saying that when her grandmother became angry she became very still and silent. Her grandmother taught her to cook, kept her at home sometimes for whole years to educate her (she had been a teacher), and was integral to the matrilineal alliance against Mead's father: she al-

[1] after symbolic theories of psychologist Carl Jung

ways agreed with her daughter-in-law. When her own son threatened to leave the family, Grandma "told him firmly that she would stay with her [the mother] and the children."

Mead reveals how the more permeable ego membrane of the woman can be beneficial to a developing girl if she has good models to internalize. At times Mead says she found it difficult to distinguish between her grandmother's life and her own. Mead heard so many stories about her grandmother's girlhood that she felt as a child she had lived them herself. The stories grandparents tell children may be a very important part of the psychic development of time and ancestral connections; many women autobiographers seem to have internalized such stories as part of their own mythos ([Maxine Hong] Kingston [*The Woman Warrior*] particularly demonstrates the power of the "talk-story" to children). Her grandmother also shaped Mead's attitudes toward being a woman and toward men. "Grandma had no sense at all of ever having been handicapped by being a woman," and she thought that boys were slower to educate and "more vulnerable." Her grandmother embodies pleasant, warm aspects of woman's physicality. Mead's love for her was sensuous and physical in a way that she never depicts with her mother; she "loved the feel of her soft skin." Most important, finally, was that her grandmother had a career of her own: "The two women I knew best were mothers and had professional training. So I had no reason to doubt that brains were suitable for a woman." When her unstable and temperamental father later refuses to educate her (due to his economic insolvency, but he uses sexism as an excuse), it never dents her sense of being bound for a career. He, in fact, incurs what she calls "one of the few fits of feminist rage I have ever had."

Margaret Mead

THE MEN IN MEAD'S LIFE

Unknowingly, Mead depicts her father in a role reminiscent of the peripheral and castrated priests of Isis [in ancient Egyptian fertility cults]. He is seen as intrusive and imperative, interrupting the real business of the household, "my mother's and my grandmother's absorption with the children," and after the mother dies, he can never find anything again. His friends and hobbies are treated by the women as irrelevant and bothersome, and he is called "impatient," "irrational and untrustworthy," "arbitrary," and "rebellious" toward the matriarchal realm about which he gyrates. Her later relationships with men seem to reflect some of this familial pattern. At a time when it was unheard of, she kept her own name when she married. She recalls that a friend in college said her future husband would have to have an Oedipal complex; Mead later remarks on the Oedipal complex of her second husband as he notes the more mature relationship she begins building with the third husband (while still married to the second one). All her husbands (except possibly Gregory Bateson) seem to have been less competent than she, and it is noteworthy how little emotional turmoil she undergoes when breakups come. She also maintains a good relationship with them and their new wives. She does not like to compete with men, nor does she seek power in the form of administrative posts. She is not destructive in any way toward men; she simply does not center her identity around her relationship with them in the way that many women do in our nuclear family oriented culture.

This is not to say that a matriarchate as almost wholly devoid of masculine influence as the Meads' is unequivocally good for everyone. Mead's brother seems to have suffered from some very specific expectations of success that her father projected onto him; Mead escapes this problem because of being a girl and is encouraged by her mother and grandmother to move into whatever realm of life she finds professionally fulfilling. The brother suffered within the family matriarchy in other ways; Mead says she projected all frailty and weakness onto him, keeping images of strength for herself. . . .

MATRIARCHAL INFLUENCES ON MEAD'S CHARACTER

There are some negative aspects to her development, though decidedly minor. Because of her constant espousal of roles of strength, warmth, and cheerfulness, she admits early that she represses negative feelings and experiences. This seems to allow a rather long-suffering acceptance of injustices, as with her father and her second husband, who appeared actually cruel in his attitude toward her. Sometimes she seems to see men mainly as Father figures, needed to complete the family constellation. She marries Luther, her first husband, mainly because she wanted to have six children, and she leaves him when she finds she cannot have children. This is a rather callous treatment of him. . . . But many first marriages are rather faceless, anonymous affairs. She also has an overdeveloped sense of responsibility, a fear of letting others down; she cannot bear being called "heartless," nor can she withhold support from friends even when it costs her too much. This, of course, is the maternal role becoming so sacrificial that it is self-destructive. Most puzzling of all, perhaps, is her sense of being "expendable" as an anthropologist in the field when she finds she cannot have children. Before that, she agreed with [anthropologist] Franz Boas and others that women who can potentially give birth ought not be exposed to dangers. (This perhaps reflects the sense of sacrality that surrounds the Persephone or Kore figure in matrilineal cults—the daughter who can give birth stands for potential fruitfulness and ongoingness. The whole culture rebels for deep and possibly healthy psychic reasons at the sight or thought of a young woman dead on the battlefield.)

But the positive aspects of her identification with the matriarchate far outweigh the negative, and no human being is free from flaws or shortcomings. For one thing, she says she was always glad to be a girl. That is a singular (and, I think, wonderful) statement for a woman to be able to make. She carries with her throughout life a system for relating with groups of people that makes her comfortable and strong. For example, in the apartments she rented as a student, she organized her college friends into kinship systems which she orchestrated; the strength of these bonds is reflected in her lifelong relationships with these women. Her desire to be a mother was apparently completely without the ambivalence that women usually bring to that experience. Her chapter on the child she finally did have, her daughter Cathy, is one of the most joyful celebrations of motherhood I have ever read. She never gives up her career or feels guilt about leaving the child with the very competent and loving nursemaids she always seemed able to find. Because of her sense of strength and self-esteem as a woman, she was apparently able to divorce and remarry without the long periods of depression, anxiety, and lack of productivity that most women go through.

In fact, her early recognition and internalizing of kinship bonds formed the framework for her whole career. She says she always preferred learning in a personal context (as with her grandmother), and she never seemed threatened by another person's prestige or knowledge. Most poignant and sad in this regard is her great depression over the period of time when she tried to get scientists to work together as "a united family" rather than becoming monomaniacally separate as they have become.

TRANSCENDENCE AS GRANDMOTHER

Finally, she experiences in her own rather prosaic way a metaphysical sense of the continuity and ongoingness of life through her sense of matrilinearism. Her last chapter (there is an epilogue, but it only "gathers threads") is called "On Being a Grandmother." The lovely pictures of Sevanne Margaret (who fittingly takes her grandmother's name) accompany a text that almost defies complete explication:

> I suddenly realized that through no act of my own I had become biologically related to a new human being . . . how strange it was to be involved at a distance in the birth of a biological descendant. . . . I have always been acutely aware of the way one life touches another. . . . But the idea that as a grandparent one was dealing with action at a distance—that somewhere, miles away, a series of events occurred that changed one's own status forever—I had not thought of that and I found it very odd.

Her syntax is often labored and twisted in this chapter, as she struggles to state the metaphysical truths she has intuited. Here is one of her clearer summations:

> Scientists and philosophers have speculated at length about the sources of man's belief that he is a creature with a future life, or somewhat less commonly, with a life that preceded his life on earth. Speculation may be the only kind of answer that is possible, but I would now add to the speculations that are more familiar another of my own: the extraordinary sense of having been transformed not by any act of one's own but by the act of one's child.

She celebrates at length the way that mothers transcend their "creatureliness" in being able to accept their unknown children, who come to them as strangers. In becoming a grandmother, she finds she has acquired a special and perhaps transient sensitivity: "It is as if the child to whom one is bound by greater knowledge and the particularity of love were illuminated and carried a halo of light into any group of children." She says that everyone needs "access both to grandparents and grandchildren in order to be a full human being":

> In the presence of grandparent and grandchild, past and future merge in the present. Looking at a loved child, one cannot say, "We must sacrifice this generation for the next. Many must die now so that later others may live." This is the argument that generations of old men, cut off from children, have used in sending young men out to die in war.

Thus, [Mead comes] full circle into the role of Grandmother, which features the mature woman's sense of transcendence and transformation. . . .

This archetype of matrilineal foothold, of a four-generation matriarchate, seems the bedrock on which the repose of the narrating, retrospective Mead rests. Her sense of transcendence, yet loving understanding of process, is consolidated by her experience of the last transformations of the Demeter/Persephone myth, in which finally the daughter (Kore or Persephone) gives birth to a child. (This archetype is imaged forth even in the patriarchal religion of Christianity by Leonardo da Vinci's painting of the Virgin Mary sitting upon the lap of her mother and holding the Christ child in her arms. "Kore" often has a baby son too.) This archetype of the endless chain of mothers/daughters underlies a woman's sense of kinship, and Mead demonstrates through her lifelong trust and adherence to this force how it helps the personality "unfold"—a metaphor which reflects the implicit assumption that human personality has its own innate nature which, if allowed to, will blossom and individuate without a great deal of struggle. The very title of her autobiography reflects Mead's sense of the importance of allowing the seasons of life to teach, to impregnate one with a sense of meaning that is at first organic, natural, allied with the unconscious. Mead's life demonstrates that one need not separate from the matriarchate in order to develop, to self-actualize fully; her life proves that a woman can individuate without rejection of the matriarchate. Indeed, rich and full development can come by remaining always rooted into it. . . . If those women who embody [the mythic] Great Mother are also fully developed, educated, and career-oriented as her mother and grandmother were, the daughter will naturally individuate and enter the community at large.

Lillian Hellman and Anaïs Nin: Masculine and Feminine Pitfalls of Liberation

Patricia Meyer Spacks

Patricia Meyer Spacks, an English professor at Yale University and the author of *The Female Imagination,* analyzes two modern women's autobiographies to demonstrate the difficulties encountered by women in search of freedom. Lillian Hellman, in *An Unfinished Woman,* assumes a tough, masculine persona, but is therefore not free to be in love, truly introspective, or even vulnerable. Anaïs Nin, on the other hand, in her diaries reveals herself constantly making sacrifices for others in life and seeking freedom through her writing. But her writing is so preoccupied with self-contemplation and self-display that she is trapped in her own narcissism.

The distinguished "emancipated" women who have written about themselves in our century often reveal the extraordinary difficulties of feminine freedom. As women approach freedom, they find it receding; as they accept limitation, it comes to look strangely like its opposite. [French author] Colette is first liberated to write when locked into her room and ordered to produce by a domineering husband who publishes her work under his name. . . . [French author] Simone de Beauvoir struggles against her sense of [Jean Paul] Sartre's superiority, hence dominance, and confesses that her lover is the center of her world. All these facts disturb students.

HELLMAN AND THE MASCULINE STANDARD

But even Lillian Hellman, whom students eagerly admire, working in a more "liberated" era and in a Hemingwayesque style which makes no apologies, exemplifies in her memoir, *An Unfinished Woman,* the degree to which feminine freedom may depend on ignorance, derive from fantasy, and produce paradoxical limitation. Miss Hellman dreams of living successfully by masculine standards: honor, courage, aggression. Her stories of triumph, considered as testimonies to the possibility of feminine freedom, thus have an ironic edge, of which she seems unaware. She relates Hemingway's praise of her: "So you have *cojones,* after all. I didn't think so upstairs. But you have *cojones* after all." Although she tells him to go to hell, she treasures the episode: Such praise, defining her difference from the rest of her sex, testifies to her distinction. She can spit in [author and longtime companion] Dashiell Hammett's eye, literally; the capacity makes her worthy of the companion. And she can endure bombardments, travel with the Russian Army, defy Hollywood moguls, the equal of any man. She sees the relation between men and women as a battle, and believes reflection on the difficulties of a woman's lot to be reprehensible weakness, "stuff proper for the head of a young girl."

However ugly her battles, she fights them. Often she wins, although her account of Hammett records his abundant victories. He asserts his power by creating a conflict and making her back away from it. By the time they reach the corner, he declares, she must decide never to discuss a certain subject again: otherwise, they will take permanently different directions. She must stop "juggling," maneuvering relationships, or he will leave her. He will not dine with a house guest who bores him; he will ignore her good friend Dorothy Parker, however embarrassing his refusals. When she rebukes him for his injustices, his insistence on his own way, he grinds a burning cigarette into his cheek to keep himself from doing it to her. "We never again spoke of that night because, I think, he was ashamed of the angry gesture that made him once again the winner in the game that men and women play against each other, and I was ashamed that I caused myself to lose so often."

Miss Hellman's shame at causing herself to lose—as women so often do—reflects the "masculine" orientation of her pride: Hemingway's praise of her for having "balls" is to the point. But it reflects also her selective blindness, a curious quality of her memoir. Although its author's interest for the public at large must depend on her reputation as a playwright, the narrative dwells hardly at all on her experience as a writer. Her accounts of her loves and of her work are

HELLMAN'S MASCULINITY

Timothy Dow Adams, author of Telling Lies in Modern American Autobiography, *argues that Hellman's personal style is actually a synthesis of the masculine and the feminine.*

Lillian Hellman repeatedly undercuts the . . . hard-boiled detective style so often attributed to her. Caught between the masculine standard for heroic action, especially at time of war . . . and its traditional feminine counterpart of fainting and feistiness, Hellman adopts a personal style somewhere in-between, an impassioned form of action in which, angry beyond control, she is hampered by traditional feminine physical weakness with a masculine twist, a literal turn, or trope: an ankle turned, not out of weakness, but in anger, almost deliberately, in an attempt to demonstrate her ability to fluctuate between the male and female worlds. . . .

Virtually every published interview with Hellman reports that her physical bearing was surprisingly feminine. Although she pictures her own body movements as stumbling and jerky, she is seen by others of both sexes as being, unconsciously, gracefully seductive. Jane Fonda, who plays Lillian Hellman in the movie version of the "Julia" section of *Pentimento,* describes her as "flirtatious and feminine and sensual." In a *New Yorker* profile, Margaret Case Harriman says of her, "Actually Lillian Hellman is neither cute nor tough. For a woman with militant undercurrents, her surface behavior is more often mild than not, and she is genuinely feminine to a degree that borders on the wacky."

In actual life, Hellman seems to have combined the apparently contradictory traits of physical gracefulness and a lack of coordination that rendered her clumsy in numerous physical activities. She is described as unable to open a safe or shoot a gun—aiming at a flying duck, she hit a wild lilac bush; aiming at a large deer right in front of her, she hit a dogwood tree behind her. Her sense of geography is often amiss, as is her sense of direction. Essential to understanding the tone of *An Unfinished Woman,* as well as her other autobiographies, is a realization of this combination of grace and awkwardness, a combination that is paralleled in Hellman's personality and that often manifests itself in an apparently boastful tone when modesty is intended, a form of self-mockery that sometimes appears to be the opposite.

Timothy Dow Adams, *Telling Lies in Modern American Autobiography.* Chapel Hill: University of North Carolina Press, 1990, pp. 138–39.

oblique, as if neither aspect of experience were vital to her (although the real meaning of the fact may be that both are too vital to be shared). Her summary comment on Hammett, with whom she spent thirty years, sounds deliberately but disturbingly flat: "He was the most interesting man I've ever met." Her most analytical comments about herself observe that she was "difficult" or "headstrong"—adjectives which classify her as her parents might, from without, but which provide little insight into her inner workings. The cumulative effect of her lack of self-penetration, her apparent uneasiness in love relationships, her reluctance to contemplate her own writing, her acceptance of a travelogue version of her experience, is to suggest that her central effort has been to create, for her own benefit as well as for others, a character to meet masculine standards. This is not a mere "image": her life substantiates it. The life of constant action (in this case "masculine" rather than "feminine" accomplishment) rests on a foundation of intense self-concentration. Lillian Hellman's work has been to make a self, rejecting in the process many traditional concomitants of femininity.

FREEDOM TO BE WEAK

She made my class nervous, despite their admiration: she didn't fit the established categories. If she exemplifies the possibilities of independence (and without working hard in school! as one student pointed out), she also suggests unexpected dangers and qualifications. For one thing, she makes more distinct the possibility that "bitchiness" goes with "doing something in the world." "None of the women we've encountered sit home and bake cookies," a student observed. True. But before Lillian Hellman, no one we read raised serious questions about the value of "niceness." Self-absorption is the foundation of Miss Hellman's freedom: the freedom to manufacture a more satisfactory self from the headstrong, difficult, unruly girl—always her father's "rumpled daughter"—so inadequate by standards of ladylike behavior. Her acquired strength appears to make bearable for her her occasional discovered weakness which, like most people, she can sometimes enjoy: another paradox troubling to the young. This truth she reveals without seeming ever to understand it. "There may be a need in many of us," she writes, "for the large, strong woman who takes us back to what most of us always wanted and few of us ever had." Strong women and strong men have clearly been important to Miss Hellman. She devotes three chapters of her memoir to describing four central figures in her life, all dominating personalities. Her yearning for dependence, her delight in discovering others, men and women, at least sometimes more forceful than she, suggest that the freedom to be weak may be as vital to a woman as the freedom to be strong. But vulnerability is dangerous—that she knows with full awareness. Only the strength of self-obsession and determination allow the memoirist space to construct a self, to make her yearning for masculine accomplishment into fact. . . .

NIN AND ORTHODOX FEMININITY

Like Lillian Hellman, Anaïs Nin writes of herself in ways that have the power to challenge standard assumptions; unlike Miss Hellman, she appears to take great pride in "losing." The published volumes of her diary emphasize her unfailing self-sacrifice, her willingness to live without so much as a pen while supplying her writer friends with typewriters, her eager yielding to others' demands. It is true that this pattern was directly responsible, Miss Nin declares, for a psychic breakdown, but her commitment to the values of orthodox "femininity" remained unchanging. Yet she is also committed to an ideal of personal freedom, which she . . . explicitly associates with the life of imagination—with "escape," the "illusory," "dream.". . .

The counterpart to the story about Lillian Hellman's "*cojones*" is an episode centered on Anaïs Nin's breasts. She complains to her analyst, Dr. René Allendy, that her breasts are too small, asking for appropriate medicine. "Are they absolutely undeveloped?" the doctor inquires. She replies no, then: "As I flounder in my descriptions, I say: 'To you, a doctor, the simplest thing is to show them to you.' And I do." The doctor begins, she reports, to rhapsodize: "Perfectly feminine, small but well shaped, well outlined in proportion to the rest of your figure, such a lovely figure, all you need is a few more pounds of it. You are really lovely, so much grace of movement, charm, so much breeding and finesse of line." Shortly thereafter, we discover that he has "lost his objectivity"; he can no longer help her. She reflects, "I asked Dr. Allendy to help me as a doctor of medicine. Was this quite a sincere action? Did I have to show him my breasts? Did I want to test my charm on him? Wasn't I pleased that he reacted so admiringly?"

Instead of Lillian Hellman's vocabulary of battle and endurance . . . Anaïs Nin uses the language of self-deprecation and self-doubt. She avoids talk of "winning" as she modestly records her victories over the succession of people who fell in love with her: Henry Miller, Henry Miller's wife, her father (he reappears after having deserted his family years before, and soon begins to fantasize that everyone will think her his mistress, then loudly to regret that she is in fact his daughter), Dr. Allendy, Dr. Otto Rank, who succeeded Allendy as her analyst, an Indian revolutionary, a French astrologer. Yet

Anaïs Nin

the need to triumph as well as the intermittent compulsion to "lose" resembles Hellman's, although the arena is different.

INTERNAL VERSUS EXTERNAL WRITING

Unlike Hellman, who claims realism as one of her virtues and berates herself even for introspection, Nin commits herself explicitly to the value of imaginative reconstruction of reality and to the centrality of writing in her life. Suffering from the twentieth-century problem of fragmentation, she solves it as a diarist, and defines her freedom as the product of her writing: "Because writing, for me, is an expanded world, a limitless world, containing all." But her real "work" appears to be self-contemplation and self-display, of which writing is only one mode. The source of her artistic energy, she believes, is her femininity. Love, service to others, those traditional forms of feminine expression, are other aspects of her self-presentation. "Yes, I see myself always softening blows, dissolving acids, neutralizing poisons, every moment of the day. I try to fulfill the wishes of others, to perform miracles." Despite her obsessive introspection, she conveys a view of herself in some ways as external as Lillian Hellman's self-portrait, because her concern centers so completely on the creation of effects. Her sense of freedom depends on her ability to manipulate those effects, to control her environment (different rooms painted different colors to encourage different moods), her clothing ("original"), and her companions, in order to show herself to advantage. When she gives birth, in agony, to a six-month fetus, dead at birth, she reports, "Towards eight o'clock I had several spasms of pain. . . . I combed my hair, I powdered and perfumed myself, painted my eyelashes. At eight o'clock I was taken to the operating room." Using all the paraphernalia of feminine attractiveness, she insists on loving and being loved, on working and having her work valued, on her symbolic position, as Woman, at the center of the universe. Demanding freedom, she declares herself to have achieved it.

Much more openly than Hellman, Anaïs Nin admits the great importance in her life of writing, publication, and relation with others. She seems willing, in fact, to admit just about anything. One does not feel that she tries to form herself in any particular mold; she quite simply loves and displays whatever she happens to be at any given moment. Yet the sense of limitation is as strong in her lengthy account of a "free" life as in Lillian Hellman's. The Hellman memoir suggests that the cost of freedom from relationship is emotional impoverishment and restriction, but the cost of relationship, for such a woman as the author, is likely to be submission, emotional limitation. Nin's diaries emphasize her resort to frequent bouts of psychoanalysis to rescue her from the desperate restrictions of an untrammeled life. Absorbed in narcissism, she flounders among the multitude of selves she perceives. Committed to fantasies of feminine power, she involves herself therefore in endless responsibilities to others. Her self-display requires an audience, her audience makes demands, her freedom eludes her. Her relationships lead her back only to herself. It seems a strangely symbolic fact that her husband has disappeared, apparently by his request, from her published diaries. The stillborn fetus might, for all we are told, be a virgin birth: the figure of Anaïs Nin, surrounded by others, exists nonetheless in a terrifying isolation of self-concern.

WRITING TO GIVE MEANING TO LIFE

All autobiography must rest on a foundation of self-absorption; men as well as women indulge in self-manufacture and self-display. What is perhaps peculiarly feminine about the autobiographical writing of Lillian Hellman and Anaïs Nin, dissimilar though the two authors are, is the obsessiveness of its implicit or explicit concern with the question of freedom, psy-chic and social, and the nature of its revelations about free-dom's limitations for women. But one may also speculate about the essential femininity of what may be called "defensive narcissism." For Ernest Hemingway or Norman Mailer, writ-ing about themselves, narcissism is a mode of aggression, a way of forcing the world to attend. In woman writers, even writers so assertive as Lillian Hellman, so exhibitionistic as Anaïs Nin, the characteristic note suggests something close to desperation: it is as though they were writing to convince themselves. The ordering of experience in memoir or diary, the implicit assertion that this life makes sense, seems in these cases a way for the author to remind herself of the value of her own experience, to hold on to the meaning of her life.

The Song of a Caged Bird: Maya Angelou's Quest for Self-Acceptance

Sidonie Ann Smith

Sidonie Ann Smith, an English professor at the University of Arizona and the author of *A Poetics of Women's Autobiography,* views Maya Angelou's autobiography, *I Know Why the Caged Bird Sings,* as a journey to self-acceptance. Angelou's journey begins with a terrible embarrassment in church as a young girl and ends with the deeply fulfilling birth of her child. In the course of this autobiographical journey, Angelou frees herself from the cage of her low self-esteem by taking control of her life and embracing her black womanhood.

A young, awkward girl child, dressed in a cut-down faded purple, too-long taffeta gown, stands nervously before an Easter congregation in Stamps, Arkansas, asking, "What you looking at me for?" The next lines refuse to escape forgetfulness, imprinting this one indelibly on the shamefilled silence. Finally the minister's wife offers her the forgotten lines. She grabs them, spills them into the congregation and then stumbles out of the watching church, "a green persimmon caught between [her] legs." Unable to control the pressure of her physical response, she urinates, then laughs "from the knowledge that [she] wouldn't die from a busted head."

But the cathartic laughter never even begins to mute, much less transcend, the real pain that is this experience, the palpable pain that pulses through her long trip down the aisle of that singing church as urine flows mockingly down her grotesquely skinny, heavily dusted legs. "What you looking at me for?" The question's physical articulation is barely

Excerpted from Sidonie Ann Smith, "The Song of a Caged Bird: Maya Angelou's Quest for Self-Acceptance," *Southern Humanities Review,* vol. VII, no. 4, Fall 1973. Reprinted with permission from *Southern Humanities Review.*

audible; its emotional articulation wails insufferably through the child's whole being, wails her self-consciousness, wails her diminished self-image: "What you looking at me for?"— "What you looking at *me* for?"—over and over until it becomes, "Is something *wrong* with me?" For this child too much is wrong.

WHITE STANDARDS OF PHYSICAL BEAUTY

The whole way she looks is wrong. She knows it too. That's why they are all looking at her. Earlier as she watches her grandmother make over the white woman's faded dress she revels for one infinitely delicious moment in fantasies of stardom. In a beautiful dress she would be transformed into a beautiful movie star: "I was going to look like one of the sweet little white girls who were everybody's dream of what was right with the world." But between the taffeta insubstantiality of her ideal vision of herself and the raw (fleshy) edges of her substantiality stands the one-way mirror:

> Easter's early morning sun had shown the dress to be a plain ugly cut-down from a white woman's once-was-purple throwaway. It was old-lady-long too, but it didn't hide my skinny legs, which had been greased with Blue Seal Vaseline and powdered with the Arkansas red clay. The age-faded color made my skin look dirty like mud, and everyone in church was looking at my skinny legs.

Wrong dress. Wrong legs. Wrong hair. Wrong face. Wrong color. Wrong. Wrong. Wrong. The child lives a "black ugly dream," or rather nightmare. But since this life is only a dream, the child knows she will awaken soon into a rightened, a whitened reality.

> Wouldn't they be surprised when one day I woke out of my black ugly dream, and my real hair, which was long and blond, would take the place of the kinky mass that Momma wouldn't let me straighten? My light-blue eyes were going to hypnotize them, after all the things they said about "my daddy must of been a Chinaman" (I thought they meant made out of china, like a cup) because my eyes were so small and squinty. Then they would understand why I had never picked up a Southern accent, or spoke the common slang, and why I had to be forced to eat pigs' tails and snouts. Because I was really white and because a cruel fairy stepmother, who was understandably jealous of my beauty, had turned me into a too-big Negro girl, with nappy black hair, broad feet and a space between her teeth that would hold a number-two pencil.

In a society attuned to white standards of physical beauty, the black girl child cries herself to sleep at night to the tune of her own inadequacy. At least she can gain temporary respite in the impossible dreams of whiteness. Here in the darkened nights of the imagination, that refuge from society and the mirror, blossoms an ideal self. Yet even the imagination is sometimes not so much a refuge as it is a prison in which the dreamer becomes even more inescapably possessed by the nightmare since the very self he fantasizes conforms perfectly to society's prerequisites. The cage door jangles shut around the child's question: "What you looking at me for?"

In this primal scene of childhood which opens Maya Angelou's *I Know Why the Caged Bird Sings,* the black girl child testifies to her imprisonment in her bodily prison. She is a black ugly reality, not a whitened dream. And the attendant self-consciousness and diminished self-image throb through her bodily prison until the bladder can do nothing but explode in a parody of release (freedom). . . .

A PATTERN OF SIGNIFICANT MOMENTS DOCUMENTED

Maya Angelou's autobiography . . . opens with a primal childhood scene that brings into focus the nature of the imprisoning environment from which the self will seek escape. The black girl child is trapped within the cage of her own diminished self-image around which interlock the bars of natural and social forces. The oppression of natural forces, of physical appearance and processes, foists a self-consciousness on all young girls who must grow from children into women. Hair is too thin or stringy or mousy or nappy. Legs are too fat, too thin, too bony, the knees too bowed. Hips are too wide or not wide enough. Breasts grow too fast or not at all. The self-critical process is incessant, a driving demon. . . . "What you looking at me for?" This really isn't me. I'm white with long blond hair and blue eyes, with pretty pink skin and straight hair, with a delicate mouth. I'm my own mistake. I haven't dreamed myself hard enough. I'll try again. The black and blue bruises of the soul multiply and compound as the caged bird flings herself against these bars:

> The Black female is assaulted in her tender years by all those common forces of nature at the same time that she is caught in the tripartite crossfire of masculine prejudice, white illogical hate and Black lack of power.

Within this imprisoning environment there is no place for this black girl child. She becomes a displaced person whose pain is intensified by her consciousness of that displacement:

> If growing up is painful for the Southern Black girl, being aware of her displacement is the rust on the razor that threatens the throat.
>
> It is an unnecessary insult.

... Thus the discovered pattern of significant moments Maya Angelou superimposes on the experience of her life is a pattern of moments that trace the quest of the black female after a "place," a place where a child no longer need ask self-consciously, "What you looking at me for?" but where a woman can declare confidently, "I am a beautiful, Black woman."

SEARCHING FOR HOME AND SELF

Two children, sent away to a strange place by estranging parents, cling to each other as they travel by train across the Southwestern United States—and cling to their tag: "To Whom It May Concern'—that we were Marguerite[1] and Bailey Johnson, Jr., from Long Beach, California, en route to Stamps, Arkansas, c/o Mrs. Annie Henderson." The autobiography of Black America is haunted by these orphans, children beginning life or early finding themselves without parents, sometimes with no one but themselves. They travel through life desperately in search of a home, some place where they can escape the shadow of loneliness, of solitude, of outsiderness. Although Maya and Bailey are travelling toward the home of their grandmother, more important, they are travelling away from the "home" of their parents. Such rejection a child internalizes and translates as a rejection of self: ultimately the loss of home occasions the loss of self-worth. "I'm being sent away because I'm not lovable." The quest for a home therefore is the quest for acceptance, for love, and for the resultant feeling of self-worth. Because Maya Angelou became conscious of her displacement early in life, she began her quest earlier than most of us. Like that of any orphan, that quest is intensely lonely, intensely solitary, making it all the more desperate, immediate, demanding, and making it, above all, an even more estranging process. For the "place" always recedes into the distance, moving with the horizon, and the searcher goes through life merely "passing through" to some place beyond, always beyond.

[1]Angelou was born Marguerite Johnson in 1928.

Stamps, Arkansas

The town reacted to us as its inhabitants had reacted to all things new before our coming. It regarded us a while without curiosity but with caution, and after we were seen to be harmless (and children) it closed in around us, as a real mother embraces a stranger's child. Warmly, but not too familiarly.

Warmth but distance: displacement. The aura of personal displacement is counterpointed by the ambience of displacement within the larger black community. The black community of Stamps is itself caged in the social reality of racial subordination and impotence. The cotton pickers must face an empty bag every morning, an empty will every night, knowing all along that the season would end as it had begun—money-less, credit-less. . . .

Suddenly Stamps is left behind. Moving on, the promise of a place. Her mother, aunts, uncles, grandparents—St. Louis, a big city, an even bigger reality, a totally new reality. But even here displacement: St. Louis, with its strange sounds, its packaged food, its modern conveniences, remains a foreign country to the child who after only a few weeks understands that it is not to be her "home." For one moment only the illusion of being in place overwhelms the child. For that moment [her mother's boyfriend] Mr. Freeman holds her pressed to him:

> He held me so softly that I wished he wouldn't ever let me go. I felt at home. From the way he was holding me I knew he'd never let me go or let anything bad ever happen to me. This was probably my real father and we had found each other at last. But then he rolled over, leaving me in a wet place and stood up.

The orphan hopes, for that infinite moment, that she has been taken back home to her father. She feels loved, accepted. Ultimately Mr. Freeman's strength, his arms, are not succor: they are her seduction. The second time he holds her to him it is to rape her, and, in short minutes, the child becomes even more displaced. The child becomes a child-woman. In court, frightened, the child denies the first time. Mr. Freeman is found dead. The child knows it is because she has lied. What a worthless, unlovable, naughty child! What can she do but stop talking: "Just my breath, carrying my words out, might poison people and they'd curl up and die like the black fat slugs that only pretended. I had to stop talking."

IN AND OUT OF HER CAGE

Now total solitude, total displacement, total self-condemnation. Back to Stamps, back to the place of grayness and barrenness, the place where nothing happened to people who, in spite of it all, felt contentment "based on the belief that nothing more was coming to them although a great deal more was due." Her psychological and emotional devastation find a mirror in Stamps' social devastation. Stamps gives her back the familiarity and security of a well-known cage. She climbs back in happily, losing herself in her silent world, surrendering herself to her own worthlessness.

She lives alone in this world for one year until the afternoon when the lovely Mrs. Flowers walks into the store and becomes for Maya a kind of surrogate mother. Mrs. Flowers opens the door to the caged bird's silence with the key of acceptance. For the first time Maya is accepted as an individual rather than as a relation to someone else: "I was liked, and what a difference it made. I was respected not as Mrs. Henderson's grandchild or Bailey's sister but for just being Marguerite Johnson." Such unqualified acceptance allows her to experience the incipient power of her own self-worth. . . .

But now there is yet another move. Once again the train, traveling westward to San Francisco in wartime. Here in this big city everything seems out of place.

> The air of collective displacement, the impermanence of life in wartime and the gauche personalities of the more recent arrivals tended to dissipate my own sense of not belonging. In San Francisco, for the first time, I perceived myself as part of something.

In Stamps the way of life remained rigid, in San Francisco it ran fluid. Maya had been on the move when she entered Stamps and thus could not settle into its rigid way of life. She chose to remain an outsider, and in so doing, chose not to allow her personality to become rigid. The fluidity of the new environment matched the fluidity of her emotional, physical, and psychological life. She could feel in place in an environment where everyone and everything seemed out-of-place.

Even more significant than the total displacement of San Francisco is Maya's trip to Mexico with her father. The older autobiographer, in giving form to her past experience, discovers that this "moment" was central to her process of growth. Maya accompanies her father to a small Mexican town where he proceeds to get obliviously drunk, leaving her with the responsibility of getting them back to Los Angeles. But she has never before driven a car. For the first time, Maya finds herself totally in control of her fate. Such total control contrasts vividly to her earlier recognition in Stamps that she as a Negro had no control over her fate. Here she is alone with that fate. And although the drive culminates in an accident, she triumphs.

This "moment" is succeeded by a month spent in a wrecked car lot scavenging with others like herself. Together these experiences provide her with a knowledge of self-determination and a confirmation of her self-worth. With the assumption of this affirmative knowledge and power,

Maya Angelou acquired the confidence to become a performing artist by overcoming the shame and guilt of her childhood.

Maya is ready to challenge the unwritten, restrictive social codes of San Francisco. . . . Stamps' acquiescence is left far behind in Arkansas as Maya assumes control over her own social destiny and engages in the struggle with life's forces. She has broken out of the rusted bars of her social cage.

But Maya must still break open the bars of her female sexuality: although she now feels power over her social identity, she feels insecurity about her sexual identity. She remains the embarrassed child who stands before the Easter congregation asking, "What you looking at me for?" The bars of her physical being close in on her, threatening her peace of mind. The lack of femininity in her small-breasted, straight-lined, and hairless physique and the heaviness of her voice become, in her imagination, symptomatic of latent lesbian tendencies. A gnawing self-consciousness still plagues her. Even after her mother's amused knowledge disperses her fears, the mere fact of her being moved by a classmate's breasts undermines any confidence that reassurance had provided. It was only brief respite. Now she knows, knows in her heart, that she is a lesbian. There is only one remedy for such a threatening reality: a man. But even making love with a casual male acquaintance fails to quell her suspicions; the whole affair is such an unenjoyable experience.

Only the pregnancy provides a climactic reassurance: if she can become pregnant, she certainly cannot be a lesbian (certainly a specious argument in terms of logic but a compelling one in terms of emotions and psychology). The birth of the baby brings Maya something totally her own, but, more important, brings her to a recognition of and acceptance of her full, instinctual womanhood. The child, father to the woman, opens the caged door and allows the fully-developed woman to fly out. Now she feels the control of her sexual identity as well as of her social identity. The girl child no longer need ask, embarrassed, "What you looking at me for?" No longer need she fantasize any other reality than her own.

SELF-DISCOVERY THROUGH AUTOBIOGRAPHY

Maya Angelou's autobiography comes to a sense of an ending: the black American girl child has succeeded in freeing herself from the natural and social bars imprisoning her in the cage of her own diminished self-image by assuming control of her life and fully accepting her black womanhood. The displaced child has found a "place." With the birth of her child Maya is herself born into a mature engagement with the forces of life. In welcoming that struggle she refuses to live a death of quiet acquiescence:

Few, if any, survive their teens. Most surrender to the vague but murderous pressure of adult conformity. It becomes easier to die and avoid conflicts than to maintain a constant battle with the superior forces of maturity.

One final comment: one way of dying to life's struggle is to suppress its inevitable pain by forgetting the past. Maya Angelou, who has since been a student and teacher of dance, a correspondent in Africa, a northern coordinator for the Southern Christian Leadership Council, an actress, writer, and director for the stage and film, had, like so many of us, successfully banished many years of her past to the keeping of the unconscious where they lay dormant and remained lost to her. To the extent that they were lost, so also a part of her self was lost. Once she accepted the challenge of recovering the lost years, she accepted the challenge of the process of self-discovery and reconfirmed her commitment to life's struggle. By the time she, as autobiographer, finished remembering the past and shaping it into a pattern of significant moments, she had imposed some sense of an ending upon it. And in imposing that ending upon it she gave the experience distance and a context and thereby came to understand the past and ultimately to understand herself.

Moreover, she reaffirms her sense of self-worth by making the journey back through her past on its own terms, by immersing herself once again in the medium of her making. Stamps, Arkansas, imprinted its way of life on the child during her formative years: the lasting evidence of this imprint is the sound of it. Her genius as a writer is her ability to recapture the texture of the way of life in the texture of its idioms, its idiosyncratic vocabulary and especially in its process of image-making. The imagery holds the reality, giving it immediacy. That she chooses to recreate the past in its own sounds suggests to the reader that she accepts the past and recognizes its beauty and its ugliness, its assets and its liabilities, its strength and its weakness. Here we witness a return to and final acceptance of the past in the return to and full acceptance of its language, the language a symbolic construct of a way of life. Ultimately Maya Angelou's style testifies to her reaffirmation of self-acceptance, the self-acceptance she achieves within the pattern of the autobiography.

CHRONOLOGY

400

St. Augustine writes his *Confessions.*

1432–1436

The Book of Margery Kempe (a spiritual autobiography) is transcribed.

1558–1566

Cellini writes *The Life of Benvenuto Cellini.*

1565

Teresa of Avila completes *The Life of Teresa of Jesus.*

1572–1588

Michel de Montaigne writes his *Essays.*

1666

John Bunyan writes *Grace Abounding to the Chief of Sinners.*

1740

Jonathan Edwards writes *Personal Narrative.*

1766–1770

Jean-Jacques Rousseau writes his *Confessions.*

1771–1790

Benjamin Franklin writes his *Autobiography.*

1789–1798

Giovanni Giacomo Casanova writes his *Memoirs.*

1796

Historian Edward Gibbon's *Memoirs* is published.

1798–1805

William Wordsworth writes the first thirteen books of *The Prelude* (a verse autobiography).

1822

Thomas De Quincey's *Confessions of an English Opium Eater* is published.

1833

J.W. von Goethe's *Poetry and Truth* is published.

1845

Narrative of the Life of Frederick Douglass, an American Slave, Written by Himself is published.

1854

Henry David Thoreau's *Walden* is published.

1855–1892

Walt Whitman's "Song of Myself" is published in nine successive editions.

1856

Victor Hugo's *Contemplations* (a verse autobiography) is published.

1861

Harriet Jacobs's *Incidents in the Life of a Slave Girl* is published.

1864

John Henry Cardinal Newman's *Apologia Pro Vita Sua* is published.

1873

John Stuart Mill's *Autobiography* is published.

1885–1889

John Ruskin's unfinished *Praeterita* is published.

1901

Booker T. Washington's *Up from Slavery* is published.

1904–1907

James Joyce writes *Stephen Hero* (an unpublished autobiographical novel) and "The Dead" (an autobiographical short story) along with other stories later collected in *Dubliners* (1914).

1907

The Education of Henry Adams is printed privately (published in 1918).

1909–1922

Marcel Proust writes *Remembrance of Things Past*, an autobiographical novel (published in 1913–1927).

1913

Henry James's *A Small Boy and Others* is published.

1914

Henry James's *Notes of a Son and Brother* is published; Maxim Gorky's *My Childhood* is published.

1916

James Joyce's *A Portrait of the Artist as a Young Man* (an autobiographical novel) is published.

1917

Henry James's *The Middle Years* is published.

1924

André Gide's *If It Die* (an autobiographical novel) is published.

1929

Mahatma Gandhi's *An Autobiography: The Story of My Experiments with Truth* is published.

1931

Emma Goldman's *Living My Life* is published.

1932

Black Elk Speaks, Being the Life Story of a Holy Man of the Oglala Sioux is published.

1933

Gertrude Stein's *The Autobiography of Alice B. Toklas* is published.

1934

Henry Miller's *Tropic of Cancer* (an autobiographical novel) is published.

1937

Isak Dinesen's *Out of Africa* is published.

1943

Woody Guthrie's *Bound for Glory* is published.

1945

Richard Wright's *Black Boy* is published.

1947

Anne Frank's *The Diary of a Young Girl* is published.

1948

Thomas Merton's *The Seven Storey Mountain* (a spiritual autobiography) is published.

1951

Alfred Kazin's *A Walker in the City* is published.

1955

James Baldwin's *Notes of a Native Son* is published.

1957

Mary McCarthy's *Memories of a Catholic Girlhood* is published; James Agee's *A Death in the Family* (an autobiographical novel) is published.

1958

Simone de Beauvoir's *Memoirs of a Dutiful Daughter* is published.

1959

Norman Mailer's *Advertisements for Myself* is published.

1961

Carl Jung's *Memories, Dreams, Reflections* is published.

1964

Jean-Paul Sartre's *The Words* is published.

1965

The Autobiography of Malcolm X, reported by Alex Haley, is published.

1966–1974

The Diaries of Anaïs Nin, 1931–1947 is published.

1967

Vladimir Nabokov's *Speak, Memory: An Autobiography Revisited* is published; Piri Thomas's *Down These Mean Streets* is published.

1968

Norman Mailer's *The Armies of the Night* is published; *The Autobiography of W.E.B. DuBois* is published; Frederick Exley's *A Fan's Notes: A Fictional Memoir* is published.

1969

Lillian Hellman's *An Unfinished Woman: A Memoir* is published; N. Scott Momaday's *The Way to Rainy Mountain* is published.

1970

Maya Angelou's *I Know Why the Caged Bird Sings* is published.

1971

Charles Mingus's *Beneath the Underdog* is published.

1972

Margaret Mead's *Blackberry Winter: My Earlier Years* is published.

1973

Lillian Hellman's *Pentimento* is published.

1974

Robert Pirsig's *Zen and the Art of Motorcycle Maintenance: An Inquiry into Values* is published; *All God's Dangers: The Life of Nate Shaw*, reported by Theodore Rosengarten, is published; Annie Dillard's *Pilgrim at Tinker Creek* is published.

1976

Lillian Hellman's *Scoundrel Time* is published; Maxine Hong Kingston's *The Woman Warrior: Memories of a Girlhood Among Ghosts* is published; N. Scott Momaday's *The Names: A Memoir* is published.

1981

Leslie Marmon Silko's *Storyteller* is published.

1983

Eudora Welty's *One Writer's Beginnings* is published.

1987

Gloria Anzaldua's *Borderlands* is published; Annie Dillard's *An American Childhood* is published.

1988

Paul Monette's *Borrowed Time: An AIDS Memoir* is published.

1992

Paul Monette's *Becoming a Man: Half a Life Story* is published; Richard Rodriguez's *Days of Obligation* is published.

1995

Mary Karr's *The Liars' Club* is published.

1996

Frank McCourt's *Angela's Ashes* is published.

2000

Mary Karr's *Cherry* is published.

FOR FURTHER RESEARCH

GENRES AND EUROPEAN LANDMARKS

Susanna Egan, *Patterns of Experience in Autobiography.* Chapel Hill: University of North Carolina Press, 1954.

Robert Elbaz, *The Changing Nature of the Self: A Critical Study of the Autobiographic Discourse.* Iowa City: University of Iowa Press, 1987.

Stephen Greenblatt, *Renaissance Self-Fashioning: From More to Shakespeare.* Chicago: University of Chicago Press, 1978.

James Olney, *Metaphors of Self: The Meaning of Autobiography.* Princeton, NJ: Princeton University Press, 1972.

———, ed., *Autobiography: Essays Theoretical and Critical.* Princeton, NJ: Princeton University Press, 1980.

———, ed., *Studies in Autobiography.* New York: Oxford University Press, 1988.

Roy Pascal, *Design and Truth in Autobiography.* London: Routledge and Kegan Paul, 1960.

Wayne Schumaker, *English Autobiography: Its Emergence, Materials, and Form.* Berkeley and Los Angeles: University of California Press, 1954.

William C. Spengemann, *The Forms of Autobiography: Episodes in the History of a Literary Genre.* New Haven, CT: Yale University Press, 1980.

Karl Joachim Weintraub, *The Value of the Individual: Self and Circumstance in Autobiography.* Chicago: University of Chicago Press, 1978.

ANGLO-AMERICAN AUTOBIOGRAPHY

Timothy Dow Adams, *Telling Lies in Modern American Autobiography.* Chapel Hill: University of North Carolina Press, 1990.

212

Thomas Cooley, *Educated Lives: The Rise of Modern Autobiography in America.* Columbus: Ohio State University Press, 1976.

G. Thomas Couser, *American Autobiography: The Prophetic Mode.* Amherst: University of Massachusetts Press, 1979.

James M. Cox, *Recovering Literature's Lost Ground.* Baton Rouge: Louisiana State University Press, 1989.

A. Robert Lee, ed., *First Person Singular: Studies in American Autobiography.* New York: St. Martin's, 1988.

Herbert Leibowitz, *Fabricating Lives: Explorations in American Autobiography.* New York: Knopf, 1989.

Robert F. Sayre, *The Examined Self: Benjamin Franklin, Henry Adams, Henry James.* Princeton, NJ: Princeton University Press, 1964.

Daniel B. Shea, *Spiritual Autobiography in Early America.* Madison: University of Wisconsin Press, 1968.

Albert Stone, *Autobiographical Occasions and Original Acts: Versions of American Identity from Henry Adams to Nate Shaw.* Philadelphia: University of Pennsylvania Press, 1982.

———, ed., *The American Autobiography: A Collection of Critical Essays.* Englewood Cliffs, NJ: Prentice-Hall, 1981.

Gordon O. Taylor, *Chapters of Experience: Studies in Twentieth-Century American Autobiography.* New York: St. Martin's, 1983.

ETHNIC AMERICAN AUTOBIOGRAPHY

William L. Andrews, *To Tell a Free Story: The First Century of Afro-American Autobiography, 1760–1865.* Urbana: University of Illinois Press, 1986.

Mutlu Konuk Blasing, *The Art of Life: Studies in American Autobiographical Literature.* Austin: University of Texas Press, 1977.

Joanne M. Braxton, *Black Women Writing Autobiography.* Philadelphia: Temple University Press, 1989.

H. David Brumble, *Native American Autobiography.* New York: Oxford University Press, 1992.

Stephen Butterfield, *Black Autobiography in America.* Amherst: University of Massachusetts Press, 1974.

King-Kok Cheung, *Articulate Silences: Double-Voiced Discourse.* Ithaca, NY: Cornell University Press, 1992.

Henry Louis Gates Jr., *Figures in Black: Words, Signs, and the "Racial" Self.* New York: Oxford University Press, 1987.

Henry Louis Gates Jr. and Charles T. Davis, eds., *The Slave's Narrative.* New York: Oxford University Press, 1985.

James Craig Holte, *The Ethnic I: A Sourcebook for Ethnic-American Autobiography.* New York: Greenwood, 1988.

Arnold Krupat, *For Those Who Come After: A Study of Native American Autobiography.* Berkeley and Los Angeles: University of California Press, 1985.

Sidonie Smith, *Where I'm Bound: Patterns of Slavery and Freedom in Black American Autobiography.* Westport, CT: Greenwood, 1974.

Valerie Smith, *Self-Discovery and Authority in Afro-American Narrative.* Cambridge, MA: Harvard University Press, 1987.

Robert B. Stepto, *From Behind the Veil: A Study of Afro-American Narrative.* Urbana: University of Illinois Press, 1979.

Hertha Dawn Wong, *Sending My Heart Back Across the Years: Tradition and Innovation in Native American Autobiography.* New York: Oxford University Press, 1992.

WOMEN'S AUTOBIOGRAPHY

Mary Catherine Bateson, *Composing a Life.* New York: Atlantic Monthly, 1989.

Susan Groag Bell and Marilyn Yalom, eds., *Revealing Lives: Autobiography, Biography, and Gender.* Albany: State University of New York Press, 1990.

Shari Benstock, ed., *The Private Self: Theory and Practice of Women's Autobiographical Writings.* Chapel Hill: University of North Carolina Press, 1988.

Bella Brodzki and Celeste Schenck, eds., *Life/Lines: Theorizing Women's Autobiography.* Ithaca, NY: Cornell University Press, 1988.

Carolyn G. Heilbrun, *Writing a Woman's Life.* New York: Norton, 1988.

Estelle C. Jelinek, *The Tradition of Women's Autobiography: From Antiquity to the Present.* Boston: Twayne, 1986.

———, ed., *Women's Autobiography: Essays in Criticism.* Bloomington: Indiana University Press, 1980.

Nancy K. Miller, *Getting Personal: Feminist Occasions and Other Autobiographical Acts.* New York: Routledge, 1991.

Sidonie Smith, *A Poetics of Women's Autobiography: Marginality and the Fictions of Self-Representation.* Bloomington: Indiana University Press, 1987.

INDEX

Adams, Henry
  on America, 108
  see also Education of Henry
    Adams, The
Adams, John, 103
Adams, Timothy Dow, 192
Advertisement for Myself
  (Mailer), 18
African American autobiography,
  12
  experience of American black
    community in, 139
  vs. Indian autobiography, 151
  individual and community in, 135
  slave narratives, 23, 134, 136-
    37, 138
  *see also Autobiography of Mal-
    colm X, The;* blues autobiog-
    raphy; *I Know Why the Caged
    Bird Sings; Narrative of the
    Life of Frederick Douglass;* tes-
    timonial autobiography
Agee, James, 21, 22–23, 28, 111
Aiken, Conrad, 74
Alford, Thomas Wildcat, 152
America
  and Henry Adams, 108
  history of, corresponding with
    American autobiography,
    160–61
America Is in the Heart (Bulosan), 122
American autobiography
  and confessional literature, 76
  dramatization of self in, 76–77
  emphasis on self in, 70, 71
  historical, 20, 74–76
  influenced by literary percep-
    tions and personal experi-
    ences, 120–21
  journalism, 21–23

literary, 21
number of, published, 121
and salvation/self-help, 73–74
and self-remaking, 71, 72–73
spiritual, 19–20
see also African American autobiography; Emerson, Ralph
  Waldo; ethnic-American autobiography; Thoreau, Henry
  David
American Childhood, An (Dillard), 13, 30
  exclusions in, 57–59
  inclusions in, 54–57
  interior landscape of, 53
  topic of, 52–53
Americanization of Edward Bok
  (Bok), 123
"American Pilgrim's Progress"
  (Bunyan), 82–83
American Revolution (1776), 18
American Scene (James), 73
American Splendor (Pekar), 31
Ancient Mariner, The (Coleridge),
  40
Anderson, Mary Jane Hill, 125,
  126
Angela's Ashes (McCourt), 30
Angelou, Maya, 124, 126, 139
  *see also I Know Why the Caged
    Bird Sings*
Anglo-American autobiography.
  See American autobiography
Antin, Mary, 123, 125, 126
Anzaldua, Gloria, 24
apology, the, 18, 19
Ariel (Plath), 28, 29
Armies of the Night, The (Mailer),
  22
  Ambassador Theatre episode
    in, 113

216

femininity, 194–95
fragmentation in, 168
on girlhood, 166–67
vs. male autobiography, 25-26, 161–62
masculinity in, 190–93
peak periods of, 160–61
self-absorption in, 195, 196, 197
see also Blackberry Winter; I Know Why the Caged Bird Sings; Living My Life

Wong, Hertha Dawn, 156
Wong, Jade Snow, 24
Wright, Richard, 23, 74, 123, 139
on his childhood, 165–66
and Malcolm X, 150
on white oppression, 140

Zangwell, Israel, 124
Zen and the Art of Motorcycle Maintenance (Pirsig), 21